Social Problems

Recent Sociology Titles from W. W. Norton

To learn more about Norton Sociology, please visit wwnorton.com/soc

Social Problems

Third Edition

JOEL BEST

W. W. NORTON & COMPANY

NEW YORK   LONDON

W. W. Norton & Company has been independent since its founding in 1923, when William Warder Norton and Mary D. Herter Norton first published lectures delivered at the People's Institute, the adult education division of New York City's Cooper Union. The firm soon expanded its program beyond the Institute, publishing books by celebrated academics from America and abroad. By midcentury, the two major pillars of Norton's publishing program—trade books and college texts—were firmly established. In the 1950s, the Norton family transferred control of the company to its employees, and today—with a staff of four hundred and a comparable number of trade, college, and professional titles published each year—W. W. Norton & Company stands as the largest and oldest publishing house owned wholly by its employees.

Editor: Sasha Levitt
Project Editor: Linda Feldman
Editorial Assistant: Mary Williams
Managing Editor, College: Marian Johnson
Managing Editor, College Digital Media: Kim Yi
Production Manager: Ashley Horna
Media Editor: Eileen Connell
Media Project Editor: Kim Yi
Media Editorial Assistant: Grace Tuttle
Marketing Manager, Sociology: Julia Hall
Designer: Margaret M. Wagner
Permissions Manager: Megan Schindel
Composition: Jouve
Manufacturing: Maple Press

Library of Congress Cataloging-in-Publication Data

Names: Best, Joel, author.
Title: Social problems / Joel Best.
Description: Third edition. | New York : W.W. Norton & Company, [2017] |
    Includes bibliographical references and index.
Identifiers: LCCN 2016016095 | ISBN 9780393283419 (pbk.)
Subjects: LCSH: Social problems.
Classification: LCC HN28 .B45 2017 | DDC 306—dc23 LC record available at
    https://lccn.loc.gov/2016016095

W. W. Norton & Company, Inc., 500 Fifth Avenue, New York, NY 10110-0017
wwnorton.com

W. W. Norton & Company Ltd., 15 Carlisle Street, London W1D 3BS

4   5   6   7   8   9   0

Contents

Figures

Boxes

A Note to the Reader

Many, many books titled *Social Problems* have been published in the past hundred years. Their tables of contents look a lot alike: they begin with a brief discussion of the nature of social problems, then consider a list of different problems. Each chapter presents more or less up-to-date information about a particular social problem: there is a chapter about crime, another about racism, and so on. If your parents, grandparents, or even great-grandparents read a social problems textbook, that book almost certainly fit this pattern.

This is not your parents' social problems textbook.

The chapters in this book do not deal with different problems. Instead, each chapter deals with a different stage in the *social problems process*—the process by which particular problems become a focus of concern. Why do we worry about, say, the risks of breast implants in one year, road rage in another, and identity theft in still another? This book seeks to explain how and why attention to different issues rises and falls.

If you're a student who's been assigned to read this book, it probably already seems long. All I can say is that it could have been a lot longer. Lots of people have written about the rise and fall of social problems; hundreds of studies have been published on the topic, particularly since the 1970s. But I have decided to cite relatively few sources. Often where I've cited one source, I could have cited dozens. In general, I have chosen to cite sources that appeared relatively recently. In addition, because this book is intended as an introduction to thinking about social problems, I have tried to hold jargon to a minimum. If you go on to read more of what sociologists have written on the topic—and I hope that this book will get you interested enough to do just that—you will find that other authors have explored the ins and outs of studying social problems in far more detail, and that they have developed many specialized terms and concepts to help us think about the social problems process. However, my goal is not to summarize everything that has been written about what I call the constructionist approach to social problems. Rather, I want to give you a basic framework for understanding this approach. This book is intended to help you become a more critical thinker; it provides some tools that can help you better analyze what you read and hear about social problems.

Acknowledgments

I particularly want to thank Karl Bakeman, Norton's editor for sociology at the time I started this book. Over the years, I had been approached by several publishers who said they wanted me to write a book about social problems. I had a standard response: "You don't want to publish the book I want to write, and I don't want to write the book you want to publish." That was enough to discourage everyone—except Karl. I appreciate his willingness to take a chance on the book I wanted to write.

When I began working on this third edition, Karl had taken on new responsibilities, and Sasha Levitt served as the editor for the revision. Like Karl, she was committed to the project, and I really appreciate her help.

Over the years, a lot of people gave me a lot of useful feedback, and the earlier editions listed all their names. I remain grateful to them, but the list started to seem unwieldy. So, this time I am only going to mention people who made comments or suggestions for this third edition: Jarl Ahlkvist, Eric Best, Kathleen Bogle, Christine Bowditch, Jennie Bristow, Kelli Chapman, Alison Diefenderfer, Steven Fazzari, Jessica Fields, Ashley Frawley, Nanette Graham, Jerry Jacobs, Joanna Kempner, Joshua Kreger, Kelsy Noele Kretschmer,

R. J. Maratea, Brian Monahan, Nicholas Parsons, Stephen Roman, Carrie Sanders, and John Vlot. Thank you all.

Finally, I want to thank the other folks at Norton who helped me pull the book together. In particular, Susan McColl did the copyediting on the third edition.

Social Problems

1

The Social Problems Process

The title of this book identifies its subject: social problems. But what are *social problems*? If asked, most people have no difficulty listing some examples: crime, suicide, racism, sexism, terrorism, climate change. Most people have a commonsense notion of what the term means, but actually defining the concept turns out to be much trickier.

Suppose we agree that suicide and climate change are both social problems. What, exactly, do the two have in common? They seem very different: we usually think of suicide as an extremely personal act, committed by individuals who feel isolated and in despair, whereas climate change involves physical warming across a whole planet. What sort of definition can cover both individual acts and global transformations?

TWO WAYS TO DEFINE SOCIAL PROBLEMS

Social Problems as Harmful Conditions: The Objectivist Outlook

The usual answer is to define social problems as conditions that somehow harm society. For example, another recent book that shares the title of this book, *Social Problems*, offers this definition: "A social problem is a condition that undermines the well-being of some or all members of a society and is usually a matter of public controversy" (Macionis, 2013, p. 5). In other words, some conditions have the characteristic of "undermining well-being" that makes them social problems. Although the precise wording of their definitions varies, most books on the topic characterize social problems as harmful conditions.

This approach to defining social problems is sometimes called **objectivist** because it tries to couch the definition in terms of objectively measurable characteristics of conditions. Once we define social problems as harmful conditions, we can look around until we spot a harmful condition and then identify it as a social problem. Most books titled *Social Problems* have chapters devoted to crime, racism, and other conditions that presumably have been objectively determined to be harmful.

Objectivist definitions seem fine—until we start to think about them. Then some problems with the objectivist approach become obvious. The first difficulty is that conditions that might be deemed harmful aren't always identified as social problems. Take sexism. Virtually all the books titled *Social Problems* and published in the United States in recent decades discuss sexism; it is widely understood to be a social problem. And yet, although social arrangements that discriminate against females have had a very long history, often they have been taken for granted, viewed as normal and natural—not at all a problem. Even today, many people around the world believe that their religions or traditions justify—even require—such discriminatory social arrangements. In fact, even American books about social problems published before 1970 rarely mentioned sexual discrimination. Only in recent decades has the term *sexism* emerged to refer to a form of discrimination seen as analogous to racism (which already was widely understood to be a social problem).

If we ask people to explain why racism is a social problem, they are likely to emphasize justice or fairness. It is, they will explain, unjust to discriminate against people simply because they belong to a particular race. Some may add that racism also harms society in that victims of racial discrimination are blocked from making all of the contributions they might make to the larger society, so that not only are those victims harmed, but the larger society is damaged because it misses out on what the victims could contribute; moreover, society is harmed further because racial tensions create conflict that makes the society less productive and harmonious. In other words, it is easy to argue that racism is a harmful condition and should be recognized as a social problem.

Obviously it is possible to make analogous arguments about sexism—that it is unfair, blocks women from fulfilling their potential, fosters conflict, and therefore harms the larger society. Thus, by objective standards, we might assume that racism and sexism should both be seen as social problems, although we know that— at other times or in other places—people have treated both racist and sexist practices as normal, even as the way things ought to be.

Note, however, that we might make essentially the same arguments about discrimination based on height. Studies show that taller people have various advantages; for example, they are more likely to be hired and more likely to be promoted. Thus, short people can be seen as victims of height discrimination (Rosenberg, 2009). Such discriminatory treatment also might be considered unfair, and ultimately harmful to society in much the same ways that racism and sexism are harmful. By objective standards, then, shouldn't "heightism" also be considered a social problem?

The first difficulty with objectivism becomes apparent: although we might argue that racism, sexism, and heightism all have analogous effects on society, as social problems these three forms of discrimination have not received anything like the same degree of attention. Racial discrimination has long been understood to be a serious social problem; sexism has only recently been added to the list of significant social problems; and heightism rarely receives mention as a social problem. As far as I know, no book about social problems includes a chapter about height discrimination. The different treatment of these three forms of discrimination makes it difficult to argue that there is an evenly applied objective standard for identifying what is or is not a social problem.

A second challenge to objectivism is that the same condition may be identified as a social problem for very different reasons; that is, people may disagree about why a certain condition is harmful. For example, some commentators argue that contemporary society discriminates against people who are overweight; heavier people find it more difficult to get jobs, are the objects of scorn, and so on. In this view, weight discrimination, like racial, gender, or—yes—height discrimination, should be considered a social problem because it is unjust and blocks some individuals from opportunities. More recently, however, attention has focused on obesity itself as a social problem. Here the argument is that heavier people are less healthy, and that obesity costs society many millions of dollars in additional health care expenditures. Critics taking this view consider obesity a social problem not because it leads to discrimination, but because it harms individuals and is a drain on societal resources (see Box 1.1).

Note that, although both arguments suggest that there is a social problem related to weight, they make very different claims: the former suggests that discrimination against overweight people is unfair (presumably, this position might lead to suggestions that society ought to become more tolerant of weight differences and that such discrimination should be discouraged); the latter views obesity itself as a source of harm (and would presumably lead to calls to reduce obesity). This example reveals a second problem with the objectivist view of social problems: very different—even contradictory—objective standards may be used in identifying a condition as a social problem.

Box 1.1 A Weighty Disagreement

Many Americans are heavy. Is this a social problem? If so, what exactly is the nature of this problem? Is it a discrimination/civil rights problem? Or is it a medical/public health problem?

The fat acceptance movement (led by the National Association to Advance Fat Acceptance) argues that weight is a form of diversity. In its view, fat people (to use the term the movement favors) are stigmatized; they are ridiculed and face discrimination in the workplace and elsewhere. Fat acceptance activists argue that this is a civil rights issue, that discrimination based on weight is no more justified than racial or gender bias. They point to research suggesting that people cannot control—and therefore should not be blamed for—their weight.

In contrast, many medical authorities and government officials warn that increases in Americans' average weight constitute an "obesity epidemic." They note that higher weight increases one's risks of heart disease and other medical problems, and that this has consequences, not only for the affected individuals who suffer more health problems, but for the larger society, which must bear the increased costs of medical treatment. In this view, obesity is a public health issue, analogous to smoking, and policies are needed to encourage citizens to maintain healthy weight.

These different views on obesity illustrate that even people who agree that a particular condition is a social problem may disagree about the sort of social problem it is.

Source: Saguy, 2013.

A third problem with objectivism has already been suggested: our lists of social problems include wildly diverse phenomena. They usually range from problems affecting particular individuals, such as suicide or mental illness, to global trends, such as overpopulation, globalization, or climate change. Any objective definition that tries to cover such a broad range of topics must be fairly vague, and speak in only the most general terms about harm, undermining well-being, or anything else. Although objectivists argue that social problems are harmful conditions, they don't specify what constitutes harm. Instead, harmfulness becomes a big conceptual umbrella, covering a huge array of phenomena, ranging from, say, the pain experienced by those who knew someone who committed suicide, through all of the economic and ecological costs that might be incurred as global temperatures rise. In practice, then, objective definitions of social problems turn out to be so vague as to be almost meaningless.

For all of these reasons, it is quite difficult to devise an objective definition of social problems that can distinguish between the things that people consider social problems and the things that they don't. So let's ask the question again: what, exactly, do suicide and climate change have in common? Once we think about it, we realize that there is really only one quality that all of the diverse phenomena considered social problems share: they are all considered social problems. The point is not so much that some conditions cause harm, but that people think of some conditions as being harmful.

Social Problems as Topics of Concern: The Subjectivist Outlook

Imagine two societies with arrangements that discriminate against women: in one, people consider these arrangements normal and natural; in the other, some people consider these arrangements wrong. From the point of view of the first society's members, sexism is not a social problem; some members of the second society, though, do regard sexism as a social problem. Of course, people's views may change. In recent decades, most Americans have come to view social arrangements that treat men and women differently as problematic, so even though sexism was formerly not considered a social problem, it has become one.

We might think of this as a **subjectivist** approach, in that it defines social problems in terms of people's subjective sense that something is or isn't a problem. If people don't think that heightism is a social problem, then it isn't one; but if height discrimination began receiving a lot of concerned attention, heightism could become a social problem. If people consider both suicide and climate change to be social problems, then both are.

Once we start thinking about social problems in terms of subjective judgments, we realize that people often disagree about what should be considered social problems. We might expect people of above-average height to dismiss arguments that height discrimination should be considered a social problem, and those of below-average height to be more receptive to those claims. Similarly, the views of individuals outside a society may differ from those of its members. When Americans criticize sexism in other countries, they are identifying a social problem, even if most of the occupants of those countries disagree. Remember, there is no objective standard that lets us declare, "X is a social problem, but Y is not." Rather, whether a condition is a social problem depends on different people's points of view—and they won't always agree.

In this view, social problems will come and go as people's subjective judgments change. Announcements of discoveries of a new disease or a new environmental threat can vault previously overlooked conditions onto people's lists of social problems. Other social problems fade away. For example, during the 1950s many commentators worried that young Americans were apathetic, but apathy stopped being considered a social problem during the 1960s, when campus demonstrations led critics to charge that students had become too concerned, too involved in political activity.

From the subjectivist outlook, it is not an objective quality of a social condition, but rather the subjective reactions to that condition, that make something a social problem. Therefore, social problems should not be viewed as a type of social condition, but as a *process* of responding to social conditions. Thus, we can define social problems as efforts to arouse concern about conditions within society. Or, to quote one influential definition, social problems are "the activities of individuals or groups making assertions of grievance and claims with respect to some putative conditions" (Spector & Kitsuse, 1977, p. 75). In other words, the study of social problems should focus not on conditions, but on claims about conditions.

At first glance, this approach may seem wrongheaded. If we're interested in, say, poverty, then shouldn't we be studying poverty as a condition? We might try to measure the number of poor people, determine the causes of poverty, and so on. In other words, shouldn't we adopt a more objectivist approach and focus on the condition of poverty, rather than on claims about poverty? Of course, it is possible to study poverty and other social conditions, and there is nothing wrong with doing so. But that has nothing to do with studying poverty *as a social problem*.

Studying poverty as a social problem requires asking how and why people came to consider poverty problematic. After all, poverty has been around for a long time; throughout history, many people in many societies have taken poverty for granted, seeing it as necessary, normal, even just. Some societies with very large populations of poor people have not viewed poverty as a social problem. In contrast, in the United States and many other modern societies, the widespread view is that poverty should be considered a social problem, and that we ought to do something about it. Studying poverty *as a social problem* requires studying how that view emerged and spread.

In other words, efforts to find a workable definition of social problems based on the objective characteristics of social conditions have proved futile. Thinking systematically about social problems requires adopting a subjectivist approach that focuses on the process by which people identify social problems. That process involves what sociologists call *social construction*.

SOCIAL CONSTRUCTION

By **social construction**, we mean the way people assign meaning to the world. People use language; language is essential to our understanding of the world that surrounds us (just try thinking without using words). One of the principal accomplishments of infancy and early childhood is learning to recognize, understand, and use words. Through language, we learn to categorize the world, to understand that some things are edible (*food*) while others are dangerous and must not be eaten (*poison*), and so on. This is obviously a social process: we do not invent our language; rather, we learn to use the language of our parents and the other people around us. The meanings of their words—their categories for classifying the world—are the ones that we learn. Children grow up speaking English, or Spanish, or whatever language the people in the group around them speak, and they learn to assign that group's meanings to the world.

Language is flexible: as people learn new things about the world, they devise words with new meanings. In this way, people continually create—or construct—fresh understandings about the world around them. Because this is a social process, sociologists refer to it as *social construction* (Berger & Luckmann, 1966).

Sociologists do not view social construction as a completely arbitrary process; it is constrained by the physical world within which people find themselves. We can imagine all sorts of ridiculous meanings that people might, in theory, construct. For instance, an imaginary society might, in theory, teach its young that rocks are edible, or that people can fly by flapping their arms, but this is hardly likely. Although this could happen, it probably wouldn't, because those lessons would prove worthless, even dangerous. In general, the meanings people construct need to make sense of the world they inhabit.

The point is not that people could assign ridiculous meanings to the world, but rather that they must assign some meanings to at least some of their surroundings. Probably every human society throughout history has categorized people as either male or female. The distinction is relatively clear-cut: we can look at virtually any newborn infant and confidently declare that it falls into one category or the other. If this doesn't seem to be a social process, remember that a tiny fraction of infants (about one in every thousand) are born with anomalous sexual organs that do challenge the simple male/female classification, and societies have to decide how to deal with those cases (Feder, 2014). These individuals, once called hermaphrodites but now termed *intersex*, pose challenges to simplistic male/female categories. There are various solutions: Many Native American societies defined these individuals as having a special status as *two-spirits*—a sort of third sex outside the standard male/female divide. By contrast, in contemporary America surgeons often "correct" the anomalies, to give the infant either a male or a female appearance, and foster an unambiguous gender identity, while some critics oppose this practice as depriving individuals of their right to be intersex.

This example reminds us that even something as apparently straightforward as sorting people into males and females is a social process of constructing meanings. Note, too, that the precise meanings assigned to these categories—the qualities attributed to males or females—vary from one society to another. Both the two-category male/female classification and the specific qualities associated with each category are instances of social construction. All meanings, including how we designate planets in the solar system and all other elements in the physical world, are socially constructed (see Box 1.2).

Sociologists sometimes illustrate social construction by pointing to problems that seem ridiculous. These examples offer a sort of analytic leverage: they lay bare the process of social construction. Witch hunts are a favorite historical example; UFO abductions and satanic ritual abuse offer more contemporary cases. Critics might argue that there is no convincing evidence that witches, UFOs, or child-abusing satanists exist (ignore, for the moment, those people

BOX 1.2   PLUTO: A PLANETARY PROBLEM?

For decades, schoolchildren learned that there were nine planets, but that changed in 2006, when astronomers demoted Pluto from the list, reclassifying it as a *dwarf planet*. Pluto is unlike the other planets in several ways: (1) It is much smaller. (2) It has a different composition; the four inner planets (Mercury, Venus, Earth, and Mars) are basically rocks, and the four giant planets (Jupiter, Saturn, Uranus, and Neptune) are composed of gas, but Pluto is basically a big lump of ice. (3) It has a less circular, more elliptical orbit than the other planets, so sometimes it is closer to the Sun than Neptune is. And (4), unlike the other eight planets, whose orbits fall more or less along the same plane, Pluto has an orbit that is at an angle to that plane.

No one denies that Pluto exists; the question is whether it makes more sense to classify it as a planet or as belonging to a different category. When Ceres—the largest asteroid—was discovered in 1801, it was initially considered a planet, but astronomers dropped that classification once they realized that there were many asteroids. Now Ceres joins Pluto in the new category of dwarf planet. These examples remind us that *planet* is a social construction, a category that people use to assign meaning to the world. Our words are social products: we create them and teach them to one another. Because we understand our world through language, sociologists view all knowledge as socially constructed.

Source: Tyson, 2009.

who remain convinced that these are real phenomena). Therefore, the sociologists declare, witchcraft, UFOs, and satanic blood cults are clearly social constructions.

This conclusion is true, but its implication is quite false. UFO abductions are a social construction, in the sense that this term was created and disseminated by people. But the implication—that only unprovable claims are socially constructed—is wrong. Poverty is just as much a social construction as UFO abductions are.

The term *poverty* is another category that people have created to make sense of the world. Just as some people have drawn attention to UFO abductions, others have campaigned to raise concern about poverty (during the 1960s, for example, President Lyndon Johnson declared "war on poverty"). Saying that poverty is a social construction does not mean that poverty doesn't exist, that it somehow doesn't occur in the real world; obviously some people have much less money than others. But the words we choose to describe those people (*impoverished*, for instance, rather than *wretched* or *depraved*—terms that were once used to describe the poor), how we explain their condition, and what we recommend doing about it are meanings that people create and use. In that sense, poverty—like everything else we know about—is a social construction.

Once we recognize that social problems are social constructions, and that what the conditions constructed as social problems have in common is precisely that construction, then it becomes apparent that social problems should be understood in terms of a **social problems process**. That is, the study of social problems should focus on how and why particular conditions come to be constructed as social problems. How and why did poverty—or UFO abductions—emerge as topics of interest and concern at particular moments, and in particular places? Why do people decide that something needs to be done about some conditions, and how do they decide exactly what should be done? This approach to studying social problems is called **constructionist**, and it is the perspective adopted in this book.

THE BASIC FRAMEWORK

The constructionist approach requires understanding a few basic terms. These will reappear throughout the chapters that follow. The first is **claim**. Constructing a social problem involves a process of **claimsmaking**: someone must bring the topic to the attention of others by making a claim that there is a condition that should be recognized as troubling, that needs to be addressed. For constructionist sociologists, social problems are defined in terms of this claimsmaking process, because it is claimsmaking—and only claimsmaking—that all social problems have in common. Note that claims may be supported by very different sorts of evidence: someone making claims about poverty might present poverty statistics, photographs of poor people, or all manner of other evidence; claims about UFO abductions tend to rely on first-person accounts by people who say they recall having been abducted. Whether other people find a claim convincing is a separate issue. At one extreme, we can imagine a claim that no one finds convincing: picture a man standing on a street corner warning passersby that invisible, undetectable aliens from planet Zorax have infested the very air that they're breathing. This may be a claim, but if everyone who hears it dismisses or ignores it, it will have no impact. The social problems process requires not only that someone make a claim, but that others react to it.

The people who make claims are, of course, **claimsmakers**. They are the ones who seek to convince others that something is wrong, and that something should be done about it. Obviously not all claimsmakers are equal: we tend to treat some claims more seriously, simply because they seem more plausible, or because they are promoted by people we respect—experts, officials, and so on. Successful claims spread, so that they become the subject of media coverage and debates over public policy.

These few concepts—claim, claimsmaking, and claimsmaker—provide a foundation on which we can build a more elaborate analysis of the social problems process. Throughout this book, we will distinguish between claims and the conditions about which claims are being made. We will refer to **troubling conditions**—that is, the conditions that become subjects of claims. The word *troubling* focuses our attention on people's subjective reactions: a condition is troubling if it bothers someone. Note that it isn't necessary for everyone to accept the claim; some people may consider UFO abductions troubling, even though others regard such claims as fantastic. We can consider both poverty and UFO abductions troubling conditions, regardless of whether we agree that they both exist.

Adopting a subjectivist stance can seem confusing at first. In particular, two sorts of confusion arise. We have already discussed the first: people sometimes wrongly imagine that *social construction* refers only to imaginary, nonexistent phenomena. Again, this is wrong—all human knowledge is socially constructed through our language, which means that all social problems are socially constructed.

The second source of confusion is that we must acknowledge that sociologists are themselves engaged in social construction. Like all other people, sociologists must use language to make the world meaningful; they devise their own categories—such as *claims* and *claimsmakers*—that they use to classify the world. This book, for instance, can be understood as a set of sociological claims about the social problems process.

Some people worry that, if sociology is one more social construction, we can't really have confidence in sociological knowledge. The response, of course, is that we can have exactly the same sort of confidence in sociology that we have in our other sorts of knowledge. When we encounter claims in everyday life—when someone gives us a compliment, politicians ask for our votes, or advertisers try to sell us their products—we neither accept everything we hear at face value nor assume that it is all meaningless. Rather, we learn to evaluate claims, to look for evidence, and so on. Similarly, sociologists can offer support for their arguments, and this book will try to suggest the nature of that support. (For more detailed discussions of various theoretical and methodological aspects of the constructionist approach, see Harris, 2010; Holstein & Gubrium, 2008; Loseke, 2003; Weinberg, 2014).

THE PLAN OF THE BOOK: THE NATURAL
HISTORY OF SOCIAL PROBLEMS

To understand the approach that this book takes toward social problems, it may help to begin with a familiar example from U.S. history: the 1960s civil rights movement against segregation. After World War II, the southern states retained customs and laws maintaining racial segregation: African Americans were blocked from voting; intermarriage was illegal; whites and blacks attended different schools; and other institutions were segregated so that the races ate in different restaurants, sat in different sections on buses, and used racially separate restrooms and drinking fountains. Organized protests against this system of segregation became more common; in particular, the 1955–56 bus boycott in Montgomery, Alabama, brought national attention to the leadership of the Reverend Martin Luther King Jr.

By the early 1960s, there were numerous civil rights organizations—including King's Southern Christian Leadership Conference (SCLC), the Congress of Racial Equality (CORE), and the Student Nonviolent Coordinating Committee (SNCC, pronounced "snick")—leading marches, boycotts, freedom rides, voter registration campaigns, and other sorts of protests. Television news programs showed dramatic scenes of police beating and arresting protesters, and public opinion—particularly outside the South—increasingly sympathized with the civil rights campaign. In 1963, the great March on Washington called for congressional action, and Congress eventually passed the Civil Rights Act of 1964 and the Voting Rights Act of 1965. By the end of the 1960s, segregation in the South had generally lost its legal standing, although of course other forms of racial inequality remained.

We can use the story of the civil rights movement's campaign against segregation to illustrate a more general phenomenon: the natural history of a social problem. The term **natural history** refers to a sequence of stages that tends to appear in lots of different cases.

While the term originally referred to observational studies of the lives of plants and animals, it has been adopted by sociologists who study social processes. Figure 1.1 diagrams the natural history of the social problems process.

This natural history identifies six stages: claimsmaking, media coverage, public reaction, policymaking, social problems work, and policy outcomes. The figure sketches a general framework. Describing a natural history helps us organize our thinking about a typical social problems process, although not every instance of social problems construction will fit this model. In fact, other sociologists have offered different natural histories of the social problems process (see Blumer, 1971; Spector & Kitsuse, 1977). Figure 1.1 is a simplified diagram intended to give an overview of what is actually a much more complicated process. In later chapters, we will expand this diagram to consider some of those complexities, but this version gives us a starting point.

Stage One: Claimsmaking

The first stage in Figure 1.1 concerns claimsmaking. During this stage, claimsmakers make claims; that is, they argue that a particular troubling condition ought to be recognized as a social problem, and that someone ought to do something about that problem. In the case of the civil rights movement, the claimsmakers were the social movement activists and demonstrators who protested against the system of racial segregation. We can distinguish between claimsmakers and their claims. *Claims* are arguments, efforts to persuade others that something is wrong, that there is a problem that needs to be solved. For example, the civil rights movement claimed that racial segregation was wrong, that it was unjust, and violated the basic American belief in equality. The social problems process always begins with claims, so we will begin this book by exploring various aspects of claims in Chapter 2.

Typically we think of claimsmakers as **activists**, members of social movement organizations such as the civil rights movement's

Figure 1.1 BASIC NATURAL HISTORY MODEL OF THE SOCIAL PROBLEMS PROCESS

Claimsmaking →	Media Coverage →	Public Reaction →	Policymaking →	Social Problems Work →	Policy Outcomes
People make claims that there is a social problem, with certain characteristics, causes, and solutions.	Media report on claimsmakers so that news of the claims reaches a broader audience.	Public opinion focuses on the social problem identified by the claimsmakers.	Lawmakers and others with the power to set policies create new ways to address the problem.	Agencies implement the new policies, including calls for further changes.	There are various responses to the new arrangements.
Example: Civil rights activists, such as Martin Luther King Jr., call for an end to racial segregation in the South, hold marches and demonstrations.	**Example:** Reporters from newspapers and television describe the conflict over the civil rights campaign.	**Example:** People become more concerned about racial segregation and more supportive of the campaign against it.	**Example:** Congress passes the Civil Rights Act of 1964 and the Voting Rights Act of 1965.	**Example:** Under the new federal laws, states and localities are forced to end formal policies of racial segregation.	**Example:** People call for additional changes to reduce racism, as well as campaigns to promote the rights of women and other groups.

SCLC, CORE, or SNCC. Lots of people want to make claims, but it is often hard to get others to pay attention. Activists must devise ways of drawing attention to their cause; civil rights demonstrators conducted sit-ins, boycotts, freedom rides, and marches as ways of attracting notice. Activists also need to recruit people to join their movement, manage the movement's operations, and maintain interest in their cause. Chapter 3 examines the role of activists as claimsmakers, as well as some of the challenges that social movements confront.

Not all claimsmakers are social movement activists. Claims also come from various sorts of **experts**, such as physicians, scientists, lawyers, and officials. These people claim to speak with special authority because they have special knowledge; for example, scientists may have done research that shows the nature or extent of a particular troubling social condition, or lawyers may argue that the law related to the condition needs to be reinterpreted. During the civil rights movement, for example, social scientists and psychiatrists claimed that segregation had harmful consequences, while lawyers devised strategies to challenge segregation in the courts. Many societies grant authority to those seen as having special, expert knowledge; Chapter 4 considers how experts can use their authority as claimsmakers.

Stage Two: Media Coverage

The second stage shown in Figure 1.1 is media coverage. Claimsmakers often seek such coverage to bring their claims to the attention of a wider audience. The nature of the media may change—from stories and photographs printed in newspapers and magazines, or reports broadcast on radio and television news programs, to social media and the endless array of sites on the Internet—but they all offer forums that can make both the public and policymakers more aware of claims. Civil rights demonstrators depended on this reporting; traditionally it had been easy for Americans outside the South to ignore segregation, but dramatic clashes between protesters and police created major news stories that focused national attention on civil rights. The media face practical considerations that affect how they address social problems, and media coverage inevitably reshapes claims. This is the topic of Chapter 5.

Stage Three: Public Reaction

The general public, then, learns about claims either directly from claimsmakers or indirectly through media reports. The public's response to these claims forms the third stage in Figure 1.1. Usually efforts to understand the public's reactions involve public opinion polls that seek to measure people's attitudes. In some cases, claimsmaking can have dramatic effects on public opinion; during the civil rights movement, for instance, polls indicated an increase in the proportion of Americans who considered civil rights a major problem, and who disapproved of the South's segregation policies. Such shifts are considered important in a democracy because voters may elect officials who reflect their changed views. Chapter 6 looks at polling, as well as other, less traditional ways of understanding the public's reactions.

Stage Four: Policymaking

The fourth stage in Figure 1.1's natural history is **policymaking**. Social policies are the means that society adopts to address troubling conditions, and such policies can be made in various ways. Most obviously, laws can be changed, as when Congress passed and President Johnson signed the Civil Rights Act of 1964 and the Voting Rights Act of 1965—the principal federal responses to the civil rights movement (over time, state legislatures and local city councils also had to modify their laws regarding segregation). But legislation is not the only form of policymaking; all sorts of bodies set social policies: government agencies establish standards for, say, clean water; schools create dress codes for their students; and so on. Policymakers respond to claimsmakers, media coverage, and public opinion, but their own considerations also shape the policies they create. Policymaking is the focus of Chapter 7.

Stage Five: Social Problems Work

Declaring that there will be a new social policy is not the end of the matter; policies have to be implemented, carried out by police officers, social workers, teachers—whoever is responsible for enforcing the particular policy. This is **social problems work**—the fifth stage in Figure 1.1. Often claimsmakers, the media, the public, and policymakers discuss social issues in fairly abstract, theoretical terms: here's what's wrong, and this is what ought to be done. In contrast, social problems workers confront these issues as practical matters. They must deal with particular cases and address a messy real world that often seems quite complicated. For example, civil rights laws had to be translated into specific enforcement practices. It is one thing to say, for instance, that an all-white police force should be integrated, but even if everyone agrees on that principle, people may disagree about practical details regarding how officers should be selected. Chapter 8 tackles the complexities of social problems work.

Stage Six: Policy Outcomes

The sixth and final stage in Figure 1.1 is **policy outcomes**, reactions to the social problems process. Several sorts of outcomes are possible. Some relate directly to the ways in which social policies are implemented. Critics may argue that the new policies are ineffective—that they don't do enough to address the troubling condition, or that the policies actually cause new problems, even making things worse. For instance, the federal civil rights laws passed in the 1960s have been criticized for not going far enough; even though the formal system of legal segregation was dismantled, all sorts of racial inequality remained (thus, blacks continue to have

lower incomes, shorter life expectancies, and so on). Other critics may argue that a policy goes too far, as with charges that the
affirmative action policies that emerged from the civil rights movement themselves create unequal arrangements. There may be efforts
to measure the policy's impact, to evaluate its effectiveness, but how
should effectiveness be judged? Often such complaints and questions lead to new claims, and the social problems process begins
anew. Such reactions to social policies are the topic of Chapter 9.

In contrast, Chapter 10 explores a broader set of outcomes
that often extend over time and space. Consider the impact of the
civil rights movement. The dramatic, heavily publicized campaign
against segregation inspired other claimsmakers, both within the
United States and around the world. Civil rights activists learned
valuable practical lessons about how to organize a social movement, attract media coverage for their cause, and so on. Veterans of
civil rights protests began to apply their new skills in other social
movements, becoming involved in protests over the war in Vietnam or campaigns to advance women's rights or gay and lesbian
rights. Claimsmakers in other nations also tried to duplicate the
success of the American civil rights movement by organizing protests over troubling conditions in their own countries. In addition
to examining how claims spread, Chapter 10 considers cycles in
claimsmaking—a pattern in which claims rise to attract a good deal
of attention, then recede, before rising again years later.

Finally, Chapter 11 uses the discussion of Chapters 2 through 10
to revisit Figure 1.1 and develop a more elaborate natural history
of the social problems process. Chapter 11 also discusses the uses
and future of the constructionist approach.

ADDITIONAL THEMES

Chapters 2 through 11 are organized according to the natural history model illustrated in Figure 1.1. In general, we will discuss
topics in the order in which they occur in the social problems

Figure 1.2 RESOURCES AND RHETORIC AFFECT EACH STAGE OF THE
SOCIAL PROBLEMS PROCESS

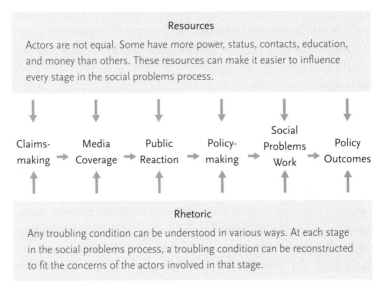

process; this is the book's central organizing principle. In addition, two other themes will run through every chapter: resources and rhetoric. As Figure 1.2 suggests, these themes influence each stage in the social problems process.

Resources

The first theme concerns the **resources** that people bring to the social problems process. A society's members are not equal; some have more money than others, or more power, more status, more education, more social contacts, and so on. These are resources that people can draw on in the social problems process. We will discover that each stage in Figure 1.1 involves competition: claimsmakers compete to attract attention to their claims, claims compete for media coverage and attention from the public and policymakers, and so on. At each stage in the social problems process, some claims succeed in moving to the next stage, while others fail to attract much notice. History is filled with claims that never attracted many adherents, and were ignored, dismissed, or discredited.

Resources affect this competition. In general, people with more money, power, and other resources find it easier to have their claims heard. The resources available to major corporate leaders give them considerable influence over social policy; they have money to spend on political contributions that allow them and their lobbyists access to policymakers. In contrast, the story of the civil rights movement is inspiring precisely because most African Americans living under segregation had such limited resources; they had relatively little in the way of money or political influence, yet they mounted a campaign that successfully changed social policy. At every stage in the social problems process, inequality—whether based on race, class, gender, or something else—means that people bring different resources to the process. It is much easier for those with ample resources to make claims and get them heard, than it is for those with fewer resources.

Rhetoric

The second theme that runs through each chapter is rhetoric. **Rhetoric** is the study of persuasion. Social problems construction is inevitably rhetorical. Whenever people make claims, they are trying to convince others that something is a problem, that it is a problem of a particular sort, and that specific action needs to be taken to deal with this problem. These arguments evolve with each stage in the social problems process; that is, every problem is constructed and reconstructed. Even people who are allied in a claimsmaking campaign may adopt different rhetoric; the claims of activists and experts often emphasize different elements. The media, when they cover claimsmaking campaigns, reshape claims to fit their needs, just as the public's awareness of social problems tends to emphasize some aspects and downplay others. Similarly, when policymakers try to devise means of addressing troubling conditions, they, too, offer their own constructions of what is at issue. And when social problems workers try to implement policies, the practical requirements of their tasks lead them to focus on particular aspects—yet another reconstruction. Finally, at the stage of policy outcomes, there are likely to be all sorts of reinterpretations of previous claims and the policies they inspired.

Rhetoric involves appeals to emotions, as well as appeals to reason. Claimsmakers try to elicit emotional reactions, such as horror or sympathy, to get people to share their concerns, and of course much media coverage encourages the audience to feel outrage or compassion. Throughout the social problems process, people invoke feelings, as well as ideas, to convince others to share their views. Thus, rhetoric is a central theme in the chapters that follow because social problems claims are not static; rather they shift and morph at each stage in the larger social problems process as the rhetoric changes.

The themes of resources and rhetoric remind us that the social problems process occurs within a broader structural and cultural context. Existing social structural arrangements—resources—give some actors advantages in claimsmaking; having more money or more power makes it easier to promote particular constructions. At the same time, the larger culture makes particular claims—rhetoric—more or less compelling. At each stage in the social problems process, then, actors compete to devise claims that others will find persuasive.

Feedback

Finally, there is a third theme that both Figure 1.1 and Figure 1.2 overlook. These diagrams oversimplify the social problems process. In both, the arrows between stages of the social problems process point in only one direction; that is, claimsmaking is shown as affecting media coverage, media coverage in turn shapes public reaction, and so on. In fact, the social problems process is more complicated, involving a great deal of **feedback**. That is, claimsmaking does affect media coverage, but claimsmakers are also affected by that coverage (for example, if the press ignored a civil rights demonstration in the 1950s and '60s, activists knew that they needed to adjust what they were doing, in order to attract better coverage for future demonstrations). Similar feedback processes can occur at every stage in the social problems process because the actors at the various stages—the claimsmakers, people who work in the media, and so on—don't just act, but also pay attention to how others react to what they have done, and then respond to those reactions by adjusting what they're doing.

At several points in the book we will consider more elaborate diagrams that illustrate some of these feedback processes; in addition, Chapter 11 will discuss feedback processes in more detail. Remember, Figure 1.1 is designed to help us start thinking about the social problems process; it is by no means the last word.

SUMMARY

This book explores the constructionist approach to social problems. Rather than assuming that social problems are conditions that share some objectively defined characteristic, it defines social problems as a process of raising subjective concerns. This process follows a typical course, a natural history that provides a framework for the rest of the book.

The chapters that follow will focus on specific stages in the social problems process. Taken together, these chapters develop a general framework for thinking about the construction of social problems. The chapters contain many brief mentions of examples that illustrate whatever principle is being discussed. In addition, each chapter features several boxes (somewhat more detailed discussions of how a specific theme in the text is related to a particular social problem), and each chapter ends with a longer case study that explores how the ideas developed in that chapter can be applied to a particular case. Of course, all of these examples are merely illustrative. The goal of this book is to give you a better way of thinking about whatever social problems strike you as interesting.

MAKING CONNECTIONS

- *A social constructionist approach to social problems focuses on the process by which people identify social problems.*

- *As you read the upcoming chapters on claims and claimsmaking, keep in mind how claimsmakers use rhetoric to convince others that a troubling condition is a social problem.*

- *In Chapter 10 you will learn how claims about troubling conditions change depending on the time period and geographic location.*

2

▦

Claims

▦

Anyone who follows the news cannot help but hear claims about new social problems. Stories on news websites announce that doctors have identified a new disease, or that scientists have discovered a new environmental threat. Television commentators warn that a dangerous new drug is spreading, or that law enforcement is battling a new crime. Bloggers discuss new problems brought on by technological developments or changing lifestyles.

Often the new problem has a catchy name, such as *road rage*, *the digital divide*, *human trafficking*, or *racial profiling*. Suddenly, the brand-new term seems to be on everyone's lips. In many cases, interest in the new problem will prove to be short-lived; people will worry about it for a time, but then their attention will wander. But other terms—think of *sexism*, which first entered the language around 1970—seem to take up permanent residence in our society's vocabulary and consciousness, and the problems they identify remain topics of concern.

Constructing a new social problem involves making claims— that is, calling attention to a troubling condition. Claims are the first element in the social problems process, and they are this chapter's focus. After examining the basic structure of claims, we will consider how audiences respond to them, how they evolve, and where they fit in the larger culture.

THE RHETORIC OF CLAIMS

Every social problems claim makes a persuasive argument; it is an effort to persuade others, to convince them that a particular troubling condition ought to be recognized as a social problem, that that problem has certain characteristics, that the problem demands attention, and that it should be addressed in a specific way. When we analyze claims as arguments or statements, it matters less whether the claims are true or false than whether the people who make the claims and the audiences for those claims find the reasoning convincing.

One of the lessons of this chapter is that claims tend to take standard forms, because people who share a culture are likely to find the same sorts of arguments persuasive. Claims need to be tailored to their audiences, but of course the people who make claims usually belong to the same society as their audience, so when they devise claims that they themselves find sensible, those claims are likely to persuade their audiences. For example, members of a highly religious society may find claims based on theological reasoning compelling, whereas members of another society may be more likely to be swayed by scientific evidence. As a result, within a given society, even claims about very different problems tend to be structured in similar ways. This means that a claim you find utterly convincing will probably contain persuasive elements that resemble those in a claim you consider completely unreasonable. Keep in mind that our topic is how claims work, and understanding this does not require knowing whether the claims are, in fact, true.

The study of persuasion is called *rhetoric*, and we can analyze the rhetoric of claims. Persuasive arguments share a rhetorical structure with three fundamental components: grounds, warrants, and

Figure 2.1 THE STRUCTURE OF SOCIAL PROBLEMS CLAIMS

Grounds ──────────────────────────────────▶ Conclusions

Information and
evidence about the
troubling condition—
typifying examples,
statistics, etc. (Also
called the *diagnostic
frame.*)

Warrants

Justifications, appeals
to values—reasons why
something must be
done about the
troubling condition.
(Also called the
motivational frame.)

Recommended
changes, new policies,
etc. to address the
problem. (Also called
the *prognostic frame.*)

Sources: J. Best, 1990; Snow & Benford, 1988; Toulmin, 1958.

conclusions (J. Best, 1990; Toulmin, 1958). In social problems
claims, *grounds* are statements about the nature of the problem, *warrants* justify taking action, and *conclusions* explain what that action
should be. Figure 2.1 illustrates the connections among grounds,
warrants, and conclusions. We will consider each in turn.

Grounds

Every social problems claim begins by identifying a troubling condition. Two sorts of statements are involved: those describing the
condition and those explaining why it should be considered trou-
blesome. The former are the grounds; the latter are the warrants
(discussed in the next section).

The Basic Rhetorical Recipe. A claim's **grounds** usually are assertions of fact; that is, they argue that the condition exists and offer
supporting evidence. Claims in the contemporary United States

often establish their grounds by following a rhetorical recipe containing three ingredients:

1. *Typifying example.* Claims often begin with a **typifying example**, a description of a particular instance of the condition. Typifying examples are, in fact, rarely typical. Usually they are chosen to illustrate the seriousness of the problem, so they tend to be especially extreme, dramatic, disturbing, memorable cases. For instance, claims about child abuse might start with an atrocity story, a description of a very young child who was beaten to death (J. Johnson, 1995). This would not be a typical case; most child abuse is not fatal. However, using a child's death to typify abuse is compelling rhetoric; the example characterizes the problem in melodramatic terms, in that it depicts a vulnerable, innocent youngster being menaced by a more powerful, villainous adult. This example suggests that child abuse is a very serious problem, because it can involve real, terrible harm. Because the example is so disturbing, people are likely to pay attention, to start worrying about innocent children being threatened by this evil.

2. *Name.* Next the claim **names** the problem. The fatal beating in our example will be transformed from a horrific *incident* to an *instance* of the larger problem of child abuse (J. Best, 1999). Sometimes a new name is attached to an old behavior: bad driving has long been a familiar problem, but calling it *road rage* is a relatively recent development. In other cases, both the name and the troubling condition are new; *sexting* could not exist before technology made it possible. Note that naming a problem is not the same as defining it. Many claimsmakers avoid defining a problem by instead focusing on typifying examples. In spite of all the attention that *child abuse* and *road rage* have received in the media, it can be very difficult to find precise definitions of either term in that coverage. Rather, the people who make up the audience for these claims probably assume that they understand the nature of these problems because they are familiar with one or more typifying examples.

3. **Statistic.** A third ingredient in the basic recipe that establishes the grounds for many claims is some sort of **statistic**, a number that suggests the scope of the problem. In our child abuse example, we might be told that authorities receive nearly three million reports of suspected child abuse annually. In contemporary American culture, statistics imply accuracy and precision—that someone must have counted something. In practice, this is not necessarily true. When claimsmakers are first trying to draw attention to a social problem, they often argue that this problem has been neglected or overlooked. But if people have been ignoring a particular social condition, they probably haven't been carefully measuring its extent, which means no one has been keeping accurate statistics. As a result, early claims often feature figures that are ballpark estimates or educated guesses (J. Best, 2013). And just as claimsmakers favor dramatic typifying examples, they usually prefer big numbers, statistics that suggest that the problem is widespread, because a big number implies there is a big problem. Particularly at the beginning of the social problems process, claims often feature big numbers that are really little more than rough estimates.

The three ingredients in the basic rhetorical recipe—a disturbing typifying example, a name, and a big number—combine to create a troubling impression. For example, a description of a small child being beaten to death, coupled with both an explanation that this death is just one instance of the larger problem of child abuse and a statement that three million cases of suspected abuse are reported each year, conveys a sense that millions of children are in danger—possibly of losing their lives. This basic recipe offers a quick, compelling case for recognizing a new social problem. It is an effective rhetorical formula, one that can be spotted in many social problems claims (see Box 2.1).

Additional Grounds. Claims often feature grounds beyond the basic recipe's three ingredients. Many different rhetorical devices

Box 2.1 The Basic Recipe: Grounds for Viewing
Prescription Painkillers as a Social Problem

A *Time* magazine cover story began by describing a conversation between a conservative Midwestern governor and the sheriff of a rural county where HIV had been spreading rapidly. The spread was caused by residents who had become addicted to prescription painkillers; they were dissolving the pills and using shared needles to inject them. The governor—on record as opposing needle-exchange programs—agreed to issue an emergency order to establish needle exchanges. This typifying example suggested that a new form of drug addiction was spreading in an unusual place (the rural Midwest) among an unusual population (middle-aged, middle-class people).

There were multiple drugs involved (the story featured a list of seven common opioids "with a similar chemical structure to heroin"). These were subsumed under the label *prescription painkillers* so that addiction to any of these drugs could be understood to be part of the same problem.

The story characterized the problem as "a national epidemic." It supported this characterization with statistics: "2.1 million are estimated by the National Institutes of Health to be hooked"; and "an average of 46 Americans die every day from prescription-opioid overdoses." Thus, within the story's initial paragraphs, readers were given a disturbing typifying example, a name for the problem, and numbers affirming that problem's importance.

Source: Calabresi, 2015.

can appear as grounds in social problems claims; what follows is just a sampling.

- *Worsening situation.* Very often, claims insist that the problem is getting worse. Words like *epidemic* and *crime wave* convey a sense of urgency: the problem is spreading, and—unless something is done—it may soon spiral out of control.

● *Familiar type of problem.* Claims often categorize a problem as being of a recognizable type, such as a crime or a disease. These types are characterized by familiar patterns: we think of crime as being perpetrated by a criminal who intentionally preys on an innocent victim, and diseases as striking vulnerable individuals who should not be considered responsible for getting sick. When a claim classifies the new problem as belonging to a particular type, the claim's audience immediately has a sense of how to think about the problem.

● *Kinds of people involved.* Most claims identify categories of people involved in the troubling condition, and explain how their involvement should be understood (Loseke, 2003). Among the most common person categories are *victims* (those harmed by the problem, who may be characterized as bearing no responsibility for their plight, and therefore meriting society's support and sympathy) and *villains* (those responsible for the problem, usually depicted as deserving blame and punishment). Typifying examples often illustrate the principal categories of people involved in the troubling condition (such as an innocent, abused child and an abusive parent).

● *Range of people affected.* Another popular ground for claims is the suggestion that the problem affects a broad range of people— rich and poor, white and black, and so on. Sometimes it is argued that the problem strikes "randomly" (J. Best, 1999). Of course, if a problem strikes at random, then it might affect anyone, including anyone listening to the claim. Such randomness suggests that each person who hears the claim has a personal interest in doing something to deal with the problem—before it affects him or her.

● *Challenge to older interpretations.* Claims also may challenge existing or alternative interpretations of the social problem. For instance, students who don't do well in school traditionally were held responsible for their poor performance, which was attributed to their inattention, lack of discipline or effort, and so on. But recent decades have featured claims about learning disabilities, arguing that many students should not be blamed because their poor performance is due to biologically based learning disabilities that deserve accommodation (Conrad, 2007). Such claims challenge older, more familiar constructions. These challenges may be quite explicit; claims may list—and debunk—what they describe as "myths," widely held beliefs about the problem that the claim dismisses as wrong. For example, claims that seek to reconstruct the problem of rape criticize "rape myths" for distorting people's thinking about that crime (Suarez & Gadalla, 2010).

Again, these are just a few of the many kinds of grounds statements found in claims. Taken together, a claim's grounds give a sense of the problem—its nature, scope, and future prospects. Effective grounds convince listeners that the condition is real, thereby setting the stage for the claim's warrants.

Warrants

A claim's **warrants** justify doing something about the troubling condition; they explain why something *ought* to be done. Warrants invoke values and emotions. That is, warrants argue that the condition identified in the grounds is inconsistent with what we value, and therefore we need to do something about it. Thus, claims suggest that the troubling condition violates our sense of justice, fairness, equality, or other values; in turn, we may experience anger, pity, or other emotional reactions.

Values tend to be expressed as vague principles that most— if not all—people can endorse. Most Americans can be expected to hold freedom, justice, equality, protecting the vulnerable, and humanitarianism as cherished values. But what does this mean in practice? It is not always clear how abstract values apply in real-world situations. It is not unusual for opponents in debates over social issues to endorse the same values, even as they support opposing policies. Thus, both those who favor and those who oppose restricting access to abortion tend to invoke *rights*: pro-life abortion opponents speak of the "unborn child's right to life," while pro-choice abortion advocates speak of a "woman's right to choose." Similarly, those who favor affirmative action argue that affirmative action programs foster equality by giving advantages to those who have been disadvantaged, yet affirmative action opponents insist that the programs subvert equality because they don't treat everyone evenhandedly. Although virtually all Americans can be expected to affirm their beliefs in rights or equality, obviously they can disagree over how those abstract values should be translated into practical policies.

Warrants rise and fall in popularity. Sometimes new warrants—new ways of justifying claims—emerge, and change how social problems are characterized. For example, in recent years the rising costs of medical care have inspired a new warrant: arguments that some troubling conditions need to be addressed because they create costly health care burdens for the larger society. For instance, laws requiring motorcycle riders to wear protective helmets have been justified by the high costs of providing long-term medical care to head injury patients, just as campaigns to restrict smoking and reduce obesity have emphasized how those conditions add many millions of dollars to the nation's medical costs.

Warrants based on medical costs seem to have emerged to counter arguments that defended motorcycle riding and other risky activities using another, older warrant: personal freedom. That is, motorcycle riders, smokers, and overweight individuals have long argued that they ought to have the freedom to make their own choices, even if those choices involve risks. American culture generally considers freedom an important warrant, particularly if the person taking the risks is not harming others. Using medical costs as a warrant tries to counter this older defense based on individual liberty by arguing that helmetless motorcycle riders and other risk takers are not just endangering themselves, but are also harming everyone else, in that their risky behavior raises health care costs across the board, and society has a right to try to discourage people from taking such costly risks.

Because people can be strongly attached to particular values, and because claims need to be compelling, claims' warrants often inspire powerful emotional reactions, such as outrage, shock, sadness, or guilt. Effective claims move people to take action. While it may be possible to assemble a claim that relies on bloodless cost–benefit reasoning to convince people that it is in their best interest to respond to a social problem, it is often more effective to arouse emotional reactions, to make them feel that something must be done right away. This is why claims favor melodramatic typifying examples: it is harder to ignore the plight of innocent victims or of those who are especially deserving. Claims can make use of a wide range of emotional appeals (see Box 2.2).

Because claims can invoke many different values and emotions, and because those values are abstract and subject to conflicting interpretations, claims often feature multiple warrants so differ- ent people may agree that something needs to be done about a troubling condition even though they disagree on the reasons for taking action.

Conclusions

Every claim, then, offers a justification for taking action: the grounds identify a troubling condition, and the warrants explain why some- thing should be done about it. Thus, all claims lead to **conclusions**, statements that specify what should be done, what action should be taken to address this social problem. The nature of the conclu- sions is shaped by the grounds and warrants. If a claim's grounds have depicted a condition that causes terrible suffering, and the warrants speak to humanitarian concerns about the need to alleviate

Box 2.2 Making Model Immigrants

The New Sanctuary movement was a campaign by religious organizations to give sanctuary to mixed-status immigrant families, in
which at least one member faced deportation and at least one other
was a legal resident. According to Yukich (2013), sanctuary might
involve housing these families on church property, or it might involve
providing legal or financial support. The campaign sought to change
public perceptions of immigrants, to portray them not as threats,
but as people who were making positive contributions to America.

The New Sanctuary claimsmakers typified immigrants by pointing to particular individuals whose stories were calculated to gain
sympathy. These typifying examples were family members with good
work records and without criminal records, whose demeanor was
polite and nonthreatening; in other words, they were people who
posed no threat, who were deserving model immigrants. The fact
that the advocates who spoke for these immigrants were religious
leaders helped affirm the morality of the cause. Immigrants whose
cases seemed more ambiguous—individuals who had criminal
records, who seemed angry, or otherwise seemed less deserving—
were not offered sanctuary.

Claimsmakers choose typifying examples to support their arguments. Thus, claims that some form of violence is a serious problem
can be supported by stories of victims who suffered terribly. Similarly,
in seeking to present the positive face of immigration, the New
Sanctuary movement chose to highlight cases of good people who
seemed trapped in a bad bureaucratic system.

suffering, then the conclusions are likely to focus on ways to help
the afflicted. On the other hand, if the grounds emphasize the
terrible nature of a particular crime, and if the warrants focus on
society's need to protect its members from such evils, then the
conclusions will probably advocate cracking down on this crime.

Often conclusions include both short-range and long-range
goals. Within the short term, claimsmakers may be trying to arouse
concern—to make others aware of the problem, to get people to

join their campaign, or to encourage the media to cover the issue. Longer-range goals typically seek policy changes by arguing that policymakers need to pass a new law, fund a program, or otherwise deal with the troubling condition in a new, more effective way. Usually the short-range goals are seen as steps toward making these long-range changes possible.

Conclusions range from vague endorsements of change to extensive, detailed agendas for action. Early in the social problems process, when claimsmakers' primary aim is to raise awareness of the troubling condition, grounds and warrants tend to receive more emphasis. At later stages in the process, when concern about the problem has become widespread, policy choices become a more central focus, and conclusions are likely to receive greater, more detailed attention.

Summary

Grounds, warrants, and conclusions, then, are standard elements in most arguments (Toulmin, 1958). In the case of social problems claims, this rhetorical structure explains what is wrong, why it is wrong, and what should be done about it. But who hears these claims? Which audiences are these claims meant to persuade, and how do they respond?

CLAIMS, THEIR AUDIENCES, AND THE SOCIAL PROBLEMS MARKETPLACE

Every claim involves communication between at least two parties: those who make the claim (*claimants* or *claimsmakers*), and an **audience** whom the claim is meant to persuade. The audience for claims can include all of the other participants in the social problems process: people who might be enlisted in the cause, other claimsmakers, members of the media who might publicize the claims, the general public, policymakers, and so on. Audiences differ in what they find persuasive, so effective claims need to be tailored to fit their audiences' concerns. How claimsmakers understand those concerns should affect their rhetorical choices. Because there is little point in presenting claims that an audience will not find convincing, claimsmakers must devise arguments that they believe will persuade their audience.

Some claims face little resistance, quickly gaining widespread acceptance among those who hear them. For example, claims about child abuse, child pornography, and other similar threats to children tend to be well received (J. Best, 1990). American culture views children as vulnerable innocents who deserve societal protection. Therefore, claims that children are being menaced by adults can arouse widespread concern. The arguments seem so compelling that it is difficult to imagine anyone opposing such claims; how could child abuse possibly be defended? Political scientists sometimes refer to claims that inspire this sort of general agreement as **valence issues** (Nelson, 1984), although what seems at first glance to be consensus may encompass different views.

At the other extreme are claims related to entrenched controversies that will probably never lead to consensus. The debate over abortion remains intense because it features people who have taken intractable, opposing positions: some pro-life advocates argue that abortion is murder and should never be tolerated, while some pro-choice proponents insist that women must be able to control their own bodies and therefore must be free to choose to have abortions. It is very unlikely that a new pro-life claim will persuade those who hold hard-core pro-choice beliefs to change their minds, and equally unlikely that pro-choice arguments can be devised that will change the opinion of those firmly committed to a hard-core pro-life position. When addressing such contested issues, or **position issues**, claimsmakers know that they cannot persuade everyone; they can expect their claims to encounter opposition from at least some people who hear them (Nelson, 1984).

The audience for claims is not an undifferentiated mass. Rather, it can be subdivided—or **segmented**—by race, age, social class, gender, region, and so on. Different segments of the audience tend to have different interests and ideologies. People may respond to a claim by recognizing that they stand to gain or lose if the claims succeed: claims probably seem more compelling to segments of the audience who perceive themselves as directly threatened by the troubling condition, while other segments may resist claims that might adversely affect them by, for example, restricting their freedom or raising their taxes.

Such perceptions of interest are often linked to ideologies or systems of beliefs; different segments of the population are likely to view the world differently, to place different emphasis on particular values, explanations, justifications, and so on. As a general rule, those who benefit from existing social arrangements are more likely to view those arrangements as just, fair, and reasonable, and they are less likely to be sympathetic to claims arguing that those arrangements need to be overturned. Thus, both their interests and their ideologies make them a tough audience, while those disadvantaged by the troubling condition are more likely to be receptive to such claims. Different segments of society, then, view the world differently, and persuasive claims need to match the various worldviews of the segments of the audience toward which they are directed.

Claimsmakers devise various methods to deal with audience segmentation. One tactic is to preach to the choir—that is, to direct claims toward those segments of the audience most likely to respond favorably. For example, abortion activists often direct their claims toward those who they believe already share their beliefs—as when they speak to sympathizers at pro-choice or pro-life rallies. Directing claims to those most likely to be supportive can be a particularly important tactic at the beginning of the social problems process, when claims are first being made: addressing a presumably sympathetic audience first can make more people aware of an issue, rally supporters to the cause, give claimsmakers a chance to hone their claims to make them as persuasive as possible, and create some momentum for carrying the claim to a broader, more diverse audience (such tactics for mobilizing supporters into a social movement are discussed further in Chapter 3).

An alternative approach is to craft claims so as to maximize their appeal to the broadest possible audience. Claims can incorporate multiple grounds, warrants, and conclusions that appeal to different people, thereby seeming to offer something for, if not everyone, at least lots of people. For instance, many advocates of vegetarianism see ethical issues as central to their cause, and they oppose meat eating as morally wrong. However, they also know that these ethical claims encounter widespread resistance; most Americans enjoy eating meat and don't consider it wrong, so moral arguments alone are unlikely to persuade a large audience (Maurer, 2002). However, other grounds and warrants are available: vegetarians can argue that eating meat is unhealthy, in that it fosters heart disease and other ailments; or they can claim that raising animals for food damages the environment. Such arguments add additional grounds and warrants to vegetarians' claims that might appeal to people who are worried about their health or the environment, even if they don't have moral qualms about eating meat. Expanding claims in this way offers vegetarians a chance to persuade people who could be expected to resist narrower ethical arguments that eating meat is wrong.

Well-crafted claims sometimes create surprising alliances among people who usually don't agree, inspiring consensus and converting potential conflict into a valence issue. For instance, political liberals and conservatives often disagree about educational policies. Yet, during the 1990s, many liberals and conservatives joined forces to promote policies requiring public school students to wear uniforms (Brunsma, 2004). Liberals argued that uniforms would make social class differences among students less visible, reduce pressure on parents to purchase expensive clothes for children, and enhance students' self-esteem; conservatives claimed that uniforms would encourage discipline and orderly behavior among students.

Both sides insisted that school uniforms could reduce violence and improve learning. In this case, people who usually disagree found themselves promoting the same solution, even though they disagreed about the precise nature of the problem.

Similarly, advocates representing a wide range of ideologies support efforts to exclude troubling material from elementary and secondary school textbooks: liberals call for excluding material that might reinforce gender or racial stereotypes, fundamentalist Christians want to block content mentioning witches or other supernatural elements, and so on (Ravitch, 2003). Mandating school uniforms and regulating textbook content are just two examples of claims constructed in ways that build broad-based consensus among people who often disagree on other educational issues (see Box 2.3).

It is important to recognize that the audiences for claims are not passive. People who hear claims react, and claimsmakers must take those reactions into account, by adjusting, revising, and fine-tuning their claims to make them more effective, more persuasive. Claims should not be viewed as one-way messages, transmitted from claimsmakers/senders to their audiences/receivers. Rather, claimsmakers need to be sensitive to their audiences' reactions, to figure out which parts of their claims are working and which are not persuasive and need to be revised. In other words, claimsmakers and their audiences engage in a **dialog** in which the audience's feedback leads claimsmakers to modify their claims (Nichols, 2003).

If a particular ground or warrant fails to elicit a good reaction, claimsmakers may strike it from their claims and substitute something that they hope will evoke a more favorable response from their audience. For instance, activists campaigning to halt impending cuts in programs that had provided support to immigrants began with general claims ("immigrant rights are human rights") that proved ineffective. However, they soon found that the media and politicians responded more favorably to claims about the vulnerability

Box 2.3 How Close Do Strange Bedfellows Get?

Alliances among claimsmakers usually bring together people who share a substantive concern (as when different environmentalists ally to raise concern about pollution) or an ideological orientation (as when conservatives rally to oppose some piece of legislation). Far less common are instances where people who usually disagree join forces—these are indeed strange bedfellows.

An antipornography campaign peaked in the 1980s, when Ronald Reagan was president. This campaign involved a collaboration between two sorts of people who usually found themselves on opposite sides of issues. Antipornography feminists argued that pornography encouraged violence against women and exemplified the media's tendency to present women as sexual objects; they were focused on how pornography harmed women. In contrast, social conservatives opposed pornography for essentially moral reasons: they saw it as celebrating lust and threatening marriage and family life. Their collaboration was in some ways unusual: feminists are usually considered part of the political left, while conservatives are, of course, on the right.

Although both groups opposed pornography, they made different arguments, and their efforts were largely separate. The 1980s saw several unsuccessful campaigns to address pornography at local and federal levels, but these were usually led by either feminists or conservatives, with minor involvement by members of the other camp. The alliance faded as technological changes—first video, and then the Internet—made pornography more readily available, but also less visible as a focus for public concern.

Source: Whittier, 2014.

of elderly, disabled immigrants, so they refocused their campaign on these more sympathetic cases (Fujiwara, 2005).

Claimsmaking is usually not a one-shot effort; it takes time to develop effective claims. Most claimsmakers have to try again and again to achieve widespread attention for their claims; they must try out claims, assess the audience's response, revise the claims, and so on, until they develop a persuasive argument. After all, claims compete within a **social problems marketplace** (J. Best, 1990; Hilgartner & Bosk, 1988). At any given moment, countless claimsmakers are struggling to get their particular claims heard—far more than can hope to capture the audience's limited attention. Moreover, it is usually impossible to control either the other claims competing to attract the audience's notice or what the audience will choose to notice. Imagine a claimsmaker who had scheduled a major event—say, a combination press conference and demonstration—for September 12, 2001. Because the 9/11 terrorist attacks monopolized the nation's attention for days, no one would have paid any attention to anything the claimsmaker had to say on the twelfth. Although extreme, this example illustrates that claims do not operate in a vacuum.

The competition to capture the audience's attention helps explain some of the features of social problems rhetoric that we noted earlier. Why do claimsmakers so often begin claims with disturbing typifying examples? Why do claims usually settle for naming the problem—often with a catchy label like *road rage*—and avoid giving detailed (and therefore boring) definitions of the problem? Why do claimsmakers favor statistics that suggest the problem is surprisingly large? Why do they favor prominent targets? Each of these rhetorical devices is arresting, eye-catching; each can draw people's attention to this claim (and away from those other claims competing for the audience's attention). The goal is to grab and hold the audience. This competition in the social problems marketplace means that claimsmakers are encouraged to devise dramatic, disturbing, easily grasped claims that will command attention over competing claims. Simpler, stronger arguments work better.

In sum, claimsmakers present what they hope will be persuasive arguments, but they must then attend to the audience's responses, and those responses and their own sense of how they need to revise their rhetoric in turn may be affected by all the other claims and events that are competing for the audience's attention in the social problems marketplace.

EVOLUTION AND OPPOSITION

Social problems claims are not static; rather, they keep evolving. This process continues even after the audience becomes concerned about the problem. Once a claim has attracted recognition and acceptance, we can consider it *well established*; that is, there is widespread agreement that this troubling condition ought to be considered a social problem. Yet this is not the end of the matter; even well-established claims need to change. However compelling claims may seem when they first gain acceptance, they tend to become familiar, stale, boring (Downs, 1972). Audiences find it easier to forget about or ignore claims that can be dismissed as old news, particularly because other, newer claims are always competing for their attention. Audiences also may become frustrated by problems that aren't easily solved—where efforts to address the problem don't seem to make much progress. Each time a claim is repeated, it seems more familiar, less interesting—and less persuasive.

Therefore, claimsmakers often find it necessary to revise and repackage their claims, just to make them seem fresh and interesting. They may add additional grounds, more warrants, or fresh conclusions to give their claims a new look. For instance, instead of simply criticizing the general problem of sexism, the women's movement has been successful at calling attention to a long series of women's issues, each revealing a different aspect of sexist practices, through claims about sexual harassment, date rape, the glass ceiling (which blocks female executives from rising to the top of corporations), and so on. Continually identifying additional forms of sexism keeps the women's movement's claims fresh.

Once a claim has gained acceptance, it is often possible to build additional claims on that foundation. One possibility is **domain expansion** (J. Best, 1990, 2015). As we have seen, initial claims often emphasize disturbing typifying examples. In the 1960s, for example, claimsmakers described the *battered child syndrome*, the problem of brutal beatings of infants or very young children. Terrible examples tend to make claims more interesting and effective; they help raise concern about an issue. In turn, once this concern has been established, it becomes possible to argue that other conditions are just as bad as—really just another form of, or the moral equivalent of—the initial problem. (Think of domain expansion as like opening an umbrella, so that more topics are covered by a social problem.)

In the case of child beating, battered child syndrome was soon renamed *child abuse*, and then the boundaries of what was considered abusive began to expand: Abuse also could affect older children and even adolescents. People began to recognize new types of abuse; beatings were now termed *physical abuse*, as distinguished from emotional abuse, sexual abuse, and so on. And advocates began applying the now widely accepted *child abuse* label to a range of other phenomena, so smoking around children, failing to strap kids into protective car seats, and circumcision, among other things, were claimed to be forms of child abuse. In other words, over time, the domain of child abuse expanded to include more and more phenomena. This sort of domain expansion can occur whenever initial claims become well established (see Box 2.4).

In a related process, claimsmakers choose to **piggyback** a new troubling condition on a well-established problem (Loseke, 2003; J. Best, 2015). Again, child abuse is a good example. The popularity of the label *child abuse* inspired other claimsmakers to characterize their troubling conditions as varieties of *abuse*—so people began speaking of wife abuse, sibling abuse, elder abuse, and so on. Similarly, the successes of the civil rights movement led, in turn, to other campaigns promoting the *rights* of various groups—such as women's rights, gay rights, children's rights, prisoners' rights, and animal rights. And mid-1990s claims about road rage (typified

---

BOX 2.4 DIFFERENT WAYS TO EXPAND BULLYING'S DOMAIN

Once social problems claims have some success, so that people are familiar with the problem's name, the domain is often expanded to encompass a broader range of phenomena. Thus, Cohen and Brooks (2014) note that school bullying's domain expanded *down* so that student behaviors that were once seen as quite ordinary and not particularly serious—such as teasing or arguments—might be redefined as forms of bullying. But, they note that bullying's domain expanded in other directions as well:

- Expanding the domain *up* involved applying the label to acts that formerly would have been understood to be serious crimes. Thus, a beating that could have been viewed as a criminal assault might also be characterized as bullying.

- Expanding the domain *out* involved characterizing ever more people as either bullies or bullying victims. Some advocates claimed that most or even all students are involved in bullying.

- Expanding the domain *across* involved designating any perceived abuse of power regardless of whether it occurred at school—everything from communism to singing Christmas carols—as forms of bullying.

In other words, the definition of bullying is not necessarily obvious or uncontroversial. All social problems claims are efforts to reshape people's thinking, to get them to redefine some troubling condition as a particular social problem. Social problems do not have established, natural, objective definitions; the term's boundaries can always be put in play, as claimsmakers seek to expand—or sometimes contract—a problem's domain.

---

as drivers becoming frustrated and violently attacking others) led journalists to begin identifying all sorts of other *rages*: air rage (among airline passengers), desk rage (office workers), even shopping cart rage (J. Best & Furedi, 2001). In each of these cases, a well-established social problem created opportunities to construct claims about other troubling conditions as being somehow analogous to the familiar original—in effect arguing that there was a sort of family resemblance among types of abuse, rights, or rages—that if the familiar case deserved to be considered a social problem, then so, too, did these other troubling conditions. (Claimsmakers can, in effect, borrow someone else's umbrella, using an existing term to cover an additional problem.)

Claims do not have to use the same terms—*abuse, rights, rage*, and so on—to piggyback on successful constructions. In some cases the rhetorical formula used to construct one social problem can be applied to other problems of the same general sort. There is, for example, a fairly standard recipe for identifying new drug problems: claims are made that a drug is particularly harmful, that its use is rapidly spreading, and so on (Reinarman, 1994). This familiar, well-established formula means that contemporary arguments about the dangers of Ecstasy or crystal meth do not look a great deal different from nineteenth-century warnings about opium smoking. Similarly, claims about new forms of victimization often use a well-established rhetorical formula arguing that victimization is widespread and serious yet remains hidden, so extraordinary measures are needed to identify it, and so on (J. Best, 1999). In other words, the structure of successful claims—combinations of grounds, warrants, and conclusions that have proved effective in bringing attention to one drug problem or one form of victimization—can be copied and brought to bear on other, analogous issues.

Claims often inspire **counterclaims**, arguments in direct opposition to the original claims. Again, think of the pro-life and pro-choice movements' struggle over abortion; or the claims that climate change is a serious problem exacerbated by humans' activities, and the counterclaims that global warming may be neither as serious as has been feared nor caused primarily by people's actions. Or the disputes may be much narrower, focused on the meaning of a particular individual's life. In all of these cases, advocates with opposing views develop full-fledged arguments—each with its own

Box 2.5 CLAIMS AND COUNTERCLAIMS CAN SHARE WARRANTS

The U.S. Army operates the School of the Americas (SOA), established to train military from Central and South American countries. In the late 1980s, SOA became the focus for claims that it was training soldiers in techniques that were used to maintain repressive regimes. This criticism led to the reorganization of SOA as WHINSEC (Western Hemisphere Institute for Security Cooperation). The protests continue, but WHINSEC makes its own counterclaims that invoke some of the same values as those of the protesters:

- The protesters warn that WHINSEC promotes a culture of military impunity, but the Army emphasizes the school's commitment to human rights training, and beneficence—the military's role in helping, rather than controlling, the populace.

- The protesters charge that WHINSEC operates in secrecy, while WHINSEC insists that its current operations are transparent and invites reporters and other observers to visit.

- The protesters charge that WHINSEC's true mission is neo-imperialism—to protect the interests of U.S. corporations in Latin America, while the Army counters that its objective is collective security against terrorism, transnational criminal organizations, and other threats.

In its counterclaims, the Army does not defend impunity, secrecy, or neo-imperialism; rather, it insists that it opposes them and shares values that the protesters promote: beneficence, transparency, and collective security. Thus, the protesters' claims and the Army's counterclaims invoke similar warrants.

Source: Gallo-Cruz, 2012.

set of grounds, warrants, and conclusions, and each trying to make the most persuasive case (see Box 2.5).

Such debates often revolve around confrontations over grounds or warrants. Each side may challenge the evidence—the grounds—

presented by its opponents, charging that those opponents have misunderstood or misrepresented the nature of the troubling condition. "Stat wars" may arise in which each side denounces its opponents' statistics and argues that its own numbers are more accurate (J. Best, 2013). Similarly, opponents may insist that some warrants ought to be more compelling than others; in the abortion debate, for example, there are sharp disagreements about whether the rights of the fetus or those of the pregnant woman ought to be considered more important.

Many claims emerge within and are promoted as linked to particular **ideologies**—that is, more or less coherent sets of beliefs, such as libertarianism, feminism, liberalism, conservatism, or specific religious doctrines. Ideologies usually emphasize particular warrants; for example, libertarianism views liberty as a central value, and feminism opposes social arrangements that block opportunities for women. Often, too, those familiar with an ideology favor particular grounds; feminists, of course, look for evidence of sexism, and so on. In addition, ideologies often recognize competing belief systems, so liberals and conservatives anticipate disagreeing over many issues. These ideological disputes make it very easy to mount counterclaims; the news that someone associated with a rival ideology is making a claim invites counterclaims.

Claims often have to be modified in response to counterclaims. Opposition means that one's arguments will be subjected to sharper scrutiny and criticism, and those elements that prove easiest to challenge may need to be changed or reinforced. A statistic that has been debunked by one's opponents may be dropped and a more defensible number added to fill the gap, and so on. At the same time, the fact that there is opposition can be incorporated into one's claims. It may be possible to characterize one's opponents as part of the problem, turning the fact of opposition into a new ground for the claims. At least for those who share our ideology, news that the opposition is making counterclaims can reassure us that we're correct.

Opposition is often predictable. There are **social problems clusters**—sets of claimsmakers who take similar positions regarding related social problems (J. Best, 2015; Griffiths and Best, 2016). When new issues emerge, many of the same people are likely to find themselves making claims that resemble those they've made in the past. For instance, claims about a new drug problem are likely to resemble those made about older drugs, with drug control advocates calling for new laws and tougher enforcement, even as advocates of drug abuse prevention and drug treatment warn that cracking down will only make things worse. There are lots of familiar social problems clusters: if you imagine some new issue related to guns, women, the environment, or race, you can probably predict some of the people likely to make claims, the sorts of rhetoric they are likely to adopt, and the interplay between claims and counterclaims.

In sum, claims are constantly in play. They evolve, and they can inspire both other claims and opposition, so new claims are almost always shaped by those that preceded them.

CULTURAL RESOURCES

Theoretically, claimsmakers are free to assemble claims in any form they choose. In practice, however, claims have to make sense—both to the claimsmakers who choose to make them, and to the audiences whom the claimsmakers hope to persuade. This means that claims must draw on the larger culture; they must be consistent with people's understandings of how the world works. In some societies, attributing misfortune to the acts of witches has been seen as a perfectly sensible explanation. In contemporary American society, however, claims about witchcraft are likely to be rejected out of hand by most people—although not by all. Most would-be claimsmakers recognize that this is the prevailing view, so they tend to avoid blaming witches or, more generally, constructing problems along lines that they and their audiences will find unconvincing.

Every culture, then, can be seen as a large repository of evolving, more or less familiar ideas about how the world works—and how it should work. These **cultural resources** are available to be exploited whenever claims are created. Our culture, for example, tends to idealize children as vulnerable innocents, and claims that warn about threats to children often elicit sympathetic reactions. This is such a widely shared view that we have trouble imagining people thinking any other way. However, New England's Puritans had a much darker view of children: they worried that children were born in a state of sinful willfulness, and they believed that children needed to have their wills broken to become properly God-fearing (Fischer, 1989, pp. 97–101).

Such different assumptions lead to quite different visions of, say, discipline. For some modern Americans, spanking is seen as harmful, even as a form of child abuse—one more way that adults inflict injuries on innocent children (Davis, 1994). Although the Puritans considered spanking a last resort, they used a variety of physical restraints and shaming devices, such as forcing a child who talked during church services to wear a wooden bit; such practices, which seem quite shocking to us, were standard ways of disciplining children, designed to teach them to be submissive and to understand God's wrath. It's easy to imagine that some claims about endangered children that might seem very powerful to us would have fallen on deaf ears among the Puritans.

Claims, then, draw on a society's cultural resources—the fund of words, ideas, images, and emotional reactions that most people understand to be reasonable. It is easier to arouse contemporary Americans' concern about threats to children or violence against women—two groups that are widely understood to be relatively vulnerable to victimization and therefore in need of protection—than to promote claims about endangered adult males. Nevertheless, although culture does limit the range of possible claims to some degree, it still offers a broad array of choices. For example, various segments of the U.S. population attribute different social problems to quite diverse causes—causes such as acts of God (for instance, to explain natural disasters), germs, conspiracies, belief systems (for example, particular religious or political ideologies), people's upbringing, and so on. Of course, part of being familiar with a culture is having the ability to predict which audiences will find which explanations appropriate for which problems (see Box 2.6).

Note that the fund of cultural resources is large, diverse, and not necessarily logically consistent. The point is not that all social problems have to be constructed in the same way, but that any culture offers various ideas and images that might be incorporated into successful claims. Just as American culture supports values that can sometimes conflict with one another, so, too, it encompasses other competing, conflicting notions.

This cultural diversity means that most social problems might be constructed in very different ways. For example, debates over poverty often feature dramatically different interpretations: Some commentators argue that the poor bear much of the responsibility for their plight, that they make bad choices (such as dropping out of school) that make poverty a likely outcome. Other critics insist that poverty is largely a product of a social structure that blocks too many opportunities, creating obstacles (such as a shortage of high-paying jobs) that make it hard for people to overcome poverty. Both the idea that individuals must bear responsibility for their own decisions, and the idea that a fair society should offer opportunities for advancement are familiar; both belong to the stock of cultural resources from which claims can be assembled. Such competing accounts of poverty's causes—although derived from the same culture—can reveal bitter differences within the culture. Claimsmakers may charge that rival claims are morally irresponsible because they apply inappropriate explanations, that they ignore God's laws, blame victims who should not be blamed, or err in some other way. Not everyone subscribes to every element in the larger culture—certainly not all of the time.

Box 2.6 Expanding the Domain of Stockholm Syndrome

Claims can have convoluted histories. For instance, Stockholm syndrome was a label originally applied to former hostages who expressed sympathy for their kidnappers. It was understood as a narrowly defined psychiatric problem, an apparently irrational response to having experienced great stress as a crime victim, for which psychological counseling was recommended.

Over time, Stockholm syndrome's domain expanded. In cases where women who had experienced domestic violence—or children who had been abused—continued to express emotional ties to their abusers, claimsmakers argued that these victims were displaying the syndrome. Later, claimsmakers applied the label to cult members, prostitutes, suicidal terrorists, and others as a way of dismissing the victims' emotional bonds to cult leaders, pimps, the leaders of terrorist movements, and so on. Eventually, Stockholm syndrome became a cultural resource for all sorts of claimsmakers seeking to criticize what they defined as inappropriate attitudes or alliances (for instance, arguing that those who do not join some popular cause are victims of the syndrome).

Notice that the claimsmakers who originally constructed Stockholm syndrome sympathized with and sought to understand and help various sorts of victims. As its domain expanded, however, the term became a resource that could be used to criticize as irrational the feelings of all sorts of people with whom the claimsmakers disagreed.

Source: Adorjan, Christensen, Kelly, & Pawluch, 2012.

Moreover, the cultural context for claims is continually shifting. Ideas, values, imagery, explanations—all the elements of culture—can go in and out of fashion. In part, this fluctuation reflects people's ongoing quest for novelty: both claimsmakers and their audiences can become bored when claims seem stale—too familiar—so claims must be continually repackaged to make them appear fresh and interesting. In addition, genuinely new elements are added to the stock of cultural resources; a scientific discovery, the spread of a new disease, a new invention, or a dramatic event can have far-reaching consequences. Such novelties can reverberate through society generally, and through the social problems marketplace in particular, in complex ways.

Consider the identification of AIDS as a new disease in the early 1980s. No sociologist could have predicted all of the consequences that derived from that development: shifts in funding priorities for medical research and reforms in the methods used to test new treatments, the promotion of AIDS prevention policies (including condom distribution and needle exchange programs), all manner of art portraying aspects of the epidemic, and on and on. Or consider how the spread of cell phones has spawned new social problems claims—about the risks when drivers are distracted while talking on their phones, about the propriety of carrying on phone conversations where they can be overheard by others, about allegations of health hazards from cell phones, and so on (see Box 2.7).

Cultural shifts are reflected in social problems claims. Many social problems—for instance, gangs, cults, racism, and poverty—have been the subject of claims going back many decades, even centuries, but the particular constructions of these problems in different periods reflect current cultural developments during those periods. This means that cultural conditions during particular historical periods affect how social problems are constructed during those times. For example, the theme of expanding individual rights during the 1960s (as reflected in the civil rights movement and the sexual revolution), or the shift toward more conservative values that began in the late 1970s (as reflected in growing concerns about sex and drugs), can be seen as having influenced claims about many different social problems (Jenkins, 2006). (Chapter 10 will have more to say about the historical context of claims.)

Cultural resources, then, both constrain and enrich claims. Claims almost always use familiar language, imagery, forms of explanations, and other cultural elements. After all, the claimsmakers are themselves

Box 2.7   Cell Phones and Driving: What's the Problem?

Early cell phone advertisements highlighted the convenience of being able to make phone calls while driving. However, as cell phones spread, so did claims that drivers using cell phones posed a social problem. However, just how that problem was understood shifted over time:

- Initially, attention focused on the dangers posed by handheld phones—drivers making calls only had one hand available to control their car. Some states responded by prohibiting the use of handheld phones while driving.

- The focus then shifted to novice drivers who, it was claimed, were too inexperienced to competently handle the unfamiliar task of driving while also making calls. Some states passed laws forbidding cell-phone use by teen drivers or those with provisional licenses.

- As texting became a more popular function, claimsmakers argued that it—and not simply talking on the phone—was the real problem, inspiring yet more state laws against texting while driving.

- More recently, traffic-safety claimsmakers have adopted new language about the problem of distracted driving. They argue that talking on a cell phone increases risk, but so do other distractions (eating, fiddling with the radio or CDs, and so on). While it is hard to argue that distracted driving isn't risky, the concept is so broad it may be hard to devise effective policies to address it.

This example suggests that technological changes often inspire social problems claims, but that it can take time for claimsmakers to settle on the most effective rhetoric.

Source: Parilla, 2013.

members of the culture, and they are almost forced to construct claims that they themselves view as sensible, claims that they also believe will receive a receptive hearing from their audiences. Thus, cultures constrain the sorts of claims that are likely to emerge. However, cultures are complex enough, multifaceted enough, that claimsmakers still have considerable leeway in choosing and shaping the arguments they present. Although we can note similarities among claims, such as cases in which new claims seem modeled on others, and we can imagine claims (about, say, witchcraft) that seem too far-fetched to succeed in our society, it is still true that claimsmakers have a lot of flexibility in devising their arguments.

UNDERSTANDING CLAIMS

This chapter has explored various aspects of social problems claims. It began by considering claims as rhetorical arguments—the ways in which grounds, warrants, and conclusions structure claims. To be effective, though, claims have to persuade audiences, so claimsmakers must understand who their audiences are and shape their arguments to fit those audiences' concerns. As a result, claimsmakers and audiences find themselves in a dialog as they respond to one another's ideas. Claims also are influenced by other claims. They evolve over time; claims need to be periodically revised to make them seem fresh. They are also shaped by the successes and failures of earlier claims: successful claims invite domain expansion or other efforts to piggyback on their success, just as claimsmakers try to avoid the mistakes of failed claims. And for highly contentious issues, claims face counterclaims, and opponents must respond to one another's constructions within the larger social problems marketplace. Finally, the broader culture provides a context for claims: language, imagery, and other cultural resources offer raw material from which claims can be built. Figure 2.2 illustrates all these various processes.

Figure 2.2 DYNAMICS SHAPING CLAIMS

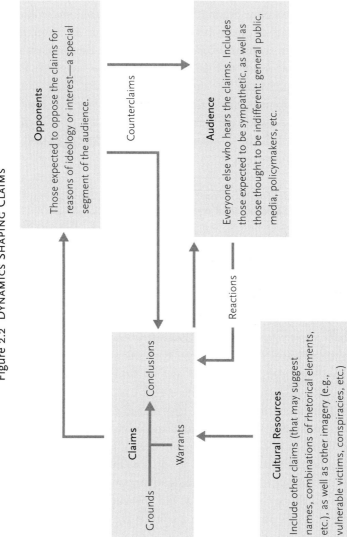

Opponents

Those expected to oppose the claims for reasons of ideology or interest—a special segment of the audience.

Counterclaims

Audience

Everyone else who hears the claims. Includes those expected to be sympathetic, as well as those thought to be indifferent: general public, media, policymakers, etc.

Reactions

Claims

Grounds

Conclusions

Warrants

Cultural Resources

Include other claims (that may suggest names, combinations of rhetorical elements, etc.), as well as other imagery (e.g., vulnerable victims, conspiracies, etc.) that can shape claims.

Of course, claims are social products; they do not exist independently of people. People assemble—construct—claims in hopes of persuading others. Although this chapter has focused on the claims themselves, the remainder of this book will concentrate on the various sorts of people who create, distribute, alter, challenge, or otherwise react to claims—the actors in the various stages of the social problems process.

MAKING CONNECTIONS

- *Claims are rhetorical arguments structured by grounds, warrants, and conclusions.*

- *The concepts of claims and claimsmakers introduced in this chapter set the stage for the next two chapters' discussion of activists as claimsmakers and experts as claimsmakers.*

- *In Chapter 5 you will learn how claimsmakers use the media to present their claims. You will also learn how the media alter the claims they present. As you read that chapter, keep in mind what you have learned in this chapter about cultural resources.*

CASE STUDY
THREATS TO THE AMERICAN DREAM AS A CULTURAL RESOURCE

In a 2013 speech, President Barack Obama (2013) warned: "The combined trends of increased inequality and decreasing mobility pose a fundamental threat to the American Dream." Googling the expression "threat to the American Dream" reveals that it has been used in claims about lots of different social problems, including civic illiteracy, sustainable development, lack of quality health care, and even—in 1999—Y2K (the now largely forgotten fear that computers would not function in the year 2000 because programmers might have used two digits to code years, so computers might not understand that "00" would follow "99").

The American Dream is a cultural resource, a familiar term that is easily invoked by claimsmakers, who can assume that it will be understood by their audiences. The term was coined by a historian, James Truslow Adams, who described it as

> that dream of a land in which life should be better and richer and fuller for every man, with opportunity for each according to his ability and achievement. . . . It is not a dream of motor cars and high wages merely, but a dream of a social order in which each man and each woman shall be able to attain to the fullest stature of which they are innately capable, and be recognized by others for what they are, regardless of the fortuitous circumstances of birth or position. (Adams, 1941 [1931], pp. 404–405)

However, he went on to warn about threats to the "quality of thought" and "abiding values" posed by inequality, materialism, and popular culture: "We have a long and arduous road to travel if we are to realize our American Dream in the life of our nation" (p. 416). In other words, beginning with the very first time the term was used, people have worried that the American Dream was endangered.

And today, claimsmakers can count on virtually everyone in their audiences to have some notion of the American Dream. This does not mean that all those people understand the term in the same way. For some people, the American Dream implies reaching a pinnacle of wealth or power—something many might aspire to, although only a few can hope to achieve. Others define it more modestly—having the proverbial family living in a house with a white picket fence. Still others think of it in terms of intergenerational mobility, of children being able to achieve more than their parents. The term lacks a standard definition.

Because the American Dream is a malleable term, it can be molded to fit a claimsmaker's purpose. When political conservatives invoke the American Dream, they tend to emphasize freedom, liberty, and protection from government interference: "There is no dream about having someone else take care of us. Indeed, that would be a nightmare. Instead we dream of being free to pursue our own dreams. . . . That is the American way. That is the American Dream" (Eccles, 2015). In contrast, when liberals use the term, they highlight ideas of equality, security, and community; protecting the American Dream, in this view, involves social programs such as good public schools and access to health care that guarantee a level of opportunity (Davenport, 2014). It is easy to spot these different visions at work: simply search online for "American Dream" plus the name of any prominent political figure.

It is almost certain that this search will turn up rhetoric about threats to the American Dream. Sometimes these claims look backward, nostalgically insisting that the American Dream once was a realistic prospect, but those once available opportunities have disappeared. Sometimes, they worry about the future, warning that the American Dream may be a reality today, but it is in danger of vanishing. In other words, the American Dream is a rhetorical device—what is sometimes called a **trope**—that is usually used as a warrant to demonstrate the importance of a social problems claim. It is relatively hard to find people expressing complacency about the American Dream; it is much easier to find claims warning that some social problem threatens the American Dream.

All sorts of claimsmakers invoke the American Dream for this purpose—everyone from presidents (and the candidates running for high office) to bloggers. Social scientists make similar claims in books with titles such as *Our Kids: The American Dream in Crisis* (Putnam, 2015). Warning that the American Dream is endangered is a way of rallying support, of getting Americans to take claims seriously.

Evidence shows that incomes in the United States are fairly fluid, that large numbers of people experience both highs and lows. One study found that both affluence and deprivation are widely shared experiences: more than three-quarters of Americans spend at least one year of their adult lifetime in a household that earns at least $100,000; however, 47 percent of Americans live in poverty or near poverty for at least one year of their adult life. While this fluidity might suggest that the American Dream is more than just a fantasy, the study also finds that whites and those with more than a high school education are more likely to achieve affluence and less likely to experience poverty than blacks and those with a high school education or less. The authors conclude: "All Americans do not have an equal chance of achieving the American Dream" (Rank, Hirschl, & Foster, 2014, p. 161). Still, there is evidence that many Americans continue to express confidence in the American Dream. Polls show that most Americans report that they have already achieved or expect to achieve the American Dream, although they also believe that achieving that goal is now harder than it once was (Bowman, Marsico, & Sims, 2014).

In other words, Americans seem to understand the American Dream as a goal, not a guarantee; they believe that improving one's lot is a possibility, although they also understand that some people face more obstacles than others. The American Dream speaks to values about equality, fairness, and opportunity. This is probably why so many claimsmakers find reason to incorporate warnings about threats to the American Dream in their rhetoric.

QUESTIONS

1. Locate examples of claims that refer to the American Dream. How do claimsmakers use these references to make their claims more compelling?

2. Is it necessary for claimsmakers to present statistics or other evidence to support claims that invoke the American Dream?

3. Are there other cultural resources that claimsmakers can draw on in much the same way as they refer to the American Dream?

3

Activists as Claimsmakers

Claims cannot exist by themselves; people—claimsmakers—must advance them. It's tempting to equate claimsmakers with activists—people like Martin Luther King Jr.—who become passionately involved with an issue, dedicate their lives to a cause, and march and demonstrate until their claims receive attention. Indeed, this is part—but only part—of the story.

When we think of activists, we envision people who stand outside the halls of power. Because they do not hold powerful political offices or have strong ties with those who do, it is fairly difficult for these **outsider claimsmakers** to get others—the media, the general public, and particularly the officials who can make policies that might actually do something about the troubling social condition—to pay attention to their claims (J. Best, 1990). This is why activists so often resort to attention-grabbing tactics: demonstrations, sit-ins, and so on. Activists hope that these activities will lead to media coverage and that attracting publicity for their cause will bring their claims to the attention of the public so that, in turn, both the media and the public will press policymakers to take action. That is, activists envision the claimsmaking process as shown in Figure 3.1a, where the thicker arrow between the claimsmakers

Figure 3.1 CLAIMSMAKING BY OUTSIDER AND
INSIDER CLAIMSMAKERS

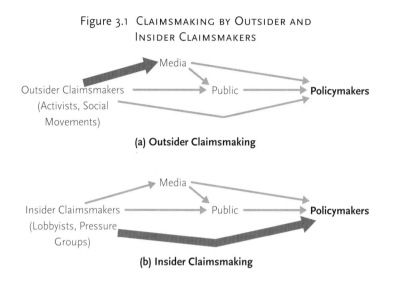

(a) Outsider Claimsmaking

(b) Insider Claimsmaking

and the media identifies the media as the most important audience for outsiders' claims.

However, there is an alternative, more direct route to successful claimsmaking. Some people already have contacts with policymakers. Such people include lobbyists, major political contributors, government officials, and well-established interest groups such as the National Rifle Association (NRA), which is concerned with protecting the rights of gun owners, or the National Association for the Advancement of Colored People (NAACP), which is concerned with advancing the rights of African Americans. Those who are already well connected to policymakers form what is sometimes called the **polity** (Useem & Zald, 1982); the polity consists of those groups whose interests are routinely taken into account by policymakers, so they are often able to influence policymaking. People with such connections can act as **insider claimsmakers**; often they pursue their claims outside the glare of the media spotlight, without arousing much public attention. The activities of insider claimsmakers are depicted in Figure 3.1b, where the thicker arrow runs directly from claimsmakers to policymakers.

The activities of insider claimsmakers will be considered in Chapter 4; this chapter will focus on outsider claimsmakers—in particular, activists such as Dr. King. Activists often belong to broad **social movements**, general causes such as the civil rights movement or environmentalism. Each social movement may contain several distinct **social movement organizations** (SMOs), such as the civil rights movement's SNCC (Student Nonviolent Coordinating Committee) and CORE (Congress of Racial Equality), or the environmentalist movement's Greenpeace and Sierra Club. As we shall see, although the larger society may view a movement's SMOs as allies that share a common cause, activists frequently think of other SMOs within the same social movement as rivals.

Social movements frequently face opposition. Movements seek to promote change, and the status quo inevitably has its defenders. The most vigorous defenses usually come from those who have vested interests in the status quo; these opponents benefit from existing social arrangements in ways that would be threatened if the changes promoted by the movement were to occur. For example, some white Southerners, who saw themselves as benefiting from legal segregation, opposed the civil rights movement. Moreover, it takes effort to change social arrangements, and even when people may not strongly oppose activists' claims, they may see no good reason to exert the effort that change requires; sociologists refer to such reluctance to alter existing social arrangements as **inertia** (Becker, 1995).

Chapter 2 described position issues—that is, topics that evoke controversy, inciting active disagreements about whether a particular condition should be considered troubling, or what that condition's causes might be, or what should be done to address the condition. In such position issues, claims inspire counterclaims, and **countermovements** may arise to promote these counterclaims.

Some sociologists associate the term *social movement* with liberal or progressive causes and prefer to restrict the term *countermovement* to more conservative causes. However, it makes better analytic sense to speak of social movements as calling for change, and of countermovements as resisting change. When abortion was generally illegal, there was a movement of abortion rights advocates, which was opposed by a countermovement that favored restricting abortion. Once abortion became widely legal, however, it became more reasonable to speak of a pro-life movement calling for change, and a pro-choice countermovement trying to defend the existing right to abortion. This example illustrates that countermovements are conservative in the sense that they seek to preserve the status quo; when political liberals support existing social arrangements (such as laws protecting the right to abortions), they may organize countermovements to oppose claimsmaking by political conservatives (such as the pro-life movement).

Because most social movements—and countermovements—promote claims about social problems, and because images of activists tend to come to mind when we think of claimsmakers, this chapter will focus on key aspects of social movements and the role of activists as claimsmakers. (Chapter 4 will consider other sorts of claimsmakers.) We will begin this chapter's discussion of activist claimsmakers by examining three recent approaches adopted by sociologists to study social movements: framing, resource mobilization, and opportunity structures.

FRAMING

Most social movements present claims; they identify a troubling condition and call for social changes to address the problem (Benford & Hunt, 2003). These claims can, of course, be studied in terms of their rhetoric—that is, by using the concepts developed in Chapter 2. Social movement scholars, however, often adopt a slightly different vocabulary: they speak of **framing** to describe how activists construct their claims.

Like the frame around a picture, activists' frames place a social movement within a larger context; frames locate the key issues and set them off so that they are easily understood. Like the wooden frame of a house, activists' frames also provide a structure, a framework around which elaborate claims can be assembled. The same issue might be framed in many different ways. Some frames emphasize morality, appealing to people's sense of right and wrong. Some frames elicit outrage or other powerful emotions that lead people to join and stick with a cause (Gould, 2009; Whittier, 2009). Other frames evoke particular ideologies or political philosophies, such as Marxism or libertarianism. Still other frames emphasize political struggles between groups with competing interests. What may seem to be a single social movement—the civil rights movement, the environmental movement, and so on—can be composed of activists who frame the issue in very different ways.

Frames encourage viewing the world from a particular perspective; they give meaning to what might otherwise seem confusing, so that once someone adopts a given frame, everything seems to be clearer, to make sense. For example, the feminist movement calls attention to the various ways in which social arrangements disadvantage women; a feminist frame gives activists a particular vantage point from which they can view women's place in the world (see Box 3.1).

There are obvious parallels between constructionist scholars' examinations of claimsmaking rhetoric (as discussed in Chapter 2), and social movement analysts' discussions of frames. Frames have three components: **diagnostic frames** identify the nature of the problem (that is, *diagnostic frame* is another term for what constructionists call *grounds*); **motivational frames** explain why action needs to be taken (akin to the constructionists' *warrants*); and **prognostic frames** specify what needs to be done (similar to the constructionists'

Box 3.1 The Name Mirrors the Frame

The term *homosexual* originated among nineteenth-century sexologists who sought to make sexual behavior a topic for scientific research; they also spoke of *sexual inversion*. Both terms seemed clinical to the people they described. Some early activists described theirs as a *homophile* movement, favoring that term because it emphasized love rather than sex.

However, a new set of activists emerged in the 1970s, and they favored *gay*. The gay liberation movement encompassed both males and females, but women complained that their concerns were treated as less important, and demanded equal billing, so it began common to speak of *gay and lesbian* issues. Over time, other sexual identities made analogous calls for mention so that the inclusion of bisexuals led to the abbreviation *GLB*, and adding references to transsexuals (later transgender) produced *LGBT*. Some expand this to *LGBTQ* to encompass either queer (suggesting a more radical, edgy orientation) or questioning (for those who are exploring their sexual identities). Others call for adding an *I* to acknowledge intersex (people with ambiguous reproductive or sexual anatomy).

We tend to take the categories and names that we use to classify people and problems for granted. But all of these terms have histories, sometimes contentious histories in which claimsmakers struggle to get a particular term accepted. In this example, individuals with a variety of identities campaigned to gain recognition as part of a larger gender-nonconforming social movement.

Source: Wilcox, 2014.

conclusions) (Snow & Benford, 1988). For our purposes, these are essentially similar classification schemes, one favored by those who think of themselves as sociologists of social problems, the other by scholars of social movements.

One reason that social movement analysts favor the language of framing is their interest in how social movements recruit new members. A key issue for most activists is enlisting supporters to their causes. Social movements need to attract new members, to convince people to share the activists' concerns and support the movement through donations and investments of time and energy. Because social movements typically promote unfamiliar ways of looking at society and its problems, they must frame issues in ways that will appeal to prospective members. In other words, activists need to align their frames with those of the people they hope to enlist in their movements.

Frame alignment refers to the ways in which social movements must address the existing frames or ways of looking at the world held by prospective members (Snow, Rochford, Worden, & Benford, 1986). Movement participants—activists—have a particular frame, with its diagnostic, motivational, and prognostic elements, but the people they might like to recruit to the movement already have their own ways of understanding the world. The goal is to bring these frames into alignment so that others will come to adopt the activists' frame (and presumably join the movement). For example, the feminist movement seeks to introduce people to a feminist frame so that they can recognize how sexism affects their lives, and so that they will support feminist efforts to challenge sexual discrimination. Frame alignment usually takes one of four forms:

1. *Bridging.* In **frame bridging**, activists seek support from people thought to hold frames similar to their own. For example, liberal activists interested in a new issue are likely to seek supporters among those already known to be sympathetic with other liberal causes, just as conservative activists generally try to bring their new concerns to the attention of known conservatives. That is, activists seek to enlist people who have already supported other, similar causes because it should be easy to build a bridge between fundamentally similar frames.

2. *Amplification.* In **frame amplification**, activists call on values or beliefs that they presume many people hold in order to rally others to their cause. Although the prospective supporters may not have been

active in other movements, they are presumed to hold basic assumptions that should make them sympathetic to the activists' cause. For instance, recent campaigns to register sex offenders and then restrict their rights have drawn on popular stereotypes about the predatory nature of sex offenses and people's sense that society ought to be protected from such predators. Frame amplification often seeks to arouse emotional reactions, such as compassion or outrage, so that people feel compelled to join the movement.

3. *Extension.* In **frame extension**, activists enlarge their frame to encompass concerns that prospective supporters are thought to have. In this case, the activists' core values or beliefs may not overlap those of their prospective supporters until they extend their frame. To return to an example raised in Chapter 2, vegetarian activists tend to be concerned with primarily ethical issues: they believe that it is morally wrong to eat meat (Maurer, 2002). However, relatively few Americans share that concern, and vegetarians have had more success gaining support by extending their frame to emphasize the health and ecological benefits of vegetarian eating—appeals that can attract supporters who worry about health or environmental issues more than the morality of eating meat.

4. *Transformation.* In **frame transformation**, activists call on prospective supporters to reject the familiar worldview that they take for granted and adopt a new and different frame. This transformation may be limited to how one thinks about a specific troubling condition (for example, the campaign to redefine drunk driving sought to persuade people to stop thinking of it as a somewhat amusing, minor offense, and start viewing it as a serious crime that all too often leads to terrible consequences). In other cases, activists may try to convert supporters to a completely different view of the world (think of efforts to recruit adherents to unfamiliar religions).

These four forms of frame alignment pose increasingly difficult challenges to activists. Frame bridging is the most straightforward task: claims are made to prospective recruits who are thought to be ideologically predisposed to being sympathetic to the claims. Frame amplification depends on emphasizing values and beliefs that the activists already share with the audience for their claims, in order to mobilize them to action; and frame extension requires activists to modify their own frame to make it more attractive to potential recruits. Frame transformation presents the greatest challenge: recruits are asked to abandon their familiar view of the world in favor of the activists' frame.

Different SMOs within the same social movement may have distinct frames that appeal to different prospective members. Often, for instance, a movement may contain both moderate and radical SMOs, the former advocating limited reforms to the existing social system, while the latter call for more significant changes. Activists from a movement's moderate and radical wings usually frame the troubling condition and its solution differently, and they may clash in **frame disputes**, disagreements over how to think about the problem (Benford, 1993). In many cases, activists from different camps within the same social movement present their frames to different audiences: as a general rule, moderates seek to appeal to older people in the middle class (who have relatively secure places within the existing social system, and who therefore are likely to resist radical calls for dramatic social change); and radicals are more likely to seek supporters among those who are younger or poorer (who have far less invested in maintaining the status quo, and who therefore should be more open to pursuing fundamental changes).

Successful framing draws on cultural resources; it incorporates familiar values, beliefs, imagery, and other cultural elements that prospective members find persuasive and convincing. Feminists, for instance, invoke familiar notions of fairness and equality, and argue that women have a right to equal treatment. But framing cannot be a one-way process. When activists interact with prospective members, they usually discover that some appeals are more persuasive than others in convincing people to join the movement. After all,

prospective social movement members have many messages competing for their attention—television shows, news reports, advertisements, and on and on. Activists cannot simply present a frame and
wait for the world to take notice; that would leave too much to chance
because it would be too easy for the activists' frame to be overlooked.
Rather, activists must seek out potential supporters, try to frame their
message in ways that others will find interesting and convincing, and
then pay close attention to what does and doesn't work. If activists
find that their claims have generated counterclaims, they may need
to reframe the issue to take this opposition into account. Similarly,
when one version of a frame fails to elicit much response, it will need
to be modified until it begins to be effective (see Box 3.2).

This need to devise frames that will attract supporters, counter
opposition, and eventually influence social policy can raise issues of
integrity for activists (Benford, 1993). Activists at the core of an SMO
often have more ideologically coherent frames than many other movement supporters have, and they may view frame extension—altering
their frame in order to make it more appealing—as a violation of their
principles, as "selling out." Frame disputes within a movement often
revolve around questions of compromise: should activists present
what they believe to be a more correct, more principled view of
the issue even if it risks rejection by many prospective supporters
who will find it too difficult to understand, or even unpalatable; or
should they frame the issue in weaker but more appealing terms
so that prospective members will find it easier to digest? Frames
inevitably reflect a combination of how activists view the world,
and what they believe will be an effective message.

RESOURCE MOBILIZATION

Adopting a frame that justifies belief in a cause is not enough to
make a claim successful; activists cannot trade on outrage alone.
Social movements also need to deal with a variety of mundane

Box 3.2 Competing Ecological Frames

A century ago, conservation was a social movement aimed at conserving American natural resources (early advocates called for establishing national parks and forests). Fifty years later, people spoke of environmentalism or ecology—a cause that combined concerns about pollution, resource depletion, and population growth. Activism related to these issues has continued, and it has adopted a variety of frames.

Pellow and Brehm (2015) describe the emergence of a new social movement frame—total liberation—that has four aspects:

- Total liberation calls for justice and anti-oppression for all—not just for all people, but for animal species and ecosystems.
- It favors anarchism; there is a distrust of governments and hierarchies.
- It is anticapitalist. It charges that capitalism is closely aligned with the state, and inevitably promotes inequalities and injustices.
- Total liberation calls for direct action, for individuals to confront injustice by taking direct action (for instance, destroying property) that, given the close alliances between corporations and governments, is likely to be treated as criminal.

Obviously, the total liberation frame is radical; it probably has relatively few adherents. It sets itself in opposition to other environmentalist/ecologist frames that it portrays as offering weak "reforms" that only allow things to get worse. While its advocates' direct actions are sometimes labeled terrorist acts, their response is to argue that the real terrorism is the continued damage humans are doing to the planet. Such competing frames force others to confront issues in new terms.

problems. Organizing a successful demonstration means picking a good time and place to maximize participation. People who might be willing to participate must be contacted and encouraged to come (demonstrations designed to attract a big crowd might require Internet postings, posters, telephone calling systems, and other ways of getting the word out); it might even be necessary to make arrangements to transport people to the event. Large demonstrations also require a lot of planning: tasks might include training people in dos and don'ts, scheduling speakers and other events, assigning monitors to supervise demonstrators, preparing first-aid stations, and possibly even arranging to post bail for people who get arrested. In addition, press releases need to be issued to inform the media that the demonstration will be taking place, and it may be a good idea to designate spokespeople to explain the demonstrators' purpose to the reporters covering the event (see Box 3.3).

In other words, one way to think about activists is in terms of the resources required by a social movement's activities. Movements need money, members, skills, and so on. These may seem like mundane considerations, especially if we think of social movements in romantic terms, consisting of plucky little guys struggling against powerful interests. But without sufficient resources, movements will have difficulty getting started, let alone enduring. Successful movements must assemble the resources they need. Sociologists refer to this gathering of resources as **resource mobilization** (McCarthy & Zald, 1977).

The resources that activists need are almost always scarce: it is hard to raise enough money, because the people who give money have lots of other ways to spend it; it is hard to get people to devote time to the movement, because there are other things they could do; and so on. The struggle to assemble resources means that SMOs—even SMOs that are theoretically allies in the same social movement—find themselves in competition with one another for the same scarce resources. They compete for members, for donations, for media coverage, and so on. If one SMO is especially effective in mobilizing resources, rival organizations are likely to find resources harder to come by.

For example, the civil rights movement—now recalled as a grand, unified movement to end segregation—was characterized by

Box 3.3   Someone Has to Ask

Mobilizing large crowds for demonstrations is a challenge. While some people may hear a media report about a planned demonstration and decide to attend, most require more convincing. After all, attending a demonstration is inconvenient and possibly even risky, and people always have other things they could choose to do.

Many demonstrators agree to participate because someone they know asked them to attend, answering their practical questions (*Where and when will the event be held?*), but also convincing them that they really should attend (*It's important that we be there*). But it is not enough to agree to attend when asked. To mobilize a large crowd, people who have been asked need to take the next step, to contact others and ask them to attend as well.

Not everyone takes that next step. Walgrave and Wouters (2014) found that individuals who went on to recruit others tended to be committed to the cause, but they also belonged to "participation-friendly" social networks—that is, they knew other people who were likely to be sympathetic to the cause, and who could be persuaded to join the demonstration. In general, while it is easiest to convince people with whom one has close ties (such as family members), successfully asking people one isn't as close to is extremely important: even if they are harder to persuade, convincing some of them spreads the message more broadly so that there is now a larger, more diverse set of people planning to attend who have a broader range of contacts they can go on to ask. The broader the base of participants, the larger the number of participants who can be mobilized.

internal competition and disagreements (Haines, 1984). Different civil rights organizations had different frames that led them to favor different strategies. For many years the NAACP had pursued a legal strategy, mounting court challenges to the constitutionality of segregationist practices. Dr. King's SCLC (Southern Christian Leadership Conference) favored high-visibility protests in communities such as Birmingham and Selma, Alabama. More radical organizations, such as CORE and SNCC, adopted riskier, more confrontational tactics such as sit-ins and freedom rides. Because potential donors could choose which organizations they wanted to support, the various SMOs were rivals for those donors' dollars. The NAACP, for instance, believed that it made sense to invest in a long-term legal campaign, and it opposed spending donors' money to bail out SNCC's demonstrators who engaged in protests that were certain to lead to their arrests. SNCC, on the other hand, argued that the NAACP's approach was too slow, and tried to rally support for its riskier activities. Establishing and maintaining alliances with other movements takes work.

In contemporary America, much social movement activity revolves not around convincing individuals to dedicate their lives to activism, or even around organizing thousands of people to march in the streets, but around fundraising. Although activists do sometimes organize large demonstrations, much of their activity focuses on seeking media coverage for their cause, lobbying policymakers, and so on. These activities cost money, and activists spend considerable time soliciting contributions from people who support the movement's cause (but may not feel they have the time or energy to work directly on movement activities). Note that we can distinguish between **beneficiaries** (who stand to benefit directly if a movement is successful) and **constituents** (who support the movement) (McCarthy & Zald, 1977). Some people belong to both categories, but many movement supporters are **conscience constituents**—that is, people who contribute money or even join demonstrations because they believe in the cause, although they do not expect to be direct beneficiaries (think of Northern whites who donated to civil rights SMOs).

The growing importance of contributions led to the emergence of sophisticated fundraising efforts using, for instance, direct-mail techniques. Mailing lists of people known to have contributed to previous fundraising campaigns were used to raise additional funds.

Fundraising efforts become more sophisticated as new technologies become available; in recent years, SMOs have begun raising funds via the Internet, using social media, websites, and e-mail to solicit donations. Of course, this emphasis on bringing in money means that SMOs become dependent on the support of constituents with whom the activists have no direct contact; most of an SMO's members act only as contributors, who may never actually encounter other members face to face. This poses a challenge: how to keep people emotionally committed to both the SMO and the larger cause and willing to continue their support when they have few direct connections to the movement. In response, SMOs maintain websites, send members frequent e-mail messages, and seek to convey a sense that their members constitute an electronic community (Eaton, 2010). Sending messages to current and prospective members turns into yet another occasion when troubling conditions must be reconstructed with compelling rhetoric—in this case, arguments that funds are needed urgently to respond to an important opportunity or, more often, to a looming threat. Both pro-life and pro-choice activists, for instance, raise money by warning that, unless supporters rally to their cause (by donating money to support their SMO's activities), their opponents are likely to win. Alternatively, SMOs may seek funding from other sources, such as foundations, but this support may come at a cost.

Increasingly, then, successful activism requires sophisticated skills—organizing, fundraising, media relations, lobbying, and the like. These skills tend to be portable: individuals who learn skills in one SMO can move on and apply what they've learned at another SMO, or even in another movement. Just as some veterans of the civil rights movement took what they had learned in that campaign and used their new skills to help organize antiwar protests, the women's liberation movement, and the gay liberation movement, people today pursue careers as activists, sometimes working for different causes over the course of their careers. Typically, these individuals do have ideological commitments, so they tend to move among social movements with which they are sympathetic: one individual may work for several liberal SMOs, while another becomes active in various conservative causes.

Resource mobilization is important because it reflects an SMO's ability to promote its claims. Organizations with more members and a bigger budget are better able to afford the services of skilled activists (who may in turn be attracted to working in campaigns that have plentiful resources and better chances of success). SMOs with money can afford further fundraising efforts, so they have better prospects for garnering future resources. Moreover, SMOs with greater resources find it easier to draw attention to their message: they are better able to gain coverage in the media; and, other things being equal, they are more likely to influence policymakers. Mobilizing resources is not glamorous, but it provides an essential base for would-be activist claimsmakers.

OPPORTUNITY STRUCTURES

Activists must worry about more than devising a persuasive frame and mobilizing necessary resources. Timing also matters. All too often, social movements face great obstacles. After all, movements seek to change existing social arrangements, and those arrangements work to the benefit of powerful people who can be expected to use their considerable resources to resist changes that might be to their disadvantage. On occasion, however, these obstacles to change are reduced, and activists must be alert for and ready to take advantage of such opportune moments. Various cultural and political circumstances can create opportunities to promote activists' claims.

Cultural Opportunities

Cultural opportunities arise when people become more willing to listen to the movement's claims (McAdam, 1994). Perhaps the most obvious cultural opportunity is the occurrence of a newsworthy event that focuses attention on a troubling condition. The September 11, 2001, terrorist attacks, for instance, suddenly moved terrorism from a peripheral concern to the central focus of national attention. Other, less dramatic events—a natural disaster, a brutal crime, and such—can have similar effects. They lead to a widespread sense that a particular troubling condition, previously neglected, must now be addressed. Activists who have been struggling to have their claims heard may suddenly find themselves in demand—reporters seek them out for interviews, legislators invite them to testify at hearings, and so on—because they are the ones who understand and have ideas for what to do about the troubling condition that is now the focus of concern (see Box 3.4).

Another sort of cultural opportunity emerges when a **master frame** becomes familiar (Snow & Benford, 1992). A master frame articulates a broad orientation that can be easily adapted for application to many issues. For instance, after the civil rights movement first drew national attention to blacks' struggle for equal rights and then succeeded in dismantling the system of institutionalized segregation in the South, the idea that demanding equal rights might be an effective way of framing social issues spread to other social movements. Within about ten years, activists were campaigning for women's rights, gay rights, children's rights, and the rights of the disabled, prisoners, and the elderly. This master frame remains influential: the abortion issue has been framed in terms of fetuses' *right to life* and women's *right to choose*; divorced men campaign for *fathers' rights*; an active *animal rights* movement has emerged; and so on. Like dramatic events, the availability of master frames creates cultural opportunities that can make it easier for activists to promote their claims.

Political Opportunities

Political opportunities to promote activists' claims arise when the distribution of power among different groups shifts so that changes that previously would have been successfully resisted can

Box 3.4 A Scandal Creates Opportunities

In 2007, it was revealed that NFL star quarterback Michael Vick had been involved in a large-scale dogfighting operation; he would be convicted on criminal charges and serve time in prison. As this scandal unfolded, it created a series of opportunities for animal-rights activists (Badano, Burgermeister, Henne, Murphy, & Cole, 2014):

- There were dozens of dogs found at the facility. Although it had been customary for animal-control officials to euthanize fighting dogs (on the grounds that they were too dangerous to rehabilitate), activists campaigned to rescue the dogs.
- In the two states that had not classified dogfighting as a felony, legislatures quickly passed tougher laws.
- Activists also kept the case in the news by demanding that Vick receive harsh punishments (he was suspended from the NFL, fined, and served time in prison).
- When Vick completed his sentence, he sought to ally himself with an animal-rights organization in an effort to demonstrate that he had been rehabilitated. Various SMOs considered working with Vick; most chose not to ally with him because they felt it would work to his advantage more than theirs.

This example reminds us that an event may create a series of opportunities for activists. The Vick scandal could be connected to a variety of animal-rights causes—opposition to euthanizing animals under any circumstances, the need for tougher laws, creating a memorable example of the consequences of violating anti-dogfighting laws, and even taking a stand on whether to align one's organization with a former offender. Opportunities can come in clusters.

now be implemented. Political opportunities may derive from shifting priorities, when formerly irrelevant concerns are redefined as relevant. One reason the civil rights movement gained momentum in the early 1960s was that former colonies—particularly the

African colonies of Britain and France—were gaining independence. The Cold War was at its height, and the United States wanted to minimize the Soviet Union's influence in these newly independent nations. The concern that African nations might be repelled by the treatment of African Americans in the United States created a new pressure to do something about the system of segregation found in the Southern states. In this case, shifting foreign policy concerns created new opportunities for civil rights activists trying to change domestic policies (Bloom, 2015).

Another form of political opportunity emerges when, for some reason, opposition to a movement becomes weaker. Those who might be expected to resist the activists' claims may be losing influence, or they may be distracted by other concerns. Perhaps more important for the social problems process is the fact that support for claimsmakers may become stronger. Successful claims lead to sympathetic media coverage, public opinion polls that reveal growing support, and political leaders' joining the cause. Support for "an idea whose time has come" can grow to the point that opponents may decide to drop their opposition. For instance, the basic principles of equal rights for African Americans and for both men and women advocated by the civil rights and the feminist movements, respectively—principles once considered quite controversial—have achieved broad acceptance.

Activists need to assess political opportunities and devise appropriate tactics for exploiting them. A tactic that is effective at one moment may be less effective at another. For instance, McAdam (1983) traces the history of tactical choices in the civil rights movement. The movement's activists devised a variety of protest tactics—sit-ins, large-scale demonstrations, and so on. Some of these tactics proved ineffective: they failed to attract media attention or to weaken the system of segregation. But others worked better, and news of these successes spread, leading activists in other communities to copy the effective tactics. Still, these successes were temporary; a tactic remained effective only for a time. News of the new tactic also inspired opposition; the movement's segregationist opponents searched for tactics of their own—responses that could minimize the movement's impact—and news of these successful opposition tactics also spread. In addition, each time civil rights activists used a particular tactic, it became more familiar and less newsworthy, so the media coverage dwindled. These processes created a cycle of tactical innovation in which a novel tactic would emerge, work for a while, then grow less effective, causing the activists to invent a new form of protest to keep the movement advancing. Similarly, activists discover that their choice of targets matters: claims that don't attract much attention when directed at an unfamiliar target may become newsworthy when aimed at a prominent target (see Box 3.5).

Just as some circumstances can improve political opportunities, others create obstacles, occasions when claimsmaking probably can't succeed. Public attention is finite; if the media are devoting their attention to other newsworthy events, they aren't likely to cover a particular social movement's claims (see Chapter 5 for a more thorough discussion of how the media choose what they will cover). In the weeks immediately following September 11, 2001, media attention concentrated on terrorism, so there was almost no chance that claims about other issues could receive much attention. Similarly, when rival claimsmakers—activists for another social movement, or even for another SMO within the same movement—are occupying center stage and hogging the limelight, opportunities for promoting one's own claims are reduced. Rather than struggling to be heard under such adverse circumstances, it may be wiser to conserve resources and wait for a more promising opportunity.

Similarly, opportunities are unfavorable when opposition to a cause seems to be growing stronger, or when support for that cause seems to be growing weaker. Under such circumstances, activists need to consider what's wrong and make the necessary changes. Perhaps the existing frame is losing its appeal; perhaps more resources need to be assembled. At these times it is better to back off and wait for a better opportunity, rather than forcing the issue and facing certain defeat.

For example, Taylor (1989) traces the history of the National Women's Party (NWP), which long promoted an Equal Rights

Box 3.5   Choosing Corporate Targets

Many troubling conditions identified by activists are large and diffuse. To be effective, social movements need to focus their efforts more narrowly to select particular targets of protests that can typify the larger problem. It is easier to construct claims about specific targets, attract interest to those claims, and apply pressure to those targets, than to try and attack the whole problem all at once.

For example, the antisweatshop movement seeks to draw attention to working conditions in factories (particularly factories in developing countries) (Bartley & Child, 2014). Obviously, there is a vast number of such factories, and they produce all manner of products. Rather than trying to denounce working conditions generally, the movement selects particular brands of goods or stores, familiar names that will be recognized by a large share of the public. Making claims about inhumane working conditions in factories that produce, say, a popular brand of clothing makes the issue visible to shoppers, who may respond to the controversy by choosing to buy a competitor's brand. (There is, of course, an excellent chance that the competitor's goods are produced under very similar conditions.) In theory, enough bad publicity—and lost sales—may lead the targeted firm to make public efforts to improve conditions, and the competitors should then follow suit to avoid becoming targets themselves.

Which firms get targeted? Big firms with high-visibility brands and good reputations make easier targets and, once a firm's name has been associated with sweatshops, it is easier to mount further campaigns. Also, media coverage of events such as a terrible factory fire with a large loss of life can draw public attention to particular firms, creating opportunities for activists to turn what may have been a previously overlooked firm into a target.

Amendment (ERA) to the Constitution that would guarantee women full equality under the law. During much of its history, and particularly during the years following World War II, the NWP confronted poor political opportunities for success. This was a period of **abeyance**; that is, the NWP maintained a modest organizational structure, continued monitoring political developments, and waited for brighter opportunities. A good opportunity arose in the late 1960s, after the civil rights movement had captured Americans' attention, making the equal rights master frame more familiar and more acceptable. In particular, new calls for women's liberation began to gain notice, and as a new wave of feminist activism began to emerge, the NWP joined the new feminists (such as the newly formed National Organization for Women, or NOW) and encouraged them to campaign for the ERA (although that particular campaign was again narrowly defeated). By tending the feminist flame during the decades of abeyance, the NWP had conserved its resources until more promising opportunities developed to use them.

Summary

Social movements can experience decades of frustration, periods when activists cannot seem to interest anyone in their cause—when they face indifference, ridicule, even repression. It helps to be patient, to wait until cultural and political opportunities develop that offer more favorable conditions for claimsmaking. For instance, the civil rights movement and the feminist movement have had long histories featuring both periods of frustration and periods of progress. These familiar examples teach other activists the importance of continuing the struggle, of hanging on until opportune moments arise.

THE ADVANTAGES OF OWNERSHIP

Activists whose efforts are particularly successful can gain **ownership** of a social problem (Gusfield, 1981). Ownership is established when particular claims or frames become generally recognized and acknowledged as the best way to understand a particular issue. It is an ambiguous status; no one receives an official certificate of ownership, but some claimsmakers become the recognized, go-to authorities on a troubling condition. If a dramatic event brings that problem back into the news, it is the owners who are asked by reporters to provide commentary and who are consulted by policymakers.

Ownership relates to framing, resource mobilization, and political opportunities. The owners' frames become influential in shaping how others approach the problem and its solution; the owners' perspective may not be the only possible way of thinking about the troubling condition, but it becomes familiar, almost taken for granted by the press, the public, and policymakers. Precisely because they are well known, owners find it much easier to mobilize resources. People who want to contribute or otherwise become involved in a cause tend to know about and turn to a problem's owners, just as reporters looking for sources to comment on an issue are likely to think first of approaching the owners. And, of course, precisely because owners find it easier to garner resources, they have an easier time maintaining their ownership in the face of competing activists. As a result, owners are well placed to take advantage of opportunity structures. When, for instance, current events draw attention to a troubling condition, owners tend to be far better prepared to exploit whatever opportunities develop: they have contacts with the media and with policymakers; they are probably better placed to assess political opportunities; and they may even be integrated into the social problems process well enough to act as insider claimsmakers.

A social problem can have multiple owners. Position issues marked by intractable disagreements often feature SMOs that own the opposing sides in the debate. For example, the NRA long ago established itself as the leading SMO speaking on behalf of the rights of gun owners and in opposition to gun control. For a long time, proponents of gun control lacked a comparably influential SMO; in recent years, however, the Brady Center to Prevent Gun Violence and the Violence Policy Center have emerged as the most visible antigun SMOs—the owners of gun control advocacy. And, as noted earlier, social movements often encompass a range of frames, from more moderate groups advocating modest reforms, to more radical SMOs pushing for more significant changes. Owners may emerge at different points along this spectrum. Within the 1960s civil rights movement, for example, the well-established NAACP favored deliberate pressure to gain favorable court decisions, while more radical SMOs, such as SNCC and CORE, became well known for organizing more confrontational activities, such as sit-ins and freedom rides. A few highly visible SMOs shared ownership of the large, broad-based civil rights movement (see Box 3.6).

Some SMOs own particular issues for extended periods. The NRA has led the fight against gun control for decades, and the NAACP has been a leading voice in the movement for African Americans' civil rights since its founding in 1909. Such owners must constantly strive to keep their issue—and their ownership— visible to the press, the public, and policymakers. Maintaining such a presence serves two purposes. First, of course, it keeps the owners' particular claims—their frame—for interpreting the issue visible and familiar so that others find it easy to continue to think about the topic in the owners' terms. Second, it helps preserve the owners' status *as owners*. Attention—and contributions—tend to go to the most familiar advocates. Although ownership is harder to achieve in the first place than it is to maintain after being gained, it must always be nurtured.

Long-term ownership requires flexibility. Narrowly focused, single-issue movements are at a long-term disadvantage; it is too easy for public attention to drift away from an issue, and once that happens, supporters, media coverage, and access to policymakers may also dwindle. It helps to develop a broader set of interrelated concerns. The NAACP, for instance, has addressed a wide array of issues related to racial discrimination during its long history. In its early years, for example, the NAACP devoted considerable attention to its campaign against lynching. But as lynching declined and then disappeared, the NAACP turned to constructing other race relations

Box 3.6 Consolidating a Cause

When the women's movement became active in the 1960s, abortion was not a central issue, either within the movement or in the larger society. At first, the National Organization for Women (NOW) was the leading feminist SMO, but some feminists saw NOW's positions as too radical, and they established more moderate SMOs (not unlike the ideological diversity among various civil rights SMOs).

By 1980, the Supreme Court had legalized first-trimester abortions, and there was a vocal antiabortion countermovement. NOW had come to redefine reproductive freedom (including abortion) as a central feminist issue, and opposition to feminism was now intertwined with opposition to abortion. Democrats were increasingly pro-choice, and Republicans increasingly pro-life.

Kretschmer (2014) explores how these developments forced two more moderate feminist SMOs to deal with abortion. The Women's Equity Action League (WEAL) began as a midwestern SMO that viewed NOW (dominated by East Coast activists) as too radical. They saw themselves as allied with NOW on what they thought of as the central feminist cause—promoting equality for women in the workplace—and they tried to avoid taking a stand on abortion, which they saw as a side issue. However, as abortion became more central to the feminist position, WEAL found it necessary to adopt a pro-choice stance to remain allied with NOW and other feminist SMOs. In contrast, Feminists for Life were by definition pro-life. They soon found themselves unwelcome at gatherings of other feminist SMOs, and they became part of the larger coalition of pro-life SMOs.

issues, such as campaigns against discrimination in education and employment, opposition to hate crimes, and so on. As political opportunities shift, it can become easier or harder to promote particular claims, but to the degree that the NAACP maintains ownership over the full spectrum of issues related to African Americans, it can remain actively involved in the social problems process.

In contrast, narrowly focused SMOs run the risk of succeeding—and thereby losing their reason for existing. Consider the March of Dimes, a charitable organization originally launched to fight the problem of polio, a disease that left children severely disabled. Once polio vaccines were developed, the threat of polio virtually disappeared, and the organization faced a crisis. It could, of course, declare victory and disband. But why dismantle a successful fundraising apparatus? Instead, the March of Dimes redefined its purpose, declaring that it would continue to operate but would now dedicate its efforts to fighting birth defects. This was not just a new but also a broader definition of the SMO's purpose: there are many different birth defects, so although further successes might result in eliminating some of these problems, the organization would continue to be needed to address the problems that remained.

When claimsmakers begin drawing attention to a troubling, previously neglected condition, there are three ways ownership of the issue might evolve:

1. **No one assumes ownership.** This situation is most likely when a newsworthy event, such as a dramatic crime, catapults an issue into the public eye. A variety of commentators may offer their takes on this troubling condition, perhaps suggesting different ways of thinking about the issue. However, it may be that none of these claimsmakers will assume ownership of the topic, work to keep the issue visible, manage a prolonged campaign to change public policy, and so on. Under these circumstances, even topics that receive a burst of intense publicity can shift away from public attention, forgotten as soon as the next dramatic event commands notice. Without owners to remind people of a problem's importance, issues can fade (this possibility is discussed further in Chapter 5).

2. **Activists establish a new SMO that can assume ownership.** A familiar example is the emergence of Mothers Against Drunk Driving (MADD). Although drunk driving had a long history, MADD gave the issue not just new visibility, but a new frame as a threat to children menaced

by drunk drivers. MADD lobbied legislators, observed courtroom proceedings, established local chapters around the country, and generally
took control over what had been an ownerless issue.

3. *An existing SMO assumes ownership of the new issue.* This can
work well for the SMO, which can otherwise become a familiar part
of the landscape and run the risk of being taken for granted. Assuming ownership of another issue, so long as it is at least tangentially
related to the SMO's original program, is a way of making its claims
seem fresh. At the same time, having an experienced SMO—which
has already found ways to mobilize resources—assume ownership
improves the prospects for keeping the issue in the public eye.

Ownership, then, affects the prospects of both an issue and the
activists who promote it. Unless someone assumes ownership, it is
hard for the social problems process to proceed; it is too easy for
public attention to shift away as soon as the next new issue arrives
on the scene. Owners are needed to tend the topic, to remind
people of its importance, and to revise their claims so that the
topic remains fresh and interesting. But ownership also benefits the
owners: their claims seem better established; their authority seems
more legitimate; and as they become familiar figures with a larger
network of social contacts, they can begin to transform themselves
from outsider to insider claimsmakers.

ACTIVISTS: PRINCIPLES AND PRACTICALITIES

Discussions of social movements often emphasize their principled
character. That is, they depict activists as individuals committed to
a particular cause, seeking to promote a higher good. But sincerity
is not enough. As claimsmakers who seek to influence the social
problems process, activists need to convey their message to, and
influence the behavior of, the media, the public, and policymakers.

That is, they need to confront the practical problems posed by social movements.

This chapter has explored four such problems (see Figure 3.2).

First, activists must develop effective frames; that is, they must construct their claims so that others will find them convincing, so that people will support the activists' SMOs. Principled statements that cannot persuade others threaten to stall the social problems process before it has really begun.

Second, activists must mobilize sufficient resources to promote their movement's goals. Activists who prove unable to attract and manage members, money, and other necessary resources probably will not be able to keep their SMOs functioning long enough for their cause to succeed.

Third, activists need to be able to recognize and figure out ways to take advantage of opportunities. Current events and the shifting political landscape can aid—or hinder—social movements. Activists

Figure 3.2 ACTIVISTS' CONCERNS IN MAKING EFFECTIVE CLAIMS

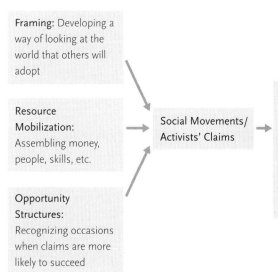

Framing: Developing a way of looking at the world that others will adopt

Resource Mobilization: Assembling money, people, skills, etc.

Opportunity Structures: Recognizing occasions when claims are more likely to succeed

Social Movements/ Activists' Claims

Ownership: A particular frame becomes recognized as the way to think about an issue, and a particular SMO becomes acknowledged as a leader on the issue need to be careful not to miss promising opportunities, just as they should avoid expending their resources when they have no chance to advance their cause.

Finally, activists can acquire and maintain ownership over an issue. Owning a social problem allows enduring influence, a means of keeping an issue—and the activists' leadership—visible so that the activists' frames remain familiar and widely accepted, resources are easier to mobilize, and the activists stay in position to take advantage of whatever opportunities develop.

Although they are the most obvious examples of claimsmakers, activists are not the only people who promote social problems claims. They often acquire allies—claimsmakers who, in addition to their commitment to principles, bring special knowledge or expertise to the social problems process. These expert claimsmakers are discussed in Chapter 4.

MAKING CONNECTIONS

- *Through framing, resource mobilization, and taking advantage of opportunities, activists attract attention to their claims in order to establish ownership over a problem and its proposed solutions.*

- *As you read Chapter 5 on the media, you will learn why ownership of a problem helps win attention from media organizations.*

- *To establish effective frames, activists rely on focus groups, polls, and other tools to measure public reactions. You will learn more about public reactions in the social problems process in Chapter 6.*

CASE STUDY
Mobilizing over Income Inequality

The Great Recession began at the end of 2007 and continued into mid-2009, when the economy began to grow again, although economic output and employment would remain sluggish for years. These aftereffects dragged on much longer than after a typical recession, and did more damage: millions of people lost their jobs and their savings, and millions of families lost their homes when they could not keep up their mortgage payments.

Most explanations for this crisis blamed banks and other financial institutions for irresponsible behavior. For instance, considerable attention focused on the adoption of policies that made larger numbers of home loans to high-risk borrowers, and then packaged those loans and sold them to investors as safe investments. When the borrowers could not repay their loans, it was the investors who took the losses; the lenders who had made the high-risk loans had already profited when they sold them. There were plenty of reports of investment firms making billions in the run-up to the collapse, even as their executives pocketed millions for arranging what the larger economy would experience as a financial catastrophe. And yet, when the dust cleared, most of the major financial institutions had been bailed out by taxpayers, and none of the executives whose actions had led to the crisis had gone to jail.

The crisis created a cultural opportunity to raise questions about the American economic order. Most obviously, the Great Recession inspired the 2012 Occupy Wall Street movement, in which protesters set up an encampment in New York's financial district. The movement attracted extensive media coverage, as well as a range of activists representing various causes, and it inspired dozens of local Occupy protests across the country (Gamson & Sifry, 2013; Gitlin, 2012). The Occupy movement was initially diffuse and confusing, with protesters promoting a range of causes: regulating banks, aiding mortgage holders, reducing student debt, and so on. In some ways, the Occupy site became the embodiment of a social problems marketplace, with claimsmakers promoting all sorts of different issues.

Over time, however, attention consolidated on rhetoric about "the 1 percent." These claims argued that Wall Street represented the interests of the wealthiest 1 percent of the population (a category that certainly included the various executives at the financial firms at the center of the crisis). There were various claims that the top 1 percent held a large share—between 35 and 43 percent—of the nation's total wealth.

Here, it may help to pause for a moment to consider just who belonged to that top 1 percent. In 2010, the U.S. population was over 308 million; this means that the top 1 percent included more than 3 million people. All of them would have been worth more than $1 million—something that could be said for about the top 3 percent (2015 estimates are that more than 10 million people have investable assets [not including the value of their homes] totaling at least $1 million), but only a few of these people—around 500— are worth $1 billion. If we consider only income, the cutoff for the top percentile is $350,000–$400,000. In other words, there is huge variation in wealth and income within the top 1 percent.

Focusing on the 1 percent provided a bit of rhetorical shorthand to draw attention to many policies that worked to the advantage of those with more money. For instance, people who earned less than $110,100 in 2012 paid Social Security tax on every dollar they earned, but those who earned more paid no Social Security taxes on income above that amount. The long-term capital gains tax (on income from investments) is 15 percent, which is lower than the income tax rates for many taxpayers; this means that someone whose income comes primarily from investments can wind up paying a lower tax rate than someone whose income comes primarily from paychecks received for working. Such arrangements help the rich get richer.

As the diffuse message of the Occupy movement became more tightly focused on the privileges enjoyed by the 1 percent, other issues fell out of discussion. Increasingly, concern concentrated on income inequality. This was not a new topic; many claimsmakers had tried to draw attention to income inequality, but the Great Recession created first a cultural, and then a political opportunity for their cause.

Social scientists think of equality as a situation where everyone has the same resources. (Imagine a group of children: if each has one cookie, they are in a situation of equality.) It is possible to measure the degree to which the distribution of resources differs from perfect equality. Of course, every society falls short of this ideal, but over the course of American history, the United States has been at various times more—and at other times less—equal. Since the 1970s, inequality has been increasing; the gap between the rich and the poor has grown. Incomes and wealth have been rising far less for those in the bottom quintile (that is, the poorest 20 percent of the population) than they have among the top 1 percent, or even the top quintile.

Such patterns raise fundamental issues. Americans like to think that theirs is an especially open society in which anyone who works hard can climb, even to the very top. This is an ideal that both political liberals and conservatives accept. But clearly, people who start out with more money have substantial advantages in life. To take just one example, higher education is widely considered to be the principal route to upward mobility, yet college costs have grown much faster than the cost of living, so greater income inequality means that low-income students find it ever harder to pay for college.

Activists with very different ideologies can agree that income inequality and restricted paths for upward mobility are a problem, although they are likely to promote different solutions. Liberals, for example, focused much of their energy on campaigns to increase the minimum wage as a direct way to raise incomes among low-income people and thereby help reduce income inequality. In contrast, conservatives argued that upward mobility could best be promoted by encouraging the poor to marry (poverty rates are much lower among married couples) and improving schools (poverty rates drop dramatically as education rises), which would in turn foster upward mobility.

The relatively severe shock of the Great Recession created an opportunity for a wide range of claimsmakers: lots of people believed that something was wrong, and they were willing to listen to claims by those who offered solutions. However, as time passed, many of those claims fell by the wayside—their frames did not attract adherents. Activists who framed the issue in terms of income inequality and the 1 percent were more successful in rallying supporters to their cause, and particular issues, such as raising the minimum wage, became the focus for public attention.

QUESTIONS

1. Opportunity is a cultural resource that is available to claimsmakers. Does the word mean different things to different claimsmakers?

2. Economies have cycles—relatively prosperous times, and relatively hard times. It might be possible to address economic issues during good times (when more money is available). Why does economic claimsmaking tend to be more vigorous during hard times?

3. Imagine that, instead of the 1 percent and income inequality, attention had concentrated on some other topic related to the Great Recession. How might the social problems process have changed?

4

Experts as Claimsmakers

Colonial Massachusetts was established by Puritans, and ministers were key figures in that society. They saw evidence of God's hand everywhere in the world, and their sermons sometimes commented on current events, interpreting them in religious terms. A bad harvest might be evidence of God's wrath, and problems among people were caused by sin, by individuals breaking God's commandments. Virtually any event could be interpreted within this religious framework. Ministers, then, were colonial New England's principal experts; their theological training qualified them to explain and evaluate most aspects of life. Their religious frame was seen as authoritative because it was promoted by professionals representing the society's leading institution.

The ministers' religious perspective seems less authoritative today. In at least public discussions of social problems, modern Americans rarely speak of *sin* (and when politicians or even religious leaders do invoke such language, they often come under criticism). Rather, contemporary Americans are more comfortable with a kind of medical vocabulary; when talking about social problems, we are more likely to speak of *diseases, syndromes, disorders,* or *addictions*—words that seem grounded in medical, scientific classifications. Consider how contemporary discussions of Aquinas's classical list of the seven deadly sins often redefine these behaviors as medical problems; for example, lust might be characterized as *sex addiction*, gluttony as *food addiction* or *compulsive eating*, anger as an *anger management* problem, and sloth as *chronic fatigue syndrome*. (At the same time, modern medicine sometimes seems to promote those same deadly sins by treating their absence as medical problems that also may require treatment; consider drugs to enhance sexual performance [lust], cosmetic surgery [pride, envy], liposuction [gluttony], or concerns about workaholism and type A personalities [sloth] or low self-esteem [pride].) At least when they talk about social issues, contemporary Americans are less likely to accept the judgments of religious leaders, and more likely to defer to doctors.

The declining influence of ministers and growing clout of doctors illustrate how constructions of social problems reflect shifting patterns of institutional influence. In societies where religious authorities hold sway, social problems often are discussed in religious language; where medical authorities are more influential, social problems tend to be understood in medical terms. At different times and in different places, ideas about which people with which sorts of knowledge ought to be considered experts vary. *Experts* are presumed to possess especially authoritative knowledge, and other people—including activists, the media, and policymakers— may defer to this expertise.

In short, experts rank among the most influential claimsmakers because they are thought to have special knowledge that qualifies them to interpret social problems. Some experts are what Chapter 3 referred to as *insider claimsmakers*; their status as experts can give them easier access to policymakers so that they are part of the polity. This chapter examines the role of experts as claimsmakers in the contemporary social problems process. It begins by exploring the central place of medical authorities in constructing social problems, then turns to other sorts of experts.

MEDICALIZATION

Sociologists who have noted the increased use of medical language to characterize social problems speak of **medicalization** (Conrad, 2007), the process of defining troubling conditions as medical problems. A century ago, it was generally recognized that some people drank too much; that is, their drinking was blamed for causing problems at work, in their homes, and so on. The common label for these people was *drunkards* (Gusfield, 1967). Being a drunkard was seen as, if not a sin, at least a moral failing; drunkards were doing something they shouldn't do, and they needed to reform (the solution to being a drunkard often involved making a pledge to practice temperance; that is, the drunkard would promise to stop drinking).

Today, the term *drunkard* has virtually disappeared from our vocabulary. Of course, there are still people who drink too much, and whose drinking is thought to cause job problems, family problems, and so on. But we call these people *alcoholics*, and we speak of the *disease* of *alcoholism*. Alcoholics may receive *treatment*, often at *clinics*, where some of the costs are reimbursed by health insurance. In short, alcoholism has been medicalized, in that we now view it as a medical problem that should be addressed through medical solutions.

Consider another example: some students do not do well in school. Traditionally, those students were blamed for their poor performance: perhaps they were of lower intelligence, or perhaps they weren't trying hard enough. Today, claims suggest that poor performance at school may be caused by medicalized conditions, that these students have *learning disabilities* or *attention deficit hyperactivity disorder* (ADHD) (Conrad, 2007). Medical language—words such as *diagnosis*, *symptom*, or *therapy*—increasingly frames discussions of students' difficulties, and doctors now prescribe drugs to large numbers of children to help them become more attentive.

Why is medicalization important? There are two obvious ways it makes a difference. The first is that medicalization seems to shift responsibility away from the individual. In our culture, we routinely hold individuals responsible for what we view as deliberate behavior—acts that people choose to perform. Drunkards were once seen as weak because they gave in to drink, and poor students used to be viewed as lazy; in both cases, the individuals were held responsible for their own problems. In contrast, we generally do not hold people responsible for their illnesses; we don't blame them for becoming sick. Therefore, saying that people have the disease of alcoholism or a learning disability means that they shouldn't be blamed for their problems, that they merit sympathy and support, rather than criticism.

A second consequence of medicalizing a problem is that it provides a familiar frame—sometimes called the **medical model**—for thinking about the issue. Medical problems are described as diseases, disorders, syndromes, or disabilities. The people with these problems are ill; they display symptoms. They need to become patients, who can receive treatment from medical personnel—doctors, nurses, therapists—who often work in hospitals or clinics, and who can be reimbursed through the patient's health insurance. In other words, medicalization is a claim arguing that some problem should be owned and controlled by medical experts and organizations.

Medicalization, then, frames troubling conditions in particular ways (see Box 4.1). At first glance, our culture seems to construct sins or crimes differently from illness: sinners and criminals are held responsible, blamed for their actions, and punished; people who are ill are not blamed and receive treatment instead. However, the medical model also focuses on the individual rather than the larger society. In a medicalized view, people have diseases or syndromes that lead them to drink too much, to eat too much, and so on; and they must confront and overcome these problems through healthy behavior. By focusing on individuals' choices, medicalization shifts attention away from the ways in which larger social arrangements, such as poverty, shape these troubling conditions.

Medicalization grew markedly during the twentieth century. In part, this shift reflected dramatic changes in the practice of medicine:

Box 4.1 Legitimizing Migraine

Migraine headaches are a familiar, common problem that affects about 12 percent of adults. Medical analyses of the disorder date back centuries. Yet both the physicians who study and treat migraine and their patients are frustrated that the diagnosis is not taken more seriously.

Kempner (2014) argues that migraine suffers from a "legitimacy deficit." People who don't have migraine often dismiss them as "just another headache" and suspect that migraine is just a psychosomatic disorder, perhaps best treated with lifestyle changes, like stress reduction. The debilitating nature of migraine is not widely appreciated.

As a result, the physicians who deal with migraine and their patients biomedicalize the condition. They point to evidence: brain scans showing that migraine has a physiological basis; disease classifications that categorize it as a disease of the brain; and pharmaceuticals that help reduce the number and intensity of migraine episodes for some patients. They hope that this evidence will give migraine more legitimacy as a "real" disease so that people will be more willing to acknowledge that migraine headaches are debilitating, rather than suspecting that sufferers are exaggerating the severity of the sort of headache everyone experiences from time to time.

Migraine reminds us that experts are not all-powerful. Although there is a good deal of evidence to support—and medical authorities who actively advance—claims that migraine is a physiological disorder, people who experience migraine, which can be chronic and totally disabling, still do not receive the sort of widespread sympathy and understanding that, say, a broken leg elicits.

doctors and hospitals became subject to tighter professional standards, so the quality of care rose; at the same time, advances in medical science led to new medications and treatments. All this meant that the chances of medical care actually helping patients rose sharply; people began to expect more of medical authorities, and the prestige and authority of physicians rose.

The rising stature of medicine encouraged the expansion of medical authority into a broader domain of social problems. In particular, psychiatrists (who are trained as physicians) began to claim that many troubling behaviors—including juvenile delinquency, unconventional sexual activity, drug addiction, and crime—should be recognized as symptoms of psychiatric problems. After World War II, the American Psychiatric Association began developing its *Diagnostic and Statistical Manual of Mental Disorders* (the so-called *DSM*), a huge catalog of all recognized mental disorders, which has continued to expand with each new edition (Kirk & Kutchins, 1992). The growing number of available diagnoses means that more and more behaviors can be understood in medical terms (see Box 4.2).

In addition to psychiatrists, whose medical training clearly placed them within medicine, practitioners in a variety of other quasi-medical professions adopted the language of *disease, symptom,* and *treatment.* Among these were clinical psychologists, licensed clinical social workers, and many others, including some with little or no professional training. Drug treatment, for instance, increasingly was provided by "professional ex-s [sic]"—recovered drug users who did not necessarily have professional credentials, but who were employed by drug treatment centers to lead therapeutic groups and who used medical language to describe what they did (J. D. Brown, 1991).

Often medicalization consists of little more than adopting a medical vocabulary. Take what is called the disease of *alcoholism*: its symptoms include drinking and getting into trouble at work, at home, and so on; there are no clear biological symptoms that distinguish alcoholics from nonalcoholic drinkers (Appleton, 1995). Similarly, treatment for alcoholism is to get people with drinking problems to choose to drink less (most often, total abstinence is recommended). The leading program for dealing with

BOX 4.2 DISPUTING AUTISM CLASSIFICATIONS

The American Psychiatric Association's *Diagnostic and Statistical Manual of Mental Disorders* is the authoritative catalog of psychiatric problems. It is periodically revised—new disorders are added, and older diagnoses are redefined. Barker and Galardi (2015) describe reactions to a 2012 *New York Times* report that the next revision (*DSM-5*) would adopt a set of diagnoses that would redefine autism in ways that might narrow the disease's definition (making it harder for a patient to receive an autism diagnosis).

While nonexperts might feel ill-qualified to comment on a news story about psychiatric experts defining their principal reference work's categories, the *Times* piece actually inspired considerable online commentary. (It is important to understand that no one—in either the news reports or the online commentary—challenged how severe cases of autism were diagnosed; the focus was on where to draw the line for people displaying less severe symptoms.) Some people argued that autism was being overdiagnosed, that what were once considered normal personality differences were being medicalized. These commentators were pleased to think that the domain of autism—the range of symptoms that might lead to a diagnosis—might contract. However, other comments—often from parents whose children had been diagnosed under the diagnostic standards set in the current *DSM*—opposed altering the diagnostic criteria in any way that might make it more difficult for them to receive a diagnosis that might let them qualify for help.

This example reveals that experts do not operate in a vacuum; nonexperts may dispute experts' knowledge, weighing in on such apparently technical issues as what should or should not be considered autistic.

alcoholism, Alcoholics Anonymous (AA), is a resolutely amateur operation. There are no professionals; all of AA's members are people who identify themselves as recovering alcoholics. Individuals attend meetings with fellow alcoholics and discuss AA's twelve-step program for achieving sobriety.

AA insists that alcoholism is a disease, but that the cure is to stop drinking, continue attending AA meetings, and follow the Twelve Steps. Note that AA's solution for alcoholism—that is, helping the individual with a drinking problem to make a commitment to stop drinking—is not all that different from the way drunkards were expected to reform by taking a pledge of sobriety, although the language of medicine seems to impart special authority to treatment as a solution. The twelve-step model has been adapted to help people deal with a variety of troubling behaviors—including drug abuse, overeating, and gambling—that have also been characterized as addictions or diseases.

In short, various medical authorities, with very different sorts of credentials, claim ownership of many contemporary social problems. As noted in Chapter 3, ownership can bring important benefits. Experts who gain ownership of a social problem usually gain a good deal: their social visibility and prestige rise, they become more powerful, and typically they stand to benefit financially from the increased business that people afflicted with the problem bring to them. This means that experts often have a vested interest in promoting claims that depict social problems from their perspective.

In a classic constructionist case study, for example, Stephen Pfohl (1977) argued that pediatric radiologists played a leading role in bringing attention to battered child syndrome—what would later be called *child abuse*. Initially this problem was typified in terms of physical injuries to children too young to explain how they had been hurt. Pediatric radiologists—specialists in interpreting children's X-rays—argued that they could distinguish fractures caused by accidents from those caused by abuse. These claims not only promised to improve the protection of vulnerable children, but also gave pediatric radiologists—who represented a small, relatively low-prestige medical specialty—ownership of a life-threatening disease, so the specialty's status rose. Expert claimsmakers often experience such gains, and thus wind up doing well by doing good.

Experts often seek to defend their professional turf and even expand their domain of ownership. The process may be gradual. Consider the changing scope of pediatrics (Pawluch, 1996). When this medical specialty emerged in the early twentieth century, pediatricians focused their efforts on problems associated with infant feeding; the milk supply was often tainted, causing many infants to become seriously ill. However, improved techniques for managing the purity of the milk supply soon made infant feeding much safer, so the major service that pediatricians had been providing was becoming less needed. In response, pediatricians began to expand their domain to emphasize the treatment of, first, other childhood diseases, and then normal, healthy childhood development. As birth rates fell, of course, there were fewer children for pediatricians to treat, but the specialists began to extend their services to treating patients in adolescence and even early adulthood (see Box 4.3).

These efforts need not be seen as cynical and self-serving. Experts generally believe that they have valuable knowledge and offer useful services, and they are continually looking for new opportunities to apply their expertise. In periods when their services are already in high demand, they have less time to extend their domain, but when business is slack, the prospect of attacking new problems becomes much more attractive. In this way, professional domains expand and the professionals' interests are advanced.

Ideally, experts' gains can be consolidated into institutionalized ownership. For instance, rising health care costs increasingly require patients to have medical insurance. But what sorts of treatments should health insurance cover? Professionals who provide different treatments want medical insurance to cover their services so that more patients will seek those services. Thus, the federal government's decision to define alcohol and drug problems as medical problems, and to require health insurance programs to cover some of the costs of their treatment, institutionalized these experts as owners of the alcohol problem (Weisner & Room, 1984). As

Box 4.3 When Experts Succeed Too Well

At the beginning of the twentieth century, childbirth was dangerous; for every 100,000 births in the United States, 850 mothers died within a month of giving birth. By 1980, this figure had fallen more than 99 percent—to 7.5 maternal deaths per 100,000 births. This might seem to be wonderful news—a serious social problem had been essentially eliminated. However, it posed a problem for those experts who had devoted their careers to studying the problem of maternal mortality, and they began to expand the domain of the problem, which allowed them to argue that their research topic remained important. They accomplished this by arguing that a death could be considered an instance of maternal mortality, not just if it was caused by an infection or some other complication of childbirth within the first month after the birth, but if death occurred from any cause within a year of being pregnant. This meant that the death of a woman who died, say, in a traffic accident eleven months after giving birth could be counted as a case of maternal mortality; indeed, a woman who died in an accident within a year of choosing to terminate a pregnancy could also be counted.

Such redefinitions allowed maternal mortality experts to argue that maternal deaths might be as high as 20 deaths per 100,000 live births, and to call for campaigns to do more to address this problem. Their claims could be made even more alarming by focusing on particular causes of death, such as homicide; such deaths might be very rare, but they could be typified as evidence of a neglected problem. It is important to remember that experts have a vested interest in the importance of their problems.

Source: K. Johnson, 2013.

Chapter 3 noted, owners have advantages in promoting their constructions of social problems; when ownership is coupled with such experts' institutionalized arrangements, experts' authority becomes entrenched.

In recent years, medicalization has taken new directions, with troubling conditions becoming subjects of **biomedicalization** (Clarke, Shim, Mamo, Fosket, & Fishman, 2003). Experts argue that biological processes are the root cause of many troubling conditions, which means that effective solutions must then address biology. For instance, the scientific revolution in genetics has led to claims that it will soon be possible to identify particular genes that cause various troubling conditions. Clearly, genetic anomalies cause some medical disorders, such as Down syndrome. But biomedical proponents argue that it will soon be possible to identify the genetic roots of all manner of behaviors, such as homosexuality or alcoholism, and research funding increasingly supports biomedical studies. This assumption that biology is at the root of many troubling conditions also fosters **pharmaceuticalization**, the process of defining prescription drugs as the solution (Abraham, 2010). Some of these claims may be borne out; others may prove false. At least for the foreseeable future, however, medicalization is likely to remain our society's leading form of expert claimsmaking.

THE ROLE OF SCIENCE

Medical authority may be seen as a subcategory of a broader form of expertise: science. As with medicine, the advances made possible by the expansion of science, particularly during the past two centuries, have given scientists considerable authority in our culture. Society has been transformed by the growth in scientific knowledge; think of the Industrial Revolution, the exploitation of new forms of energy (steam, electricity, petroleum), faster transportation, speedier communication, and so on. Increased scientific knowledge made these changes possible.

Science depends on an appreciation of evidence. A scientific theory must generate falsifiable predictions; that is, those predictions must be able to be tested, and if they are proved wrong, the theory is rejected. Scientists do research to produce evidence that can support or challenge their theories' predictions; the more supportive evidence they find, the more confidence scientists have in their theories. This system of reasoning has proved very powerful and has provided the foundation for all sorts of technological and medical advances, and in our society scientists are considered to have considerable authority when speaking about matters for which they have gathered evidence.

This is not to say that scientific evidence is infallible. Science is socially constructed; it is one of the ways people make sense of the world. To be sure, we have considerable confidence in well-established scientific findings, but it takes time for findings to become well established. Research can be flawed, and evidence can be incomplete or incorrectly interpreted. Scientists may debate issues among themselves, questioning one another's reasoning and evidence. Scientific progress can be a slow process; such debates can continue for years, even decades, until the evidence compiled becomes sufficiently compelling for a consensus to emerge among scientists.

Unfortunately, the deliberate pace of science is not well suited to news media eager to report on dramatic scientific breakthroughs. For instance, the media may publicize reports of the initial study on a particular topic, even though that research may eventually prove to have been flawed. A dramatic example was the media's reaction to a 1989 report by two researchers who said that they had observed a cold-fusion reaction in their laboratory. The implications were staggering—harnessing cold fusion would provide limitless, inexpensive energy—and the media began to speculate about the social changes this discovery would bring. Alas, other scientists soon concluded that the researchers had misinterpreted their results—that they had not found a way to produce cold fusion—and the media quickly dropped the topic.

Scientific experts' claims derive much of their rhetorical power from the understanding that scientists have special knowledge and access to particularly strong evidence, so their views deserve respect.

The media's tendency to treat the results of a single piece of research as definitive leads to confusion in the case of ongoing scientific debates. Until sufficient evidence becomes available, scientists— like other experts—do not necessarily agree. Their evidence and interpretations may differ, even conflict. The press, the general public, and policymakers often find such disagreements frustrating, because they tend to look to scientists for not just authoritative, but correct, information. Apparent contradictions call scientists' authority into question.

For example, one week the media might report that a medical journal has published a research report concluding that drinking alcohol increases the risk of contracting a particular disease. The following week the media might announce that another group of researchers has concluded that moderate drinking improves one's health. What should people think? It is possible that both reports are correct—that is, that drinking raises the risk of contracting a particular disease but generally improves health. Or perhaps one of the studies is flawed (or even both are flawed). Over time, additional research is likely to lead to an eventual scientific consensus, but it is important to recognize that disagreements are normal within science and many other expert communities. Experts may disagree about which are the important questions to ask, about the best way to arrive at answers to those questions, about how to interpret the available evidence, and so on.

In general, research questions and answers are most clear-cut in the physical sciences (such as physics and chemistry), less so in the biological sciences (such as medicine), and the least so in the social sciences. The physical sciences have fewer disagreements about what constitutes compelling evidence, and debates among physical scientists often can be settled decisively; in contrast, social scientists often cannot agree about what constitutes convincing evidence. In addition, it is important to appreciate that disagreements among scientists can center on very different sorts of questions, and that the authority of science depends on the sort of question being asked.

Consider, for instance, the debate over climate change. At the most basic level is the question of whether the planet's temperature is indeed rising. Scientists have devised various ways of measuring temperatures going back through time. Although there may be some disputes about the accuracy of particular measurements, or about which methods of measuring temperature changes are most accurate, these are relatively technical matters, and there is considerable scientific consensus that cycles of global warming and global cooling have occurred in the past and that temperatures have risen about 0.74°C over the past one hundred years or so. Accurately measuring changes in temperature presents a relatively clear-cut research challenge—the sort of question that scientists are clearly qualified to answer. It is, of course, more difficult to predict what will happen in the future, although again there is fairly widespread consensus that temperatures are likely to continue to rise over the next century (but considerable disagreement about how much they are likely to rise, with estimates ranging from 1.8°C to 4.0°C).

A second issue—over which there is more debate—concerns the causes of climate change. Although some argue that the current global warming may be a natural process—just part of the long-term cycle of planetary heating and cooling—most scientists agree that at least some of the warming is due to humans' impact on the planet. Most commonly these claims focus on the role of greenhouse gases (for instance, emissions of carbon dioxide from vehicles and smokestacks) in retaining heat in the atmosphere. Note that these explanations are not mutually exclusive; perhaps the planet would be warming naturally in any case, but human activities are exacerbating the trend. At this level, the scientific issues are not as straightforward, and even experts who agree that global warming is occurring may disagree over the extent to which people's activities contribute to this process.

The debate's third level is far more contentious. Even if we assume for the moment that everyone agrees that human activity plays a substantial role in causing climate change, what should be done?

Here, debates can address many different issues, including what the consequences of global warming might be, what sorts of policies might reduce climate change, what the costs of those policies might be, whether the prospective benefits justify those costs, who should bear the costs, and so on. At this stage, purely scientific issues are less central; science may offer fairly compelling evidence about the extent and causes of climate change, but scientific knowledge cannot specify the correct course of policy. Consider nuclear weapons, for example: scientists were able to design and build nuclear weapons, but the decisions to use—or not use—those weapons were made by political leaders, not scientists. Scientific knowledge ordinarily is not sufficient to set social policy.

In short, we need to understand that when scientists participate in debates over social issues, the relevance of their expertise varies, depending on the particular questions being considered. While people—including some scientists—may like to imagine that scientific findings are sufficient to guide policy, in practice policymaking is shaped by other considerations, especially values (Pielke, 2007). In addressing a question such as how much the planet's temperature has increased during the past century, scientific expertise is likely to play the central role. However, many commentators would argue that science cannot provide authoritative answers to questions such as whether the prospective benefits of implementing a particular policy to reduce greenhouse gases will justify the policy's costs, or how the costs of controlling emissions should be distributed among richer and poorer countries. The willingness of audiences to grant authority to scientists is likely to depend on how relevant they believe the experts' knowledge to be (see Box 4.4).

Contemporary debates over scientific authority often focus on constructions of risk. The modern fascination with risk can be dated to the 1960s, when the surgeon general announced that smoking was hazardous to health, activist Ralph Nader drew attention to unsafe automobiles, and author Rachel Carson warned that pesticides were causing significant environmental damage (Meyer & Rohlinger,

Box 4.4 Conservatives Losing Confidence in Science

Expertise confers social status, for it is not enough that experts claim to have special knowledge; it is also necessary that other people ratify that expertise, and defer to the experts' judgments. For decades, surveys have asked the public to rate the amount of confidence ("a great deal," "only some," and so on) they have in various institutions. These data make it possible to track changes in the level of confidence of both the public overall, and in various subgroups of the population, such as people who describe their political orientation as conservative, moderate, or liberal.

In 1974, there were only modest differences in how people with different political orientations rated their confidence in science; if anything, conservatives expressed slightly more confidence in science than the other two groups. However, in the intervening years, the levels of confidence expressed by liberals and moderates remained essentially stable, while conservatives' confidence in science fell until they were the group least likely to say they had a great deal of confidence in science.

Such shifts have consequences for the social problems process. To the degree that there is general agreement about the authority of some type of expert, claims from such experts need not be divisive. However, if views of experts become politicized—as when conservatives have less confidence in scientific authority—then experts' claims have less power. In particular, conservatives' skepticism about the scientific findings regarding climate change have made policy debates much more contentious.

Source: Gauchat, 2012; McCright & Dunlap, 2011.

2012). These highly visible claims led to concerns about other risks, which in turn produced all manner of warnings—about the dangers of cholesterol, secondhand smoke, toxic waste, and so on. Such claims often couple scientific evidence (suggesting, for example, that a particular chemical may be carcinogenic) with warnings that the danger is widespread and the issue urgent. Increasingly, the media cover scientists' warnings that this or that condition poses risks to individuals' health, to environmental safety, and so on. Although the evidence regarding some risks—such as the link between smoking and lung cancer—is overwhelming, scientists disagree about the extent and significance of other risks.

It can take time for scientists to agree on assessments of risk. The most compelling scientific evidence comes from experiments, but it is usually impossible to design experiments to study risk. We cannot take identical groups of infants and make sure that they have identical experiences going through life—except that we can expose the experimental group to a particular risk and keep the control group from being exposed to that risk. Such a study might produce very strong evidence, but it would be time-consuming, expensive, and unethical. In practice, researchers must settle for much weaker evidence; they might, for example, identify people exposed to a particular risk, try to match them with similar folks who have not been exposed to that risk, and then study whether the two groups have different rates of particular diseases. It is always possible to challenge the results of such studies—for instance, were the two groups matched on every relevant variable?—and it takes a great deal of evidence (such as the countless studies on smokers' health) to make a convincing case.

It is difficult for nonscientists—a category that includes most activists, members of the media, the general public, and policymakers—to assess claims about risk that refer to scientific evidence. Debates over social problems often ignore such issues as comparative risks (for instance, the number of people at risk, the number of people likely to be harmed, and so on). All kinds of activities (for example, driving to work) carry risks. Often we take these risks for granted and ignore them, even though they may be far greater than are the heavily publicized dangers of, say, exposure to secondhand smoke. Scientific evidence—particularly calculations of risk—is not well understood, and such issues often lead to confusion in the face of what is thought to be expert claimsmaking.

EVIDENCE, INTERESTS, AND ADVOCACY

A major reason why people defer to experts is their presumption that experts command knowledge that other people don't have. Although all knowledge is socially constructed, we consider experts' knowledge to be more likely to be accurate than gossip, rumor, or other less authoritative sorts of knowledge that, we know from experience, often prove to be wrong. Thus, we tend to consider expert knowledge to be relatively correct. We defer to medical authorities because we assume that they know how to diagnose diseases, are able to understand the causes and workings of those diseases, and can recommend the best possible treatments. Similarly, we presume that scientists have done careful research and compiled evidence that offers the best available information about how the world works.

In other words, we turn to experts for sound information based on high-quality evidence, and experts' status as relatively authoritative claimsmakers depends on such understanding. Experts are commonly assumed to be impartial judges—their medical diagnoses or scientific findings grounded in facts rather than opinions. Yet experts often have an interest in promoting claims, and when they become advocates for particular positions or policies, they are not necessarily guided solely by their expert knowledge (see Box 4.5).

We have already noted that experts stand to benefit from the ownership of social problems; recall how the status of pediatric radiologists rose after they drew attention to battered child syndrome. Experts also may have social ties to parties with interests in social issues. Scientific research can be extremely expensive, and many scientists derive funding from corporations, government agencies, and so on. These funders may have an interest in the researchers' findings. For example, both medical researchers and their pharmaceutical company sponsors may have financial stakes in a new drug, and they may hope that the drug proves safe and effective, just as scientists employed by a corporation may be under pressure to affirm that the firm's waste disposal practices are safe. Other

---

BOX 4.5 MAKING HAPPINESS AN EXPERT PROBLEM

Obviously, happiness is a very old idea. But happiness has recently emerged as a social problem under the ownership of experts. As the twentieth century came to a close, there were claims that increases in income did not correspond to increases in measures of happiness (these measures typically asked people to rate how happy they were). The notion that happiness could be measured objectively made it a subject for expert assessment, with psychiatrists, psychologists, and economists becoming the principal owners of the happiness problem.

The experts' claims that prosperity and programs to promote social welfare through improving material conditions do little to enhance happiness invite a romantic critique: materialism will not lead to happiness; the roots of true happiness lie within the individual. In their view, public policies should worry less about emphasizing the importance of economic growth, and more about enhancing mental health; educators should teach "happiness skills"; and individuals should be encouraged to pay more attention to nonmaterial values and to take care of their health. Thus, inner welfare should be more important than social welfare in ensuring what really matters—happiness.

Experts play active roles in constructing many social problems. We assume that doctors know what ails us, that economists know how to improve prosperity, and so on. The construction of happiness—traditionally viewed as a personal emotion—as a social problem best understood by experts reveals our increasing readiness to allow experts to intrude into and offer guidance for our private lives.

Source: Frawley, 2015.

---

scientists may be closely associated with particular social movements, such as environmentalism.

Even though we tend to idealize scientists as objective, impartial observers, they may have allegiances that help shape their conclusions.

Some legal trials feature psychiatrists hired as expert witnesses by the prosecution and the defense, who testify, respectively, that the defendant's mental state was such that the trials should or should not proceed. The point is not that experts' social ties make science illegitimate—a very large share of scientists have such commitments—but that scientific knowledge is not produced or disseminated in a social vacuum.

In some cases, scientists' allegiances may be to the particular perspectives or approaches that characterize their disciplines. For instance, sociologists and other social scientists also act as expert claimsmakers. Just as medical authorities bring their professional training to bear when they medicalize troubling conditions by characterizing them using the language of diseases, symptoms, and other medical concepts, social scientists have their own orientations and conceptual tools. Economists, for example, argue that people can be understood as rational actors who make choices to maximize their own satisfaction. This proves to be a powerful underlying assumption, in that it can be extended to analyze all manner of choices. Thus, economists tend to see social problems as the products of people's choices, and to promote policies that will encourage people to make particular choices. For example, one way to discourage smoking is to raise tobacco taxes; if tobacco is more expensive, at least some people may choose to stop smoking.

Sociologists, too, apply their discipline's perspective to the analysis of social problems in their works (including this book). Sociologists argue that people shape one another's actions, and that social problems are products of particular social arrangements. Thus, where a psychiatrist may approach a social problem in terms of individuals whose thinking is disordered because they suffer from a syndrome of some sort, or an economist may see it in terms of arrangements that reward some choices more than others, sociologists are more likely to point to the way culture and social structure constrain and shape people's activities. C. Wright Mills (1959) called this mode of thinking the *sociological imagination* (discussed further in Chapter 5). This book, for instance, emphasizes understanding the social problems process through which actors socially construct social problems.

In other cases, experts may have allegiances to particular ideological positions. Liberal and conservative experts can approach social problems in very different ways: they focus on different causes, and they recommend different solutions. So-called think tanks—private nonprofit organizations dedicated to policy analysis and advocacy—often have an ideology that shapes their experts' recommendations (see Box 4.6). These experts maintain connections with media outlets and politicians who share their ideological orientations, so advocates from different positions have access to expert knowledge that can be used to buttress their claims.

Although we might like to imagine that experts are completely independent, impartial authorities, without interests or ideological commitments, this perfect objectivity is, in practice, impossible to achieve. Experts are part of the larger social order. At a minimum, they believe in the value of their professions: psychiatrists consider psychiatry a valuable perspective, just as sociologists promote the value of the sociological imagination. Experts can further be expected to believe that the problems they have chosen to study are important and worthy of their attention and that the solutions they have been working on are promising. They may also have more obvious interests (such as a financial stake in the outcome of their research) or ideological preferences. Such social connections do not necessarily mean that the experts are wrong, but they do suggest that experts may be less than perfectly objective, and may think less critically when they confront ideas that fit their prejudices, so their claims should not be automatically accepted.

Expert knowledge is imperfect because it is produced by scientists, physicians, and other experts who are themselves actors in the larger society. It should be no surprise that experts' ideas evolve as new information becomes available. But it takes time for novel ideas

Box 4.6 Constraints on What Think Tanks Think

Think tanks are organizations of experts designed to promote claims and policy responses. Typically, they represent particular ideological positions; thus, the Brookings Institution often adopts liberal stands, the American Enterprise Institute and the Heritage Foundation promote conservative positions, and the Cato Institute presents libertarian views.

Claimsmaking is a central purpose of think tanks. Their experts try to identify troubling conditions, construct them as particular sorts of social problems, and devise proposals for policies that might solve those problems. Think tank experts operate as insider claimsmakers, trying to bring their concerns to the attention of legislators and officials in government agencies, so as to directly influence the policy process.

To maintain their influence, think tanks' experts are dependent on their connections to others (Medvetz, 2012). To get members of Congress and other government officials to pay attention to their claims, people at think tanks need to consider what concerns those officials; think-tank proposals are more likely to receive officials' attention when they address problems those officials already consider important. Think tanks are largely funded by substantial gifts from corporations and foundations; those donors have their own ideas about which issues deserve the think tanks' attention, and they may withhold funding if they sense that think tanks don't share their concerns. It also is important to maintain contacts with members of the media who can choose to cover or ignore the claims think tanks produce; a well-connected think tank can get more coverage for its claims. Think tanks, then, do not operate in a refined intellectual vacuum.

to emerge and gain acceptance. As evidence accumulates, consensus is likely to develop, but this process cannot occur overnight. This is why expert knowledge is best understood as a special type of claim, part of the larger social problems process.

OFFICIALS AS EXPERT CLAIMSMAKERS

Another important category of expert claimsmakers consists of officials, particularly those employed by government agencies, such as the Centers for Disease Control and Prevention (CDC) or the Environmental Protection Agency (EPA). Such agencies have various responsibilities: they may compile information (collecting data to measure the crime rate, the unemployment rate, and so on); they may administer regulations (regarding workplace safety, pollution, or other issues); they may fund research through grants to experts outside the government; they may disseminate information to the citizenry; and so on. The work of many agencies bears on one or more social problems. Because the federal government spends billions on the budgets of its various agencies, these officials can draw on substantial resources. Usually they are able to compile more and better information about troubling conditions than unofficial claimsmakers can, giving officials' claims special authority in many social problems debates. Official agencies often achieve a level of ownership for social problems.

Agencies compete with one another for budget allocations and other scarce resources. Often multiple agencies have an interest in the same social problem. For instance, alcohol issues are the concern of several federal agencies: the Bureau of Alcohol, Tobacco, Firearms and Explosives (ATF); the National Institute on Alcohol Abuse and Alcoholism (NIAAA); the National Highway Traffic Safety Administration (NHTSA), which is concerned with alcohol-related traffic fatalities; and on and on. Imagine how many federal agencies must be concerned with a particular aspect of racial inequality. Just as social movement organizations find themselves competing with one another, officials—at least some of the time—view other agencies as competitors, both for resources and for ownership of particular social issues.

Protecting and, if possible, expanding an agency's turf becomes a central concern for officials, and claimsmaking provides one weapon for bureaucratic infighting. That is, drawing attention to a particular troubling condition, devising a program to deal with the problem, and then administering that program can serve two ends. On the one hand, it is easy to imagine that most officials are sincere, that they have joined an agency because they believe that it does important, valuable work. Like other claimsmakers, officials probably believe their own rhetoric and adopt the frames they promote. At the same time, officials have instrumental reasons to promote claims: successful claimsmaking is likely to serve the agency's interests, to increase its power, influence, and budget. Whatever their convictions, officials often have an interest in the claims they promote. For example, officials of the U.S. Bureau of Narcotics undoubtedly saw marijuana as a dangerous drug when they first called for a federal law against it in the 1930s, but that law also helped protect the bureau from further budget cuts (Dickson, 1968).

Officials may recognize that their agencies could address certain additional troubling conditions if they could help launch the social problems process. Indeed, agencies often control significant, flexible resources that can be used to jump-start the claimsmaking process. In the 1960s, for instance, the U.S. Children's Bureau (CB) was under fire from critics and losing control of some programs that were being shifted to other agencies (Nelson, 1984). At the same time, CB officials had long been in contact with the American Humane Association, an organization that had historically been concerned with the physical abuse of children. The CB began funding the research that drew national attention to what was initially called *battered child syndrome*, soon to be renamed *child abuse* (Pfohl, 1977). Child abuse became a visible, dramatic subject of considerable public concern, and in the process helped restore the CB as an important agency of the federal government. As an owner of the child abuse problem, the CB could extend its programs—funding further research, helping develop legislation requiring doctors and other professionals to report child abuse, and so on.

Although the expert claimsmakers in these examples were federal officials, analogous processes can occur in state or local governments, wherever officials become involved in drawing attention to troubling conditions. In some cases, national attention on a problem may lead local officials to call for action in their communities; in other locales, officials may be slower to acknowledge that the problem exists in—and requires action in—their jurisdictions. The policies of different cities toward homelessness, for instance, depend on how local officials respond to the issue (Bogard, 2003). In other cases, claimsmaking by officials may focus on purely local issues—such as whether an old building should be demolished to permit new development, or be preserved as part of the community's historical heritage (Lofland, 2003).

Officials working in government agencies usually have special knowledge or expertise that justifies their participation in claimsmaking. They are insiders, and their activities often occur behind the scenes, out of the public view. In sharp contrast are the claimsmaking activities of elected officials—presidents, senators, and the like—who may seize on an issue and become active claimsmakers. These officials may lack special expertise, but their visible positions make it much easier for them to attract media attention and help publicize a cause.

EXPERT CLAIMSMAKERS IN THE SOCIAL PROBLEMS PROCESS

Chapter 3 explored the role of activists and social movements in claimsmaking; this chapter has concentrated on the claimsmaking of experts—particularly medical authorities, scientists, and public officials. In many cases, claimsmaking campaigns feature alliances between activists and experts. Activists often contribute enthusiasm, passion, and whatever organizational resources their movements may control, whereas experts provide authoritative knowledge.

(This is obviously an oversimplification: many activists become quite knowledgeable, and experts can become highly dedicated to claimsmaking campaigns.)

Knowledge is an important commodity in claimsmaking. Remember that social problems claims begin with grounds statements—that is, statements about the facts concerning the troubling condition. When claimsmakers are trying to draw attention to a neglected condition—one that hasn't attracted much attention—often they discover that little information is available and no experts are studying the problem yet. One solution is for activists to begin to collect their own information. For instance, it was only after gay and lesbian activists in some cities tried to gather reports of homosexuals who had been assaulted that official efforts to collect hate crime statistics started (Jenness & Grattet, 2001). Similarly, residents living near toxic waste sites may begin to collect their own evidence of health problems as a way of arousing concern about the risks they face (P. Brown, 1992). In such cases, amateurs try to generate the sort of knowledge that experts have failed to collect, in order to fill what would otherwise be a gap in their claims. Figure 4.1 illustrates how both trained professionals and those without formal training as experts can make use of professional knowledge when making claims.

Just as activist claimsmakers must be alert to the responses of others—particularly the media, the public, and policymakers—so, too, must experts be concerned with feedback from other actors in the social problems process. Because experts are likely to consider the knowledge that they contribute to the social problems process especially valuable, they may be disappointed that their statements are not more influential. Audiences may have trouble interpreting what experts have to say, particularly when the experts present their findings using a professional, technical vocabulary. To bridge the gap, experts may discover that they need to popularize their work, to translate their findings into lay language.

Another problem is that audiences may have impossibly high expectations for experts' contributions; as we have suggested, experts

Figure 4.1 EXPERTS' ROLE IN THE SOCIAL PROBLEMS PROCESS

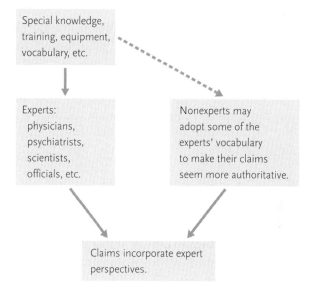

may add to our understanding of a troubling social condition, but their knowledge usually is not sufficient to identify policies that can make the problem disappear. Ultimately, whether experts' claims— or, for that matter, the claims of activists—are widely understood depends on the treatment they receive in the media.

MAKING CONNECTIONS

- The role of experts in the policymaking process is discussed further in Chapter 7.

- The media rely on experts to make claims about social problems. In the next chapter you will learn how experts and the media collaborate in the social problems process.

- In Chapter 9, the role of experts in evaluating the outcomes of social problems and making new claims about problems will be discussed.

CASE STUDY
Forecasting the Future

While social problems claims usually focus on troubling conditions in the present, they often warn about how those conditions will only get worse. That is, they offer constructions of the future (J. Best, 2011). But claims about what is going to happen some time in the future can always be challenged: "How can you claim to know what is going to happen?" In some societies, people might turn to oracles, soothsayers, or others who claim to have some sort of supernatural expertise, an ability to foresee what will happen. Today, of course, we are likely to turn to various sorts of experts.

Consider predictions that Social Security will run out of money. These are based on relatively straightforward calculations. At present, an individual can qualify for "full" Social Security payments when they reach age sixty-six (the law already in place states that this will rise to sixty-seven in 2027). Thanks to the census, we already have a pretty good idea about how many Americans will turn sixty-six and qualify for Social Security in, say, 2018. Population records also let us predict the percentage of seventy-year-olds who will die before they reach their seventy-first birthday, and so on. So it is a fairly simple matter to add the people entering the Social Security rolls and subtract those who are expected to die, which lets us predict with considerable accuracy how many Americans will be receiving Social Security in any particular year and, based on current arrangements, we can figure out how much money will be needed to pay them. These figures are not really in dispute; there aren't many Social Security skeptics.

We can also imagine ways in which the laws regarding Social Security might be changed: for example, we could raise the age at which individuals become eligible, alter the formula used to calculate cost-of-living increases, raise Social Security taxes by raising the tax rate (which would mean that everyone would pay more on the first $118,500 of their income [the figure when this book was written]) or by increasing the amount of income subject to Social Security taxes (which would mean only those earning more than $118,500 would pay more), or reduce payments for high-income recipients. All of these are ways to postpone Social Security's running out of money, and we have enough information to make reasonably good predictions about the effects of any of these changes.

Contrast these predictions with the difficulties of predicting climate change. There is general agreement that global temperatures have been rising, and there is nearly as much agreement that this change is due, at least in part, to humans' effects on the environment, but there is much less agreement about how much further temperatures are likely to rise in the next fifty or one hundred years. Predicting temperature increases is much more difficult than predicting the future costs of Social Security. Social Security's future involves a relatively small number of variables: how many people are expected to qualify for the program in each coming year; how many people are expected to leave the Social Security rolls; how much people are expected to pay in Social Security taxes, and so on. In contrast, there are thousands of variables thought to affect climate. Scientists develop elaborate computer models that specify the effects these variables are thought to have on one another. These models change over time as experts incorporate more knowledge about climate processes.

The result is that climate change predictions vary; some models predict larger and faster temperature increases than others, so there are a range of estimates—some higher, some lower—for how much temperatures will increase by, say, the year 2100. Scientists may disagree about which models they prefer. This is not unusual in debates among scientists and other experts; science advances by proposing hypotheses, testing them, and gradually accepting some ideas while dropping others. Scientific knowledge is constantly changing in the face of new evidence; we should not be surprised when scientists disagree.

Still, it is possible for claimsmakers to point to such disagreements as a means of raising doubts. A notorious example is the decades-long campaign waged by the tobacco industry against antismoking activists. For decades, scientists had argued that smoking increased the risk of lung cancer and a host of other medical problems; thousands of studies supporting this conclusion accumulated. In response, the tobacco industry mounted a public relations campaign and hired scientists as spokespeople to question the generally accepted conclusion that smoking was dangerous. In effect, they argued that the evidence was not all in, and therefore policymakers should not take action.

A somewhat similar campaign questions the scientific consensus about climate change. Because the most promising way to slow climate change involves reducing the emission of greenhouse gases, industries that generate those gases (such as the petroleum industry) have resisted climate-change claims. In the United States, Republicans have been more allied with these businesses, and they have argued that policies should not be changed until the science is settled. This campaign has reshaped public opinion: where once Republicans and Democrats, and liberals and conservatives, were about equally likely to report that they respected scientific authority, in recent years Republicans and conservatives have been more likely to express skepticism about predictions of climate change, even though there is widespread scientific agreement that temperatures are rising (Gauchat, 2012; McCright & Dunlap, 2011).

Notice some differences between expert claims about Social Security and climate change. First, predictions about Social Security are more precise because the relevant factors are well understood and easily measured, so there is less disagreement about what is likely to happen. With climate change, scientists generally agree that the planet is warming, but their models disagree about how fast this is occurring and what the effects are likely to be. Second, it is relatively easy to "fix" Social Security by some combination of raising taxes and/or reducing benefits; while none of these options is painless, it is easy to imagine that some compromise solution could be crafted. In fact, the history of the Social Security program is a series of these compromises, generally agreements that put off the crisis for a few decades. In contrast, proposals to address the global problem of climate change are likely to be extremely costly, so that the stakes are higher, making it harder for the many different nations involved to agree on a solution that they all find reasonable.

Society depends on expert claimsmakers to make knowledgeable recommendations about social problems, but experts' claims are only one element in the social problems process, and experts' recommendations do not automatically overcome all objections. Patients can challenge doctors' diagnoses and prescriptions, and so on. This is particularly true when experts make claims about the future. A prediction is not a certainty, and uncertainty invites doubts and resistance.

QUESTIONS

1. Identify another current prediction about a future social problem. Who makes the claim, and how much confidence should we have in the prediction?

2. Can you think of predictions about the future that were made in the past? What was the societal reaction to those predictions? Were those predictions accurate?

3. Predictions vary in how far they peer into the future—a year, a decade, even a century. Does this time span make a difference in how people respond to future claims?

5

The Media and Claims

Analyses of the mass media's role in the social problems process often focus on the issue of **bias**. Conservative critics charge that the media systematically present a liberal point of view:

> The argument over whether the national press is dominated by liberals is over. Since 1962, there have been 11 surveys of the media that sought the political views of hundreds of journalists. . . . And the proportion of liberals to conservatives in the press, either 3-to-1 or 4-to-1, has stayed the same. That liberals are dominant is now beyond dispute. (Barnes, 2004)

Meanwhile, liberals counter that the media have a conservative bias:

> Even the genuine liberal media . . . [are] no match—either in size, ferocity, or commitment—for the massive conservative media structure that, more than ever, determines the shape and scope of our political agenda. (Alterman, 2003, p. 11)

These critiques address the news media that report information (such as newspapers, newsmagazines, and radio and television news broadcasts), but also the entertainment media (such as television dramas, novels, or movies) and so-called infotainment that uses entertaining formats to discuss social issues (such as television talk shows, or "reality" shows that depict police at work).

All forms of **media coverage** tend to alter how social problems are constructed, although not necessarily in the ways that critics of media bias imagine. The social problems process typically begins with claimsmaking that precedes the media's involvement; usually activists or experts present the initial, or **primary**, **claims** (J. Best, 1990). Unless these claimsmakers are insiders who have ready access to policymakers (see Chapters 3 and 4), they probably hope that the media will cover their claims, thereby bringing those claims before a larger audience than the claimsmakers could hope to reach on their own. Newspaper stories, talk show episodes, or movies with plots involving troubling conditions can bring claims to the attention of millions of people in the general public, as well as policymakers. However, media coverage almost inevitably alters the claims that it presents.

Media workers face their own constraints: they work under deadlines, so they rarely have time to become thoroughly familiar with the claims they cover; their presentations are usually constricted (for example, newspapers can print only so many inches of news per day [journalists call this the *newshole*], and television news programs have only so many broadcast minutes available); and they need to make their coverage interesting enough that the audience won't stop reading or watching. The media, then, translate and transform claimsmakers' messages into what we will call **secondary claims**, typically by making them shorter, more dramatic, and less ideological than the original primary claims.

Because there are many claimsmakers and the media can cover only a limited number of stories, claimsmakers find themselves competing for media attention. Savvy claimsmakers realize that they need to package their claims so as to interest the media in covering them. The media prefer to cover new, seemingly fresh material, so it is important to present claims in novel ways (the first sit-in or peace march may get a lot of coverage, but each additional sit-in or march is likely to get less, unless it offers an interesting new angle). The media like to be able to plan their coverage in advance, so it helps to issue press releases and schedule press conferences so that reporters know when and where they can find someone willing to talk with them. The media favor claims presented by interesting people, so claimsmakers need to find spokespersons who seem engaging (note how often claimsmaking campaigns use either celebrities—interesting in their own right—or highly dramatic figures, such as parents who have suffered the loss of a child, to present their claims). Television seeks visually interesting material that can accompany a story, so claimsmakers favor marches, demonstrations, and other easy-to-film ways of presenting their claims. In the competition for media attention, claimsmakers who take the media's needs into account have an advantage (Sobieraj, 2011).

Hilgartner and Bosk (1988) suggest that the marketplace for social problems can be understood as composed of multiple **arenas**. Each arena is a venue where social problems claims can be presented; the pages of a newsmagazine, a TV talk show, or the hearings of a congressional subcommittee are all arenas. Each arena has a limited **carrying capacity** for presenting claims: magazines have only so many pages per issue, talk shows schedule a set number of episodes per season, subcommittees hold only a limited number of hearings, and so on. In Chapters 3 and 4, we considered the perspective of claimsmakers, who understand that they are competing for attention in various arenas. In this chapter we will adopt the perspective of those who work in the media. We can think of them as managing different arenas and having the job of sorting through all the competing claims and choosing which ones will receive attention in their arena.

In general, sociologists who have observed how news reporters and editors decide which stories to cover and how to cover them conclude that bias—in the sense of an underlying political ideology—is less important in shaping how the news is covered than the nature of the work that reporters and editors do. This chapter begins by considering the nature of those jobs—and the parallel considerations that shape how social problems are treated in entertainment media—before examining the forms that secondary claims tend to take. The chapter ends with a caution against exaggerating the media's influence.

WHAT'S THE NEWS?

The term **news work** draws our attention to the fact that reporters and editors have the job of locating and presenting news to the larger public. Like all other occupations, news work has constraints (Schudson, 2011; Tuchman, 1978). Some constraints are economic: it costs money to collect and produce news, and news workers operate within budgets, so newspapers and television news operations can afford only so many employees; the newshole (that is, the number of available column inches or broadcast minutes) can contain only so many stories; and so on. Other constraints are cultural. News workers have their own understanding of what they should do; that is, their sense of professionalism also shapes their coverage.

News workers operate under pressure. They have schedules and deadlines; newspapers and magazines need to reach the printer on schedule, just as radio and television programs need to be ready in time for their broadcasts. News workers cannot simply sit back and wait for news to happen and come to their attention; rather, they must try to plan ahead, to anticipate what might be and ought to be covered. Many news organizations assign reporters to beats—types of news that are expected to generate suitable stories; for example, a reporter on the police beat covers stories about crimes. News workers also are drawn to predictable events; a scheduled demonstration or even a press conference can be attractive precisely because reporters and editors have some sense in advance of what sorts of stories those events might generate.

News workers also judge some stories as being more deserving of coverage than others. Most obviously, they consider some stories to be more important, or, as they say, more newsworthy. Important stories involve consequential events, things about which people need to know. But importance depends on the news workers' audience. Imagine a passenger jet crashing and killing, say, 150 people. How much attention should a newspaper give that story? If the crash occurred in the city where the newspaper is published, we can imagine this dramatic local story consuming most of the front page. If it occurred, say, in a city a thousand miles away, and if there were other compelling stories competing for the paper's attention, the crash story might well be pushed off the front page. If the crash occurred in a foreign country (and especially if no Americans were killed), it is likely to receive no more than a paragraph or two, somewhere well inside the paper. In other words, it is not just the death toll that makes a story seem important, but also the story's perceived relevance to the paper's readers.

In addition to being of varying importance, stories strike news workers as being more or less interesting to their audience. Television news, for example, favors stories that can be accompanied by videotaped footage showing something happening. The earliest television news broadcasts featured newscasters facing the camera and reading stories to the audience. Television workers soon realized, however, that theirs was a visual medium, and that audiences found these "talking heads" boring. There is, then, a strong preference for having some sort of videotaped action to illustrate the story, even if the activity shown is mundane; this explains why stories about ongoing trials—where cameras are often forbidden in the courtroom—routinely feature footage of trial participants walking into the courthouse to accompany the sound of a reporter describing what happened in court that day.

There are, of course, other ways of making stories interesting. Like claims generally, news stories often begin with typifying examples. For example, a story on homelessness might begin by describing the experiences of one or two particular homeless individuals; such an introduction puts a human face on the story and gives the problem "human interest." Stories that seem less interesting can easily lose out in the competition for media attention; news workers will favor covering stories that can be presented in an interesting manner (see Box 5.1).

Another quality of an attractive story is novelty. Notice the very word *news*—that is, "what's new." In general, news workers prefer stories that are current (especially "breaking news") and that seem different. "Fresh" news is preferred to stories that seem too familiar, that have grown "stale." After all, if there isn't something new to report, why should news workers expect the audience to pay any attention? This means that familiar, troubling conditions that affect many people—such as world hunger—may not attract nearly as much media attention as the latest sex scandal or lurid murder.

In assembling the stories they report, news workers apply other professional standards as well. For example, when the story's subject is clearly an issue about which people disagree, many news workers consider themselves obliged to *balance* their coverage by reporting the views of "both sides." This expression reveals an assumption that most issues have only two sides—pro and con, liberal and conservative, or whatever. The news media often resist reporting complex stories in which there are more than two competing positions; they prefer to construct the issue as a straightforward, two-party disagreement. Note, too, that news workers do not feel the need to balance coverage when they perceive a general unanimity of opinion (concerning what Chapter 2 called *valence issues*). If there is general, widespread agreement that, say, child pornography is bad, then reporters will not consider themselves obliged to balance their coverage by reporting the views of child pornographers.

Because most news workers keep track of coverage by rival news organizations, they often feel obliged to *follow one another's lead.*

Box 5.1 Framing Veterans of Iraq and Afghanistan

News coverage of social problems often involves constructing the types of people involved in those problems—as heroes, villains, victims, or whatever. Those images make a difference: throughout American history, they have shaped social policies designed to reward or support war veterans. Kleykamp and Hipes (2015) examined how major newspapers reported on veterans of the conflicts in Iraq and Afghanistan, and found patterns in how veterans are depicted.

Most of the articles examined portrayed veterans as deserving. The articles described them as generally worthy in that they had made sacrifices to serve their country, and they linked that worthiness to policies designed to provide benefits for veterans. Notably, no article suggested that veterans were not deserving. At the same time, an even larger share of articles depicted veterans' victimization. These included not only references to physical or psychological harms incurred during their service, but also to the challenges veterans faced in returning to civilian society, such as difficulties in finding housing and employment. Bureaucratic failings in programs designed to help veterans also received coverage.

The two themes of deservingness and victimization worked well together; articles criticized circumstances that victimized individuals who could be portrayed as especially deserving. Even acts of violence by veterans could be constructed as evidence of the failure of social policies to do enough for individuals who unquestionably deserved strong social support. This example illustrates how moral assumptions are warrants that underpin news coverage.

The very fact that another newspaper or newscast is covering a story suggests that that story must be newsworthy. When several news organizations rush to follow the same lead, the result can be a wave of news coverage. This often happens with social problems coverage, which is why criminologists have long understood that crime waves are not so much waves in criminal activity as waves in news coverage (Vasterman, 2005).

Considerations such as importance, interest, novelty, balance, and what other news organizations are covering shape how news workers construct the news. These are inevitably matters of judgment, with editors making choices—deciding which stories deserve more attention, which deserve less, and which can be ignored. In some cases, news workers may act as primary claimsmakers; that is, they might originate the claimsmaking through their coverage.

For social problems claimsmakers, the challenge is to construct claims that will strike news workers as sufficiently important and interesting to merit news coverage. Sophisticated claimsmakers learn to take the news workers' concerns into account: they make it easy to cover their claims by, for example, staging demonstrations and other events that will seem interesting and therefore newsworthy; they schedule these events and press conferences in advance so that news workers will know when and where to go to get their stories; they designate articulate spokespersons who can present the claims, answer reporters' questions, and help them identify suitable typifying examples; they devise novel, visually interesting ways of presenting their claims—new forms of demonstrations, new evidence, and such—so that their message seems fresh and the story well suited for television; and so on. For instance, a small San Francisco prostitutes' rights movement managed to attract a great deal of media attention by organizing the "First Annual Hookers' Ball" (Jenness, 1993). Understanding the news media's concerns allows claimsmakers to package their claims in ways that will appeal to news workers, and thereby makes it more likely that those claims will, in fact, become the subjects of news coverage.

News workers are not naive; they understand that experienced claimsmakers tailor their campaigns to attract news coverage. On the one hand, news workers may be wary of being manipulated; they particularly want to avoid wasting time covering a story that will strike them and their audiences as familiar and boring. They want to be convinced that the information they're being given is fresh, accurate, and interesting; they have no interest in attending yet another press conference where the same speakers make the same old claims. Still, depending on what rival stories are under consideration, it may be easier to cover a well-packaged story. There are, after all, "slow news days" when there seems to be a shortage of newsworthy stories, just as summer has long been known among journalists as the "dog days" or the "silly season"—months when the federal government and other news-generating institutions are less active, so competition for coverage is less intense and it is easier for offbeat stories to attract news coverage. A well-assembled claim can become very attractive to news workers if there aren't strong alternative stories competing for attention.

Geography also plays a role in this process. News workers are not evenly distributed across the country; rather, they are concentrated in larger cities (J. Best, 1999). In particular, three cities have exceptionally large concentrations of news workers: New York is the nation's largest city, and it remains the traditional base for such important news media as the *New York Times*, the *Wall Street Journal*, and the three major television network news broadcasts; Los Angeles is the second-largest city, and as the center of the entertainment industry, it has its own concentration of news media; and Washington, D.C., is, of course, the center of the federal government and attracts a vast army of news workers devoted to covering the government's actions. Events that occur near such concentrations of news workers are more likely to attract coverage.

Such geographic concentrations of news workers are important because where there are more reporters, there are more opportunities for claimsmakers to get their claims covered. There is nothing to keep people from making claims in a small town in a remote rural location, but it is more difficult to get news workers to travel there to cover the story. It is far easier for a claim to gain widespread attention if the claimsmakers bring their case to a major media center, to a location where many news workers will have convenient access to the story. Thus, even claimsmakers who begin in distant places tend to migrate to larger media centers.

All of this is to say that the news is a social construction, produced by news workers operating under various constraints that force them to make choices—to prefer stories that can be covered in ways that fit their sense of what good news ought to be. Claimsmakers who ignore these considerations do so at their own peril.

CHANGING NEWS MEDIA

Note that the news media's forms shift over time. During television's first thirty years, the great majority of Americans relied on broadcast signals; even those living in fairly large urban centers might receive signals from only half a dozen stations. The three major networks (ABC, CBS, and NBC) originally ran fifteen-minute news broadcasts on weekdays, which were expanded to thirty minutes in the early 1960s, then later to six days per week; in addition, local stations offered their own news broadcasts a couple times a day.

Today, most households receive either cable or satellite television signals offering access to dozens, if not hundreds, of channels. Several channels offer round-the-clock news coverage. This shift has had all manner of consequences: the audience for the networks' evening news broadcasts has grown smaller as viewers turn to all-news channels at more convenient times; the audience for print journalism—both newspapers and weekly newsmagazines—has also declined as more people rely on electronic media for their news; and some cable networks have begun to adopt overt editorial stances (as the emergence of Fox News as an unabashedly conservative network illustrates) (see Box 5.2).

For claimsmakers, one important consequence of these changes in the media is that competing twenty-four-hour news channels have a colossal appetite for fresh stories. In television's early years, when the networks broadcast five fifteen-minute news shows per week, it was far tougher to get an issue covered on national television than it is today. Television's carrying capacity for news has increased vastly.

Box 5.2 Prime-Time Pundits on Problems

During evening prime-time, the twenty-four-hour cable news channels feature commentary by so-called pundits (e.g., Anderson Cooper on CNN, Bill O'Reilly on Fox News, Rachel Maddow on MSNBC). Typically these pundits give their opinions about current stories in the news; their programs are a form of infotainment, packaging news coverage in an entertaining format. Each episode frames opinions within a series of segments that give a predictable structure to each pundit's program. Most often, pundits talk about current political stories, but sometimes they also discuss social problems.

Letukas (2014) examined how cable news pundits dealt with two stories: the huge British Petroleum oil spill in 2010, and the H1N1 flu pandemic in 2009. Because it took some weeks to contain the spill and address the flu, both issues remained topical news stories for several weeks, and they received a great deal of attention on cable news.

Pundits manage to comment on the news, which is of course constantly changing, by packaging their opinions with a set of assumptions about an ideal society. Thus, Fox News tends to promote the idea that government should have a small, limited role in society, while favoring unfettered free-market capitalism; in contrast, MSNBC tends to argue in favor of government involvement and regulation, while worrying about the risks of unfettered capitalism, and CNN tends to adopt a middle ground, favoring government involvement that is neither too intrusive or too slow, and in particular, some level of regulation of business. With such principles in mind, pundits on each cable news channel find it possible to craft a response to most social problems stories that is consistent with that channel's orientation.

(On the other hand, as their advertising has declined, newspapers and newsmagazines have been shrinking in size, so their carrying capacity has grown smaller.)

As television channels have increased in number, they have increasingly aimed at targeted audiences. Theorists once worried about the "mass media" that would turn society into an undifferentiated mass receiving the same media messages (Turow, 1997).

In practice, the media find it more profitable to practice **audience segmentation**, to aim at particular demographic groups; because people fitting a particular demographic profile (defined by age, sex, income, and so on) are more likely to watch programs aimed directly at their interests, the audience for those programs will be relatively homogeneous, and advertisers who believe that their customers will be concentrated in that segment of the larger audience will prefer—and even pay a premium—to place their ads on those programs. Thus, there are cable channels aimed at women, Spanish speakers, people in particular age groups, and so on, just as websites are aimed at people with distinctive interests or concerns. (A similar process changed magazine publishing: general-interest magazines such as *Life* that once sought to appeal to huge mass audiences have folded; the titles that remain aim at people with particular interests.)

Audience segmentation affects the media's role in the social problems process. Because different television channels or magazines seek to appeal to demographically distinct audiences, their coverage of claimsmaking will reflect their sense of which issues will strike their viewers or readers as interesting and relevant. Because advertisers often favor more affluent customers who can afford their products, the news media are less likely to target poorer audiences, which means that social problems coverage tends to downplay claims of greater concern to the poor and the powerless. Newspapers' economic reporting, for instance, tends to devote far more attention to the concerns of corporations than to those of workers or the unemployed (Kollmeyer, 2004). The consequence of audience segmentation for social problems claimsmaking is that, although it is becoming easier to gain media coverage for claims, that coverage often is tailored for the particular audience that follows the television programs or magazines that choose to cover the claims.

The obvious example of changing media is the emergence of the Internet. The Internet is a boon to claimsmakers in that websites, discussion groups, and blogs can be established quite easily, and at minimal cost. Claims of all sorts can be posted and made accessible to anyone who knows how to use a search engine; in effect, the

Internet has an unlimited carrying capacity. Because there is little in the way of filtering, the Internet offers a forum for even the most controversial claims, and sites can be *cloaked* so as to conceal the posters' identity (Daniels, 2009). However, it becomes difficult for news workers to evaluate the various claims that wind up posted in cyberspace. (In contrast, those working in print and broadcast journalism routinely sort through prospective stories and have standards for rejecting some claims.) Moreover, posting a claim does not guarantee that it will gain a large audience; bloggers have learned to encourage traffic to their sites by providing mutual links to other sites. Still, it seems likely that the Internet will have a long-term effect on claimsmaking. In some instances already, websites or bloggers have forced more established news media to cover particular issues by breaking stories about those issues (see Box 5.3).

Thus, the news media's structure is changing: Some media, such as newspapers and magazines, are losing part of their audience, shrinking their coverage, and becoming less influential. Others, such as television news, are expanding their coverage and shifting forms (by, for example, becoming more openly ideological). At the same time, new Internet-based forms such as blogs, websites, and electronic discussion groups are emerging. Thus far, these changes seem to make it easier to gain some sort of media coverage of claims, although, because the target audiences for different media tend to be smaller and more homogeneous, it is not necessarily easier to bring claims to the attention of a broad, general audience.

PACKAGING SOCIAL PROBLEMS IN THE NEWS

In short, the nature of news work and the structure of the news industry shape which stories are covered and the form that coverage takes. In particular, news about claimsmaking tends to display some fairly clear patterns.

Box 5.3 Does the Internet Change Everything?

Cyberoptimists argue that the Internet has had dramatic effects on society and, moreover, that these effects are largely positive. In particular, they insist that the Internet serves to democratize public debate: it takes little money for an individual to establish a website or blog and begin to comment on social issues. It is possible for nearly anyone to make claims that can reach any of the billions of people who go online.

Indeed, the Internet has transformed news media. Print journalism—primarily newspapers and newsmagazines—began to see its audience shrink once television news established itself, and that process has continued for decades. Fewer people read newspapers and magazines, and many news publications have gotten smaller or even stopped publishing.

Instead, a growing proportion of people get their news online. But this does not necessarily mean that they are surfing the full range of content on the net. Instead, people tend to get their news from the websites of established news organizations—those of newspapers, newsmagazines, or television news operations—that have reputations for reliability. Some established bloggers do have considerable audiences that enjoy their posts or share their interests. But most blogs and other commentaries by individuals usually reach large audiences only when one of these established news organizations picks up their views and repeats them.

Source: Maratea, 2014.

The Advantages of Issue Ownership

First, remember that particular claimsmakers sometimes assume ownership of their social problems. That is, they become widely recognized as *the* authorities on the problem, as especially knowledgeable. One of the principal benefits of such ownership is that, when news workers find themselves covering a story related to a certain social problem, they routinely turn to the problem's owners for comments. This status is self-reinforcing; once the media have used particular activists or experts as sources for one story, they are more likely to seek out the same sources for future, related stories.

Of course, achieving ownership is easier for some people than for others. The news media frequently turn to government officials as sources for their stories, and other experts have credentials that make their comments seem particularly authoritative. The news media also favor covering people who are already well known; thus, when movie stars or other celebrities enlist in claimsmaking campaigns, they often draw press attention. (Another way to claim ownership and control the media message is for corporations or other interest groups to run advertising that presents their claims [Silver & Boyle, 2010].) In short, the news media prefer to collect their information from those who already have high status.

The flip side of ownership arises when the media define some claimsmakers as lacking the legitimacy to deserve coverage. We might call these *dispossessed* claimsmakers (that is, they are the opposite of owners). News workers may view people who are poorer—who lack power, wealth, or high status—as less news-worthy, and claimsmakers representing these people find it hard to get their claims covered. Similarly, those with views considered too far outside the mainstream—too unpopular or too radical—find it much harder to gain media coverage for their claims. Remember, the media often try to balance their coverage by presenting "both sides" of an issue—typically understood to mean liberals and con-servatives, or Democrats and Republicans. Those who adopt other, very different positions—who are too radical or too reactionary, who hold unpopular beliefs or values—usually find it difficult to break into the news media that have the largest audiences. As a result, claimsmakers whose rhetoric strikes news workers as too far out-side the mainstream—think of vegans, hate groups, or unfamiliar new religions—may find themselves ignored by the major media. Those newspapers, newsmagazines, and television networks with the largest audiences tend to concentrate their coverage on less controversial claims.

Dispossession also reflects the news media's efforts to appeal to their target audiences. Although we might imagine that newspapers or television news broadcasts want to gain the largest possible audience, audience segmentation leads them, in practice, to be more concerned with reaching some people than others (Hamilton, 2004). Advertisers are more likely to place their ads in media that reach particular types of consumers, and editors may favor stories that will appeal to their target audience. To the degree that social problems claims address troubling conditions thought to be of concern to that target audience, it is easier to get coverage; claims that may be of more concern to people outside the target audience have a tougher time getting covered. Again, advertisers—and therefore the news media—tend to be especially interested in reaching more affluent audience members and less interested in attracting poorer readers and viewers; therefore, claims about problems that face the poor may have a harder time gaining news coverage.

Not all social problems come to have owners, because claims-makers must themselves choose which issues are most important (J. Best, 1999). Consider the media coverage of school shootings that began in 1998; there were several heavily publicized incidents (most notably, of course, at Columbine High School in 1999). Various claimsmakers sought to explain these episodes, but the cacophony of explanations was remarkable. School shootings were blamed on insufficient gun control laws, violent video games, the Goth subculture, bullying, theaters admitting those under seventeen into R-rated movies, the gun culture, and so on.

This is a common pattern: reports of novel sorts of violent crime often lead to all kinds of commentators offering competing explanations and solutions. In the case of school shootings, none of these explanations emerged as dominant; that is, no single set of claimsmakers assumed ownership. Why not? Probably because school shootings were not central to the causes of any of the commentators who spoke out on the issue. Gun control activists, for example, saw school shootings as just one small part of the larger gun problem; they wanted to continue to draw attention to all of the aspects of that problem, rather than focus on school shootings. The emergence of ownership requires claimsmakers who are motivated to continue promoting an issue, as well as news workers who treat those claimsmakers as authoritative.

The Dominance of Landmark Narratives

Second, particular typifying examples—what are called **landmark narratives**—often come to dominate news coverage of a topic (Nichols, 1997). That is, a particular case may become the central focus of media coverage of a social problem—the subject of more newspaper and magazine articles than other, similar cases, or represented in more of the video clips that accompany numerous TV news stories on the topic. Just as the typifying examples chosen by claimsmakers are often quite atypical—more serious, dramatic, or troubling than most cases—so news workers choose landmark or iconic narratives not because they accurately reflect the larger problem, but because they are the stuff of compelling news. These cases serve as landmarks in two senses: they guide news workers' thinking about the nature of the problem and how it should be covered, and they shape the terms by which the news audience understands the problem.

Constructing Packages

Third, landmark cases often belong to larger constructions called **packages** (Beckett, 1996; Gamson, 1992; Gamson & Modigliani, 1989). A package is a familiar, more or less coherent view of a social issue, including its causes and what ought to be done about it. A package has a core idea, or frame; for example, arguments that climate change is substantially caused by humans' activities, that it poses a serious threat, and that steps need to be taken to minimize the problem are at the core of one familiar package. Similarly, arguments that climate change is not necessarily caused by humans' activities and may not constitute a serious threat are the frame for a rival package. Within a package, there is room for disagreement: people may accept the same basic frame yet disagree about specifics, such as the exact processes causing the problem or what needs to be done. Not everyone who shares the basic concern about climate change has to agree on every aspect of the package.

In addition, packages offer **condensing symbols**, shorthand elements—landmark narratives, typifying examples, slogans, visual images, and so on—that evoke the package. Editorial cartoons in newspapers depend on the fact that readers will understand such symbols; a figure in a Klansman's robe and hood denotes racism, a smokestack belching smoke symbolizes pollution, and so on. Similarly, a bumper sticker's slogan—"When Guns Are Outlawed, Only Outlaws Will Have Guns"—can encapsulate a larger package of ideas about guns and gun control. Condensing signals remind people of the larger package, which presents claims that define the nature of the problem, its causes, and a vision of what ought to be done about it.

Note that packages draw on the larger stock of cultural resources. Like primary claimsmakers designing their claims, news workers want to assemble coverage that seems sensible to them, and that also will seem sensible to their audiences. Their stories, then, incorporate the culture that they take for granted—values, symbols, worldviews, and so on. These underlying assumptions are invisible to those who share them, although they may seem quite glaring to others. Consider Americans' shock when they discovered that during the hostage crisis of 1979–80 (perhaps the first time serious tensions with the Muslim world became apparent), Iranian media had described the United States as the "Great Satan." In most cases, however, the way news coverage draws on cultural resources that are taken for granted goes unnoticed.

Media packages help organize people's thinking about social problems. News workers sort through many, if not all, of the available claims, select some as worthy of coverage, and give that coverage shape. The packages they choose may change over time. News workers' choices are influenced by the nature of the claims they encounter, but also by other considerations, including the need to produce news under the pressures of news work, the range of available stories competing for coverage, the desirability of tailoring coverage to the target audience, and so on. Social problems packages are one outcome of this process; they give the news media's secondary claims a sense of coherence: among all the things that might be said about race or crime or anything else, these become the most visible positions. It is relatively easy for the public to become familiar with the packages presented by the news media, and considerably harder for people to learn other ways to think about social problems.

Packages help make the media coverage of social problems seem more coherent; they turn a lot of information into a *story*—a word that is significant, because it reminds us that news is often presented as narratives (Nichols, Nolan, & Colyer, 2008). In the process, some elements are highlighted, while others are pushed to one side. This helps explain why analyses of media content regularly find that the depictions of people or events mirror popular images of problems, and are a less accurate reflection of official measures of a problem's dimensions. Our notions of who is likely to be victimized by a hate crime or what it is like to be poor not only derive from images presented in the media, but also shape the imagery the media choose to present.

It is possible to exaggerate the media's role in packaging social problems; they do not have a completely free hand. News workers have to derive and present packages that they believe will make sense to their audiences. American culture, for example, places great weight on the idea of individual responsibility; this idea runs through much commonsense thinking about life. We tend to hold individuals responsible for their circumstances; people who are poor, overweight, or addicted to drugs bear, most Americans agree, at least part of the blame for their troubles. It is, then, relatively easy to devise frames and packages in which individual responsibility plays a key role, but much harder, for instance, to present explanations that argue that individuals' actions are largely determined by social forces.

IS IT JUST ENTERTAINMENT?

We assume that the news media will cover social problems; after all, it is their job to report on serious matters. But social problems claims are also picked up by a wide range of entertainment media and are portrayed in what is called **popular culture**. Television talk shows, for instance, often present episodes focused on particular sorts of relationship problems, addictions, and the like. But even fictional genres, such as mystery novels, adopt topics from the news: when missing children became a national concern, fictional detective heroes tried to find missing kids; once stalking attracted notice, some of those same heroes confronted stalkers; and so on. And just as the demands of news work shape how the news media cover social problems, entertainment media are constrained by conventions that affect how they construct social problems.

Every pop culture genre has its own conventions and constraints—a formula that it follows. Television situation comedies need joke-filled scripts that will last about twenty-three minutes (thirty minutes less time for the commercials and the opening and closing credits), in romance novels the main characters fall in love, and comic book superheroes confront and defeat supervillains. The people who produce popular culture follow these formulas because they are known to work; that is, they appeal to each genre's respective audience. Romance authors, editors, and publishers, for instance, doubt that their readers want stories about people who can't find love.

These formulas shape how entertainment media deal with social problems claims. Although popular culture often reflects current social problems claims, with stories "ripped from the headlines," its depictions of those claims must conform to the different formulas' requirements (Gitlin, 1983). For example, to be dramatic, a confrontation requires an uncertain outcome; this means that the hero must face a villain who seems capable of winning. For instance, detective heroes—whether on television or in mystery novels—must be matched with powerful lawbreakers. As a result, fictional criminals tend to be far more powerful than their real-world counterparts: fictional child molesters belong to organized rings of wealthy abusers, drug dealers are millionaire industrialists, or gang leaders command hundreds of highly trained, well-armed followers. In comparison, real-life offenders, often people with very limited resources, offer poor material for entertaining plots (see Box 5.4).

Sociologists often complain that popular culture's conventions focus on individuals rather than on social forces. Novels, movies, and television series tend to match good people with heroic virtues against bad people with villainous vices, instead of exploring how social problems emerge from social arrangements. Thus, when racism appears in popular culture, it is often treated as a sort of personality defect: villains and other unsympathetic characters express racist sentiments, thereby affirming their poor character. Where sociologists view racism as a widespread problem with roots in social arrangements and consequences for the larger society, popular culture often treats racism as a personal characteristic of flawed individuals, because the formula requires

Box 5.4 What's Entertaining about Date Rape?

Above all else, popular culture needs to entertain its audience: the content needs to seem fresh and novel. Early in the social problems process, simply incorporating claims may strike audiences as unusual and interesting. For instance, Polletta and Tomlinson (2014) examined the treatment of date rape in television dramas aimed at young viewers. In 1988, there were two afterschool specials with plots focused on date rape (afterschool specials were a genre on the major networks that dealt with teen pregnancy, drug and alcohol use, and other issues facing youth). These programs wove a good deal of information into their plots, so characters learned about the nature of date rape and appropriate responses to it.

Later programs shifted the focus from date rape to how characters in the dramas responded to date rape. Presumably the people writing and producing these episodes now assumed that their audience had basic information about date rape and no longer needed instruction. Instead, date rape—which was often portrayed as attempted but interrupted—became the device that set a plot about characters and their relationships into motion. Even later shows featured characters who seem jaded, who certainly did not approve of date rape, but who viewed it as just one of the awful things that occurred in an amoral world.

Such shifts in how popular culture treats social problems are almost inevitable given the nature of media work, in that the people who create pop culture must continually keep its content seeming fresh and sufficiently interesting to hold their audiences' attention. Unable to stand still, pop culture must reconstruct social problems.

a hero triumphing over a particular villain. Similarly, talk shows and other genres that mix elements of news and entertainment feature the same emphasis on flawed individuals. They present problem gambling as a psychological compulsion that affects some individuals, rather than emphasizing how social institutions, such as government and the gaming industry, exacerbate the problem by promoting gambling.

In other words, the formulas used in entertainment media highlight stories about individuals (Berns, 2004). This individual focus is found in both fictional pop culture genres (such as mystery novels) and the quasi news of infotainment (such as talk shows). Entertainment media may address social problems claims, but regardless of whether primary claimsmakers view a problem as widespread and systemic (think of claims about racism, environmental degradation, or climate change), entertainment tends to translate those claims into stories about the struggles and successes of particular people. This focus on telling compelling stories about individuals is central to the formulas for many entertainment genres, and the people who work as creators and producers within the media understand the need to focus on typifying individuals.

This means that entertainment media have an especially difficult time adopting what C. Wright Mills (1959) called a **sociological imagination**—that is, viewing the world in terms of social arrangements and social forces. Mills noted that, in everyday life, people focus on their private troubles, such as not having a job. Adopting a sociological imagination requires seeing those private troubles in terms of larger public issues; for example, whereas an individual may have trouble finding a job, the larger society confronts the more general problem of unemployment. Sociologists, then, tend to downplay the experiences of individuals and focus on larger social patterns. (To use concepts from Chapters 3 and 4, the sociological imagination can be understood as the frame that sociologists as experts use to construct social problems.) No wonder sociologists—as well as many primary claimsmakers—often criticize the entertainment media's portrayal of social problems; by translating claims into dramatic tales about individual suffering and redemption, the media favor constructions that run counter to more sociological interpretations (see Box 5.5).

Box 5.5 Complaints about the CSI Effect

The popularity of *CSI: Crime Scene Investigation* and other television dramas that depict forensic investigators uncovering key evidence needed to solve crimes has led some critics to warn about a "CSI effect." Prosecutors worry that these programs lead jurors to expect that the evidence in a criminal case should include the presentation of scientific evidence, even as defense attorneys complain that the shows exaggerate the certainty of such evidence so that jurors give too much credence to forensic evidence.

Dramas about forensic investigations necessarily distort how criminal investigations work: in real investigations, there often is no forensic evidence present, or the evidence that is collected is ambiguous or insufficient to resolve the issue. Moreover, critics also warn that—television entertainment aside—experts' testimony often exaggerates the strength of the forensic evidence presented in criminal trials.

Claims about a CSI effect illustrate how both news and entertainment media construct the nature of expert knowledge. Not just courts and jurors, but the media as well, idealize knowledge as being "really" true, and then criticize those who fall short of that ideal, including scientists whose investigations fall short of producing certain knowledge, television dramas that exaggerate those scientists' certainty, and jurors who are insufficiently critical of those televised portrayals. Thus a reminder of a basic constructionist principle: Everything that we know is filtered through a process of social construction.

Source: Cole, 2015.

WHAT ABOUT SOCIAL MEDIA?

Do social media (think Facebook, Twitter, and the like) belong in a chapter on media coverage of claimsmaking? This chapter has been using the word *media* as shorthand to refer to what were traditionally called *mass media*, that is, methods of communicating messages to very large audiences, such as newspapers, television, film, and the like. So, the question becomes, are social media a form of mass media? Certainly lots of people participate in social media; Facebook reports having more than a billion active users, and there are individuals—mostly entertainers—with tens of millions of Twitter followers. So the total social media audience is huge. However, it is also diffuse. Facebook is individualized; each user maintains a set of friends. The median number of Facebook friends is 200, meaning that half of all users have fewer than that number, which is about the number of followers that the average Twitter user has. These are hardly mass audiences.

Social media are most likely to affect the social problems process as a means of drawing attention to claims. In addition to entertainers, those with vast numbers of Twitter followers include a few political leaders (who may use Twitter as a platform for making brief claims) and major news organizations (such as the *New York Times* and CNN Breaking News) that hope to redirect their Twitter followers to some of their coverage on their websites. We might think of these as institutional participants in social media. But of course, most communication via social media occurs between individuals, and they, too, can draw attention to claims. In a few spectacular cases (usually involving a good deal of deliberate marketing), a claim can "go viral" and reach millions of people (Madianou, 2013). In other cases, claimsmakers may try to package claims in ways that will maximize their chance of spreading widely (see Box 5.6).

In other words, there is evidence that social media can become a factor in the social problems process, although social media are such a new phenomenon that relatively little research has been done on this topic. We will return to social media in Chapter 6, when we consider their uses in assessing public reactions to claimsmaking.

Critics worry that media constructions—whether in news or entertainment genres, or in social media—are important because they are influential. That is, it seems obvious that people who follow the news, consume entertainment, or surf the web must be affected by how these media portray social problems. But is this true?

Box 5.6 Using Social Media to Prepare for the
Zombie Apocalypse

The rapid spread of social media has inspired arguments that they are altering societal arrangements. Thus, there are claims that social media will transform or even replace traditional mass media. Social media are still a relatively new and imperfectly understood phenomenon, and it is difficult to assess their impact, but some research suggests that they have limitations.

In 2011, the Centers for Disease Control and Prevention (CDC) launched a campaign to help people prepare for a zombie apocalypse. Obviously the government was not worried about a zombie outbreak, but officials were interested in trying to help people anticipate and prepare for other, more likely public health crises—disasters, flu outbreaks, and the like. And, since zombie-themed movies and television programs were popular, officials reasoned that it might be possible to take advantage of that popularity and attract people to a zombie preparedness website offering advice that would be applicable to improving citizens' readiness for all sorts of potential problems. That is, the preparations for a zombie outbreak would also be useful in getting ready for more likely crises.

When Fraustino and Ma (2015) examined the CDC campaign, they discovered that it did in fact receive a lot of exposure: the campaign was publicized both through coverage in traditional media and via social media, and lots of people checked it out. However, exposure to the site did not increase disaster preparedness. Apparently, a humorous campaign was not the best way to convince people to take disaster planning seriously.

THE MEDIA'S IMPACT

Commentators often assume that the media are extremely powerful and influential, that members of the audience are regularly affected by media messages. To be sure, most of us would deny that we, personally, are easily manipulated by the media. We are made of stronger stuff; we take an attitude of healthy skepticism toward the messages in news, entertainment, and especially advertising. But others, we worry, must be easily bamboozled by the media and may require protection. The media's powerful influence may seem obvious, but it turns out to be fairly difficult to document. Consider claims that televised violence leads to violent behavior. Television is nearly universal in our society (which makes it difficult to construct experimental studies of its effects, since there is no natural control group lacking exposure to television), yet most people do not engage in violent acts. Similarly, most people who view commercials do not rush out to purchase the advertised products. Although claimsmakers often insist that media exposure has damaging effects, it is hard to observe and measure these consequences. Clearly, the media don't have the same effects on everyone.

If we are to understand the media's role in the social problems process, we need to specify what forms its influence might take. One thing we might mean is that the media can bring a social problem to public attention. As we have already noted, this is a central goal of many claimsmakers. When claimsmakers are calling attention to a new problem—that is, to a troubling condition that has been generally neglected or ignored, one that is unfamiliar to many people—getting media coverage can bring the topic out in the open. Media attention can make the public aware that the issue exists or encourage the public to think that something ought to be done to remedy the problem. This is sometimes called **agenda setting** (McCombs, 2004).

Just as a meeting may be guided by an agenda—a list of topics to be addressed, usually in order of importance—we can envision a society's members as needing to prioritize their concerns. All people have countless topics competing for their attention. Many of these concern the individuals' personal lives—routine errands, conversations with friends and relatives, and on and on. The media—particularly the news media—provide some sense of what's occurring in the larger world, suggesting what else deserves people's notice. Media coverage, then, can make people aware of a social problem—get it on society's agenda. Agenda setting can affect both public awareness (as will be discussed in Chapter 6) and policymakers' sense of what deserves their attention (a topic covered in Chapter 7).

Note that the media do not have a free hand in agenda setting. They are constrained. First, some events—say, a major disaster— may demand media coverage. Second, the media can be influenced to cover particular topics—by claimsmakers who convince the media that a problem deserves their attention, by officials who herald a particular new policy, even by other media outlets whose coverage suggests that a topic must be worthy of coverage. Third, as we have already noted, people working in the news and entertainment media are limited by the resources available to them, by their sense of the sort of coverage they ought to produce, and so on.

Nevertheless, in one sense the media make choices that are consequential. We have already noted that the media translate and transform social problems claims. In the case of contentious issues, topics (such as abortion) about which claimsmakers may advance contradictory claims, media coverage can structure the debate by assembling a small set of claimsmaking packages. Although the media cannot force people to adopt particular ideas, they make some constructions readily available, so it is easier to come to understand social problems in particular ways. In some cases, media coverage may give individuals a new perspective on their personal lives, to help them redefine their personal troubles as part of larger social problems.

The public and policymakers pay attention to what the media cover for a couple of reasons. First, they use the media as a source of information: media coverage may be how the public and policymakers first learn about particular social problems. Second, policymakers may begin to hear from members of the general public who, having learned about the problem via the media, may call for action. Although the media are by no means all-powerful, they do help shape the social problems process.

THE MEDIA IN THE SOCIAL PROBLEMS PROCESS

Part of the reason why commentators exaggerate the media's power is that the media play an especially visible role in the social problems process. Outsider claimsmakers view media coverage as almost essential for making the public and policymakers aware of their claims. More powerful people use press conferences and other public relations techniques to attract and shape coverage for their activities. Meanwhile, much lobbying and other insider claimsmaking is hidden from the public (unless an enterprising reporter draws attention to it). Media coverage remains the easiest way for most people to learn about social problems.

This chapter has argued that the media must also be understood in terms of their social arrangements. Figure 5.1 illustrates some of the key features of these arrangements. First, note the distinction between news and entertainment media; the figure portrays news coverage as occurring first and often shaping the entertainment media's coverage of social problems. Second, the figure draws attention to the role of cultural resources. News workers' sense of what is newsworthy, as well as how news stories should be assembled and reported, depends in part on their understanding of how the larger culture will make sense of claims; a parallel set of considerations will shape what will be considered entertaining. Finally, note that both news and entertainment media have their own organizational constraints—operating budgets, production schedules, established conventions and formulas, and so on—that also influence what the media produce.

In addition, the media constantly receive feedback. Most obviously they worry about the reactions of their audiences: Are people

Figure 5.1 THE MEDIA'S ROLE IN THE SOCIAL PROBLEMS PROCESS

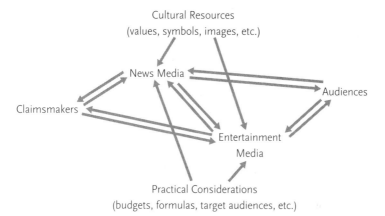

interested in the news or entertainment they produce? If not, the media are likely to modify what they're doing. The media may also hear from claimsmakers who offer congratulations or complaints about coverage, from segments of the general public who are not in their target audiences (and who often have their own criticisms), and from policymakers who may endorse or challenge what the media have done. The people who work in the media, then, should not be seen as all-powerful, as able to dictate what others think. Rather, they are connected to—and influenced by—the other actors in the social problems process. And just as the media transform and translate primary claims into the secondary claims presented in news coverage or entertainment, the media's audience—the public—reworks those messages for its own purposes.

MAKING CONNECTIONS

• *The media are eager for new claims and fresh ways of framing problems. Chapters 3 and 4 explain how activists and experts frame their claims to attract the most media attention.*

- *Claimsmakers use the news media to encourage recognition of a problem. In Chapter 7 you will learn about the essential role that the media play in introducing a social problem into the policymaking process.*

- *In the next chapter you will learn how the public responds to media coverage of social problems.*

CASE STUDY
DEMOCRATIZING THE MEANS OF MEDIA
PRODUCTION AND REPRODUCTION

At the end of World War II, media production was firmly in the hands of journalists and other professionals. But the intervening decades have seen the spread of a long series of relatively inexpensive technological innovations, beginning with photocopiers and cassette tape recorders, to whatever new devices were introduced last week. Today, a large share of the population has access to personal computers, smartphones, and an array of other gadgets that allow them not just to access media content produced by professionals, but also to produce their own content. These developments have reshaped media in several ways that affect the social problems process.

To begin, the professional media have been transformed—often in unexpected ways. Print journalism—newspapers and magazines—may have been damaged by the rise of television news, but it has been devastated by the Internet. As readers have drifted away, the advertising that accounted for the largest share of print journalists' profits has declined, which creates a vicious cycle: print cannot afford to employ as many journalists, which means there is less news reported, which pushes even more readers away, and so on. Similarly, the news operations at the three original broadcast television networks (ABC, CBS, and NBC) have also dwindled, as their audiences—and advertising revenues—have shifted to twenty-four-hour cable news networks and other media. The old news media in most cities were in a few hands: one or two newspapers and perhaps three network affiliates, a public TV channel, and maybe a couple other independent television stations. Aside from the possibility of writing a letter to the editor and seeing it published in a newspaper, ordinary people had no way of addressing the world from a media platform.

This relatively small number of news outlets has been replaced with the boundless choices offered by the Internet. Most old news outlets—newspapers, magazines, and broadcast TV networks—have established their own websites, as have their counterparts on the hundreds of TV channels now available on cable and satellite television. But the Internet is a forum for countless other websites, many of them appealing to distinct demographic slices of the population—people who subscribe to particular religions, share some political ideology, or simply have a common interest. It takes little in the way of equipment to establish a website, start a blog, post a video, or simply open a Facebook page. Anyone with a computer can check out what CNN considers important news—or find out what their Facebook friends are thinking.

All of this means that the media have been democratized, at least in the sense that virtually anyone is able to post his or her views online. They can make social problems claims, or comment on claims made by others; these can take the form of text, sound, images, or video. To be sure, CNN probably gets more hits in a day than your blog, and CNN doubtless has access to more sophisticated hardware and software, so its claims probably seem more professional or polished, but access to the media is no longer restricted to professionals. The means of media production are now in everyone's hands. This is not to say that everyone will take advantage of these possibilities; age affects how comfortable people are with these changes, with younger people readier to learn about and adopt new technologies.

The new media environment is reflected in several different sorts of social problems claims. First, there are concerns, not just about the ability to produce, but to reproduce content. Intellectual property is far less secure than in the past. Books have been protected by copyright, just as inventions have been protected by patents, but these protections were designed to prevent large-scale unlicensed copying. Thus, before there were international agreements about copyright, authors complained that a printer in another country might produce unauthorized copies of their books (for which the author would receive no royalties). But notice that it is now possible for anyone with access to a photocopier or a scanner to make a personal copy of any book at minimal cost and no risk. Parallel technologies make it possible for individuals to gain access to and make copies of music, movies, and other copyrighted works. Major media industries are concerned about piracy involving those making and selling lots of counterfeit copies, but also about millions of computer users downloading their own individual copies of songs, films, and so on.

Second, there are claims about the risks involved in posting online. Almost from the beginning, people have worried that youth who go online might be vulnerable to harm from sexual predators, identity thieves, and other menacing adults lurking on the Internet. Such warnings began almost as soon as ordinary people started having home Internet connections.

Third, there are claims about the uses of technology to mobilize activism. Social movements have increasingly relied on electronic means to organize demonstrations, protests, and the like. The proliferation of smartphones in particular has allowed people to communicate by e-mail, text, and tweet; accounts of large-scale political protest in Iran, the Arab Spring, and Hong Kong—to give only a few examples—often emphasize the role of technology in mobilizing contemporary social movements (Adorjan & Yau, 2015; McGarty, Thomas, Lala, Smith, & Bliuc, 2014). There are also reports of networked youths mobilizing to specific locales in order to engage in disruptive behaviors (Houston, Seo, Knight, Kennedy, Hawthorne, & Trask, 2013).

Fourth, there are a host of claims about the unexpected uses of technology to expose troubling conditions in unexpected ways. An early example was the violent arrest of Rodney King in 1991, when a man who was trying out his new video camera happened to tape Los Angeles police officers beating King; that video ultimately led to a major riot. More recently, there have been many examples of videos of police making arrests, shooting at fleeing individuals, and so on. These videos provide a documentary record of behaviors that the officers presumably never expected to be recorded. Sometimes, the photos or videos are taken by the people themselves, presumably for their own amusement—the photographs of prisoners being mistreated at Abu Ghraib is perhaps the most famous example, but there have been other cases of fraternities hosting racially themed parties and the like. One of the risks of posting on the Internet is that what is easy to put up may prove difficult to take down, so that people are surprised when their provocative sexts reach a wider audience, or when prospective employers make hiring decisions in part based on photos that applicants posted on their Facebook pages.

All of this suggests that the democratization of the media has many facets. It has already inspired a range of social problems claims, and there is every reason to expect that new sorts of claims will continue to appear.

QUESTIONS

1. Consider some earlier technological revolution, such as the invention of the telegraph or the telephone. How might that change have affected the social problems process?

2. Has technological change led to more troubling conditions, more solutions to social problems, or both?

3. Identify a technological change that you imagine may arrive in the near future. How might it affect the social problems process?

6

Public Reaction

Discussions of the social problems process usually assume that, at some point, claims reach and influence members of the general public. Sometimes there's a direct connection between the primary claimsmakers and the public, as when people hear a claimsmaker give a speech, or find themselves listening to a claim during a conversation. More often, of course, claims reach the public via the media; people encounter secondary claims on television or radio, or through reading newspapers, magazines, web pages, or books. All this simply reflects the media's ability to reach very large audiences; claimsmakers who receive media coverage can be exposed to a far larger segment of the general public than they can hope to reach through face-to-face contacts.

As part of the audience for claims, members of the public are not completely passive; they can react in various ways. They may be energized and moved to action by some claims, deciding to contribute to a social movement organization, participate in a demonstration, write their legislators, or relay the claims to others they know. Some may treat a claim as interesting information— something to talk over with friends and acquaintances. Others may be indifferent, apathetic; they may find the claim boring and ignore it. Still others may react negatively, disagreeing with the claim and opposing its conclusions. Probably all claims elicit all of these possible reactions in different people.

Because the public is both large and diverse, because people can respond to claims in different ways, and because many of those responses are relatively private (in that people may keep their opinions to themselves or share them only with others they know well), interpreting the public's role in the social problems process poses special problems. Nonetheless, the other actors in the process want to understand the public's reactions. Claimsmakers use the feedback they receive from the public to modify their claims, in hopes of making them more persuasive; the media also attend to feedback from the public, in order to better devise news and entertainment that will capture the audience's attention; and policymakers may respond to public pressure to do something about a particular social problem. Thus, many people want to learn what the public is thinking, in spite of the difficulties in doing so.

This chapter will focus on the methods that claimsmakers, the media, and others involved in the social problems process—as well as sociologists—use to assess public reactions. It will consider several of these, beginning with the most familiar method—public opinion polls or surveys.

MEASURING PUBLIC OPINION

Public opinion polls have become a taken-for-granted part of our political landscape that we take for granted. We are used to hearing news reports that polls show one candidate favored to win the upcoming election, that the president's approval rating has risen higher or fallen lower, that the public is more or less concerned about particular issues, and so on. Before considering how public opinion figures into the social problems process, we need to consider how the very methods of polling can affect a survey's results.

The Impact of Polling Methods

Efforts to measure public opinion through polling came of age during the early twentieth century. Usually this research involves conducting a **sample survey**. Because it would be prohibitively expensive to contact, say, all voters or all citizens (what statisticians call the **population**), the poll approaches a **sample** of people within that population and asks them questions. The responses to the poll can be tallied to reveal, for instance, the proportion of sampled voters favoring Candidate A in an election; in turn, the sample's results provide a basis for generalizing about the population by projecting the likely outcome of the election.

Many people are suspicious of sample surveys because the samples seem too small to promise accurate results. National surveys often use samples of 1,000 to 1,500 respondents. How, critics ask, can such a small number of people accurately represent the huge U.S. population (over 300 million)? However reasonable this question might seem, it emphasizes the wrong issue. A relatively small sample—say, 1,000 people—can produce fairly accurate results, as long as it is a **representative sample**—that is, as long as the sample is not selected in ways that make it more likely that some sorts of people will be chosen than others. (Statisticians calculate that, for a population of 300 million, a poll with a representative sample of 1,000 will produce results accurate within about 3 percent, 95 percent of the time. Thus, if a survey shows that 54 percent of voters favor Candidate A, there is a 95 percent probability that between 51 and 57 percent of the population favors A's candidacy. Moreover, larger samples aren't that much more accurate: a 10,000-person sample—for which collecting the data would cost about ten times as much—will produce only slightly more accurate results: accuracy within 1 percent, 95 percent of the time [de Vaus, 1986].)

However, statistical theory's assumptions about representative samples often have to give way to the realities of survey research. It is both difficult and expensive to design perfectly representative samples, and unrepresentative samples can lead to inaccurate results. Consider some sampling problems that affect today's pollsters: an increasing number of households screen calls using answering machines or caller ID, and some of those people may choose not to answer the pollsters' calls; in addition, a growing proportion of the population has only cell phones (which the law requires must be hand dialed, making them more expensive to contact) (Link, Battaglia, Frankel, Osborn, & Mokdad, 2007). Can we assume that people who refuse to answer—or who can't be reached via landlines—have the same distribution of opinions as those who pick up the phone, or should we suspect that those who don't respond or can't be reached may have somewhat different opinions from those of the respondents? Refusal to take the pollsters' calls or having only a cell phone—like any other factor that may make the sample less representative—can damage the accuracy of a survey's results.

In addition, survey results are sensitive to many other influences. Pollsters know that the wording of a question can affect the results. Polling is expensive, and often the costs are covered by claimsmakers who hope to use the results to support their campaigns. As a result, many polls ask questions worded in ways that encourage people to produce the answers that the poll's sponsors favor. Of course, when the claimsmakers or sponsors release the poll results to the press, they tend to ignore the questions' wording, while emphasizing the favorable results.

Another important problem is that surveys usually try to distill people's thoughts about complex, multifaceted issues into one or two questions. The result is inevitably crude and oversimplified. For example, many discussions of abortion attitudes imply that people can be classified as either pro-life (opposed to abortion under any circumstances) or pro-choice (in favor of women having complete freedom to choose whether to have abortions) (J. Best, 2013). But the largest proportion of Americans' attitudes fall somewhere between those extremes: these people favor permitting abortion for

Box 6.1 Partisanship and Public Opinion

The Great Recession was the most severe economic crisis since the Great Depression of the 1930s, and many commentators expected public opinion to express widespread increased support for government policies to address the crisis. Instead, Brooks and Manza (2013) report that surveys revealed partisan cleavage: Democrats had always resisted claims about too much government regulation, and their attitude did not change markedly; but Republicans became much more concerned about government overreach even while the recession began and continued. The growing gap in attitudes parallels the growing partisan divisions in Congress (and we might suspect it also reflects the emergence of cable news networks such as Fox News and MSNBC that frame issues in unapologetically ideological terms).

Public opinion is never uniform across groups; we expect liberals and conservatives to hold somewhat different views, so that liberals will tend to be less concerned about government regulations than conservatives. The question is the degree to which these responses differ: the evidence shows that the gap between the views of liberals and conservatives is growing. We can imagine this having important implications for the social problems process, as it may become harder for claimsmakers to construct problems in ways that appeal to the entire population, and harder for policymakers to identify the "will of the people." The impact of partisanship doubtless varies among different social problems, but notice that the Great Recession was an issue that presumably affected a large share of the population, yet there was no agreement about what caused the problem or how it ought to be addressed.

"good" reasons (such as pregnancies resulting from rape or incest, or cases in which continuing the pregnancy might endanger the woman's life), but they have reservations about allowing abortions for less compelling reasons. A simple question asking whether the respondent favors or opposes abortion cannot hope to accurately measure these complicated attitudes (see Box 6.1).

We should also remember that answering a survey is a social situation. That is, respondents who are interacting with a pollster usually want to make a good impression, to be a good respondent. This means that some respondents may try to say whatever they believe the pollster might think they ought to say. For example, if a pollster asks whether X should be considered a serious problem, the very fact that the question is being asked suggests that at least some people consider X a problem, and some respondents may feel that they ought to agree that, yes, X should be considered a serious problem. But responding in that way to a question does not mean that the respondent actually spends much time thinking about—let alone worrying about—X.

In short, a variety of methodological issues—who is polled, how the questions are phrased, and so on—can affect the results of survey research. Every survey's results have been shaped by the choices that the people conducting the surveys have made, and those people may have designed their poll to produce particular results. This doesn't mean that all survey results are meaningless, but they need to be viewed with some caution. After all, media coverage of poll results is fairly common, and this measure of public opinion often becomes a factor in the social problems process.

Constructing the Meaning of Public Opinion

Typically, discussions of the role of public opinion in the social problems process have two distinct themes. First, analysts argue that public opinion is a product of claimsmaking and media coverage of social problems, that effective claims can make the public aware of and concerned about some social problem. Second, policymakers are assumed to be responsive to public opinion; that is, it is assumed that high public concern about a social problem will in turn lead policymakers to try to do something about that problem.

Factors Affecting Public Opinion. Some evidence suggests that public opinion can be affected by media coverage. However, it is important not to exaggerate the media's influence; people are not passive recipients of media messages who automatically must accept whatever the media tells them. The media are probably more effective at agenda setting than at communicating particular messages. That is, they may be better able to influence what topics people are thinking about than what exactly people think about those topics.

For example, one study (Beckett, 1994) found that the proportion of people who expressed concern about crime in polls did not correlate well with official crime rates—concern for crime might rise even when the crime rate was falling; similarly, public concern about illegal drug use did not correlate closely with official measures of drug use. In other words, the shifts in public concern about crime and drug use revealed in surveys do not seem to have been responses to changes in the actual levels of those conditions. However, public opinion did correspond fairly closely with media coverage of crime and drug use, and particularly with officials' announcements about anticrime and antidrug policies (which were, of course, covered by the press). The media coverage tended to rise first, with public opinion following somewhat later; that is, opinions lagged behind media coverage. Thus, increased media coverage of crime and drug problems led to higher proportions of poll respondents expressing concerns about crime and drugs.

This example suggests that the public can be influenced to at least pay attention to heavily publicized social problems. And naturally the perception that this is true affects the behavior of claims-makers, who work hard to promote their constructions of social problems by gaining media coverage, in hopes of arousing public concern. Of course, concern is not spread evenly throughout the population. On most issues, opinions vary with the respondents' characteristics: differences in race, social class (as measured by education or income), age, gender, and region often influence people's opinions. The media cannot affect everyone equally, but they can sometimes arouse fairly broad public concern about a particular troubling condition.

The Impact of Public Opinion. Survey results contribute to the social problems process in two major ways. First, polls offer feedback at earlier stages in the process. Claimsmakers use polls to determine whether their claims are effective or ineffective, hoping that their efforts—particularly if they have received a reasonable amount of media coverage—will cause public opinion to shift in the direction the claimsmakers favor. For instance, imagine that gun control advocates mount a campaign to promote a new law restricting guns. They may organize demonstrations, testify before legislators, appear on talk shows, and so on, in an effort to make the public aware of the issue. If polls taken following this effort suggest that a growing portion of the public is aware of and favors the proposed gun control law, the claimsmakers will view this result as evidence that their campaign has been effective. But, of course, if the poll results do not reveal a substantial shift in public opinion in support of their position, the advocates may look for ways to alter their claims, in hopes of making them more effective. Polls, then, provide feedback to claimsmakers.

The second major way polls affect the social problems process is that policymakers often follow poll results. In particular, elected officials may view evidence of widespread concern about a troubling condition as an indication that they need to take action, to develop a new policy to address the problem. This is not an automatic response. Poll results are one of the considerations that may influence officials, but they are by no means the only one. Still, it is possible to track poll results as "the voice of the people," and to justify policymaking as a response to what the public wants. Polls become one element in the construction of policymaking—a topic that will receive further attention in Chapter 7.

FOCUS GROUPS AND OTHER INTERVIEWS

Survey questionnaires are limited by the questions asked. Sampling does allow analysts to measure the relative distribution of opinions in large populations, but each respondent's views tend to be reduced to relatively simplistic responses to particular questions; moreover, as we have noted, those responses can be affected by precisely how the questions are worded, the order in which questions are asked, and so on.

Sometimes researchers try to circumvent these problems by organizing **focus groups**. Focus groups are sets of people to which a moderator poses questions that stimulate discussion on a particular topic. Group members may be chosen so that the group has a particular racial composition, level of education, and so on. Sometimes the members are acquaintances, who presumably will feel comfortable talking with one another about controversial social issues. Focus groups have several advantages over surveys. Individuals have more freedom to express their ideas about the topic, to qualify their remarks and explain what they really mean. In addition, the group is a social setting in which people can respond to one another's comments.

Focus groups often reveal that the public's views about social problems are more complex than the simple pro/con disagreements revealed by many surveys. Analysts tend to imagine that the public's views are internally consistent, and that they reflect the sorts of ideological consistency that claimsmakers often bring to the social problems process. Compared with these expectations, the views of members of the public often seem confused, ambivalent, or uncertain. These apparent inconsistencies can become evident in focus group discussions. Focus groups also allow individuals to express emotional reactions to issues (see Box 6.2).

Studies of focus groups reveal that individuals tend to draw on at least three sorts of information when discussing social problems (Gamson, 1992; Sasson, 1995b): First, they use popular wisdom— "commonsense" understandings about how the world works as expressed in aphorisms, stereotypes, and so on. Second, people refer to personal experiences—things that have happened to them or others they know. Third, they may adopt various information and ideas derived from media messages about the larger world, including not just news reports, but also the various forms of infotainment

Box 6.2 Focusing on Flash Mobs

The term *flash mob* originally referred to a form of prank or performance art in which people contacted through e-mail or other electronic means came together in some public place for some brief activity, and then dispersed. More recently, the media have applied the term to urban youth gathering in some location, and then sometimes engaging in vandalism or other criminal activities. In other words, definitions of flash mobs vary from benign to more troubling.

Houston, Seo, Knight, Kennedy, Hawthorne, and Trask (2013) wanted to understand how youths in Kansas City—the scene of some disorders attributed to flash mobs—understood the term. Using a survey would have required figuring out how to word questions that could be asked of all respondents—a difficult task, considering the various meanings people assign to the term. Instead, they organized small focus groups of young people who participated in youth programs in the central city. The conversations in these groups revealed a range of views of flash mobs. Some saw them as planned, yet apparently spontaneous, events that might be organized for good (having fun) or bad (disruptive) purposes; others conflated flash mobs with gangs and more serious criminal activity; and still others saw them as just instances of large groups of young people hanging out together. As might be expected, these different definitions were related to different attributions of motives for flash mob participants, as well as different interpretations of flash mobs' causes and consequences. Focus groups provided an effective way to capture a wide range of views about the complex meanings of flash mobs.

and popular culture that depict the workings of the world beyond our personal experience. Popular wisdom, personal experiences, and media discourse are resources that can be used to construct public definitions of social problems, and focus group conversations reveal how people weave these elements together. In general, groups that are able to integrate all three sorts of information—to combine their personal beliefs and experiences with information about the larger world—are more confident that their constructions are correct and more willing to defend their views.

Given the importance of experiential knowledge in focus groups, it should be no surprise that people with different backgrounds construct issues differently. Such background characteristics as race, social class, gender, age, and education affect how people think about social problems. For example, among groups given the task of discussing crime, references to racism in the criminal justice system were relatively common in all-black groups, but relatively rare in all-white groups (Sasson, 1995b). In some cases, African American group members presented conspiracy theories, arguing that powerful whites supplied guns and drugs to poor black neighborhoods as a means of keeping them disadvantaged (Sasson, 1995a). Such findings illustrate a strength of focus groups; survey researchers might not even think to ask questions that could reveal whether their respondents hold such views.

The results of focus groups can, in turn, influence claimsmakers. Like political consultants trying to understand voters' views during election campaigns and firms seeking to market their products to consumers, activists sometimes use focus groups to better understand what the public is thinking. Identification of the frames that emerge within focus groups can be used to revise claims so that they are tailored to influence the public more effectively. For example, when opponents of abortion successfully campaigned against public funding for abortions during the 1980s, abortion rights advocates organized focus groups that revealed that people who opposed such funding also objected to government intrusion in their lives (Saletan, 2003). Abortion rights advocates used this knowledge to craft a new argument—that the right to have an abortion was tied to a broader right to privacy; in this view, restrictions against abortion became another form of government interference in people's private lives. This new pro-choice campaign proved relatively effective.

As a source of information about public reactions, focus groups obviously have limitations. They are relatively costly in terms of time and money, and it is impossible to know how representative particular groups may be. Much depends on the moderator's skill in directing the conversation, making sure that the various participants have their say, and so on. Still, focus groups can be an important way of discovering what ordinary people think about social problems.

SOCIAL MEDIA AS AN INDEX
OF PUBLIC OPINION

Beyond surveys and focus groups, there are other ways to examine claims made by ordinary people about troubling conditions. These may involve access to some media platform intended to let members of the public express their views. The classic example—more common in the past than now—is writing a letter to the editor for publication in a newspaper (see Box 6.3). This is hardly a random sample: people who wrote these letters had to care enough about an issue to put pen to paper; and they had to be literate enough and have enough time and money to spend on the project. Probably only a tiny fraction of the population ever expressed themselves in this way. It also is important to appreciate that the newspaper editors must have been selective in choosing which letters to publish; they might have had all sorts of reasons—everything from objecting to a letter writer's views, to not having enough space to print a letter—for deciding not to publish all the letters they received. Still, such letters can tell us something about how members of the larger population thought about the issues of the day.

While people still write letters to the editor (probably most often via e-mail), the Internet now offers all sorts of new platforms that allow members of the public to express their views. Increasingly, physical newspapers are being replaced by news websites, and readers of a news story on a site may be invited to post their reactions.

Box 6.3 LETTERS TO THE EDITOR ABOUT INTERMARRIAGE
IN BLACK NEWSPAPERS

The challenges of assessing public reactions become even greater when studying the past, and particularly when studying attitudes among specific groups within the larger population. To try to understand how African Americans viewed intermarriage in the decades before the civil rights movement, Doering (2014) examined letters to the editor published in major black newspapers between the 1920s and the 1960s. This is an imperfect sample: only some people write such letters, and the papers' editors chose which letters to publish (and presumably excluded others). Still, the letters capture ordinary African Americans, members of the public, exchanging views with one another.

Although the letters studied all focused on intermarriage, they reflected a larger debate among blacks between two positions. Integrationists argued that racial boundaries needed to be eliminated, and they saw intermarriage as one way those barriers could be diminished—it was a solution to a problem. In contrast, separatists argued that intermarriage damaged the cohesiveness of the black community; they constructed intermarriage itself as a problem. Of course, a parallel debate over integrationism versus separatism can be found in the rhetoric of the more visible African American leaders who figure in black history.

Such analyses cannot measure how many blacks supported or opposed intermarriage, but they can reveal something about the range of views among African Americans, and thus demonstrate that disputes among leaders were reflected in the thinking of the larger black public.

A story may elicit hundreds of these comments; it is not uncommon for the original story to fade into the background as people begin to add comments giving their reactions to some earlier comment. News organizations track these comments, and post lists of the stories eliciting the most reactions. Presumably this alerts readers to stories other people have found interesting, and also provides valuable feedback that the site can use to decide what to cover and how to cover it in the future. Similarly, websites keep track of how often particular items are forwarded as another way of identifying what the public finds interesting.

Such discussion threads appear across the Internet—appended to blog posts as well as news stories, and on various website forums organized to attract people who share some particular interest or point of view. Many of these sites focus on hobbies, celebrities, and other matters of only fleeting interest to hard-core enthusiasts, but others have been established to address social issues, often for people who subscribe to a particular ideology, and can be seen as part of the social problems process. Analysts are struggling to devise methods of assessing public reactions using these various electronic forums.

Thus, the emergence of social media has led some commentators to try to discern public attitudes from tweets, Facebook posts, and the like. This turns out to pose difficult problems; it is hard to know how to measure social media content, or to know how accurate those measurements may be. The simplest method is to selectively quote individual comments to suggest a sense of the sort of things people are thinking, as when a television news program takes a moment to present comments from members of their audience. But it is impossible to know whether the few comments shown accurately reflect ideas in the larger public. A second method is to measure the frequency with which some term is used—whether it is "trending." But such counts may ignore a good deal of diversity among the various comments; the fact that a lot of people are using some word hardly tells us what they are thinking.

A more promising alternative is **semantic polling** (Anstead & O'Loughlin, 2015). This involves software that tries to interpret the meanings in large numbers of social media messages, to categorize them as reflecting particular sentiments. The difficulties here are obvious: the messages are not all being read and classified by people, but by computers that may have imperfect methods of interpreting what a particular set of words means. People promoting semantic polling argue that by having humans review a portion of the messages being classified and recoding those that the software seems to have misinterpreted, the computers can be taught to make more accurate assessments. And, even if they aren't completely accurate, semantic polls have the advantage of speed—results are available in close to real time. Traditional survey researchers are skeptical of analyses of social media content. The people participating in these forums cannot be assumed to statistically reflect the general population, nor do we yet know very much about how well social media posts reflect—or affect—public attitudes. Like other methods used to understand public reactions, analyses of social media content produce imperfect results that need to be examined with considerable care.

LEGENDS, JOKES, AND OTHER FOLKLORE

Public opinion polls, focus groups, and even social media posts involve somewhat artificial, formalized situations in which people know that their opinions are presented for analysis, and this knowledge may affect what the people who participate are willing to say. But talk about social problems also is the stuff of everyday conversations. It would be nice to know how members of the public construct social problems when they are not self-conscious about being observed. Studying folklore offers one way of examining such everyday constructions.

The term *folklore* refers to information that is disseminated informally, among the *folk*—that is, among ordinary people. Traditionally folklore was transmitted orally, rather than through writing: people told one another folktales, or taught each other folk songs, folk dancing, or folk crafts. You may have a mental image of a folklorist seeking out old folks living in remote corners of society, hoping to capture traditional folk wisdom that is in danger of disappearing as the last generation to have this knowledge fades. This common image equates folklore with an elderly person perched in a rocking chair on a rickety, unpainted front porch, talking about the old days.

This is a mistaken image because it is far too narrow. *All* people have folklore—young people, people living in cities, everyone. Contemporary folklore spreads in new ways—in photocopied bits of humor posted in offices (Dundes & Pagter, 2000) or through faxes ("faxlore"), e-mail messages, and posts on social media—as well as by the traditional means of word of mouth. And some of the time, this folklore expresses ordinary people's reactions to social problems claims. Let's consider two common folklore genres: contemporary legends and joke cycles.

Contemporary Legends

Sometimes called *urban legends*, **contemporary legends** are stories that people tell one another (Ellis, 2001; Fine, 1992). In general, contemporary legends lack supernatural elements; they are far more likely to feature criminals than, say, ghosts. Typically the teller claims—and the listener believes—that the story is true, that the events in the story really happened. Often the teller offers evidence of the story's truth, such as identifying the place where it happened (perhaps a nearby shopping mall), or explaining the teller's connection to a person who witnessed or experienced the events: "This really happened to my roommate's cousin's neighbor." Folklorists refer to this sort of attribution as a *FOAF* (for *Friend Of A Friend*). Efforts to trace the story back to the FOAF inevitably fail; the roommate's cousin's neighbor may agree that the story is true but explain that "it actually happened to my mother-in-law's brother's friend."

As legends spread, the details tend to shift. A story about a horrible crime at a shopping mall may be revised so that it is relocated at the local mall; the shocking thing that someone said on a TV talk show may be said to have occurred on several different programs, and so on. Folklorists call the differing versions of the same tale **variants**. Variants often make the story more interesting to the audience; for example, the story is better if, instead of having happened at an unknown mall somewhere, the events are described as having actually occurred at a nearby mall.

Contemporary legends must be good stories—good enough for people to remember them and want to repeat them—in order to spread. Thus, effective legends tend to evoke strong emotional reactions, such as fear or disgust (Heath, Bell, & Sternberg, 2001). People are more likely to recall—and repeat—stories that pack a punch. Often legends warn that the world is far more dangerous than we might imagine: that gang members lurk beneath our parked cars or in our backseats, that terrible crimes occur in the mall where we shop, that having a drink with an attractive stranger may lead to having a kidney stolen, and so on (see Box 6.4).

What is the difference between a rumor and a legend? The distinction is somewhat blurry. Basically, *rumors* tend to be specific, confined to a particular time and place. They spread in conditions of uncertainty; they report "improvised news" when more authoritative information is not available, and they tend to be short-lived, one-of-a-kind stories (Fine, Campion-Vincent, & Heath, 2005; Shibutani, 1966). Rumors tend to have local relevance: they refer to a case of corruption by a local official, a local business in trouble, and so on.

In contrast, *legends* can survive over decades—they may lie dormant for a time, only to be revived. A story may pass through a city, disappear for years, but then reappear. Though a legend may include local references ("It happened at our mall"), the same story may be told as having occurred in many places. Legends often invoke familiar **motifs**; that is, the same elements recur in many legends. For example, many contemporary legends involve maniacs with sharp objects—the escaped killer with a hook replacing his missing hand, the man (disguised as an old lady) with a hatchet,

Box 6.4 Legends about Kids out of Control

The Internet not only makes it easy for contemporary legends to spread, it lets us track how they spread. J. Best and Bogle (2014) examined two recent tales about sexual misbehavior among the young: that elementary school–age children used sex bracelets to demand sexual favors from one another; and that junior high school students participated in oral sex (rainbow) parties. Although there was little hard evidence of either practice, both stories spread widely online.

The dates of posts reveal that legends spread in short, intense bursts of just a few weeks. This makes sense. Legends trade on their novelty: people ask one another: "Have you heard about _____?"; once the response starts being: "Yes, I've heard that story," the topic becomes less interesting, and it drops out of their conversations. It is also possible to identify the country of the media covering some legend, which reveals something about the geography of legend dynamics. The sex bracelet story, in particular, spread in different places at different times—first in North America in 2003–04, and then in Europe in 2009–10.

Although most folklorists think of legends as spreading informally, the evidence shows that media reporting of these stories tends to occur during the same brief periods when individual posts are most frequent. They seem to reinforce one another: media coverage may make a legend seem more plausible and therefore worth repeating, even as a story's popularity online makes it seem like a legitimate topic for the media attention. Everyone knows that legends spread, but examining legends online helps us understand that process better.

Halloween apples laced with razor blades, and such—just as a surprising number of contemporary legends involve terrible crimes at shopping malls. Legends can supply raw material for rumors; that is, familiar legendary elements, such as villainous conspiracies, can easily be reworked to become the stuff of a new rumor.

What do rumors and contemporary legends have to do with social problems? They often reflect contemporary claimsmaking: when the media report on the dangers of drugs, stories circulate about drug dealers giving small children LSD-laced lick-on tattoos; when gangs become a hot news story, tales of vicious gang initiation rites circulate; and so on. Many contemporary legends respond to current claims, but they also reconstruct those claims to fit the constraints of legend. Their need to be memorable means that legends tend to be melodramatic; these stories feature innocent, vulnerable victims preyed on by villains whose evil nature explains their crimes. Why would drug dealers distribute LSD to preschoolers? That's just the sort of bad thing those bad people do. Just as news and entertainment media reshape primary claims to fit the demands of their respective genres, legends rework the topics of the media's secondary claims to make them disturbing, dramatic, and memorable—the qualities of successful legends (see Box 6.5).

Rumors and legends often revolve around social conflicts. Many tales, for example, center around racial or ethnic conflict (Fine & Turner, 2001). Typically, these stories circulate within one ethnic group and describe the nefarious activities of people of another ethnicity. In the United States, for instance, there is a long history of both whites spreading tales about blacks, and blacks telling stories about whites. Sometimes these stories are mirror images of one another—the same story, only with the races reversed. A major race riot in Detroit in 1943 featuring open conflict between blacks and whites, for example, was inspired by rumors that a woman and her baby had been thrown off a local bridge (Langlois, 1983). But the story whites told one another featured a white woman and baby thrown off the bridge by blacks, while blacks shared a story of a black woman and baby thrown off the bridge by whites. In either case, the incident was apparently imaginary; there was no evidence that anyone had been thrown off a bridge.

Stories based on ethnic tensions do not necessarily have such precise counterparts. Several stories circulating among African

Box 6.5 Fiends on Facebook

A friend e-mailed me a link to this story; she found it posted on a friend's Facebook page:

> A guy sends you a friend request. You don't know him, but he's got a cute profile picture, so you accept his friend request.
>
> It's your baby girl's first day of school. She looks SO cute in her new outfit you just have to take a picture and put it on Facebook so all your friends and family can see.
>
> You're so excited dropping her off that you 'Check in' to her school on FB saying
>
> 'I can't believe how big she's gotten. Time sure flies. One proud momma/daddy right here.'
>
> Meanwhile, the mystery guy whose friend request you hurriedly accepted earlier this morning is saving that picture you posted of your daughter in her cute new outfit to his phone and texting it to 60 other grown men across the world with the caption—
>
> 'American Female. Age 5.
>
> Brown hair. Black eyes.
>
> $5,000-.'
>
> Not only did you provide a picture of your little girl to a child trafficker, you've handed him the name and exact location of her school on a silver cyber platter. You go to pick her up at 3:00 this afternoon, but she's nowhere to be found.
>
> Little do you know, your precious baby girl was sold to a 43 years old pedophile before you even stepped foot off campus this morning, and now she's on her way to South Africa with a bag over her head, confused, terrified and crying because a man she's never seen before picked her up from school, and now she doesn't know where her parents are, where she's going, or what's gonna happen to her.
>
> STOP ADDING STRANGERS ON FACEBOOK
>
> and STOP posting everything about your life on Facebook.
>
> Avoid keeping children's pictures as profile picture.

Please SHARE it for the sake of all kids and parents.
Source: Facebook

Notice that this posting features standard contemporary legend motifs—children menaced by deviant adults; dangers lurking in apparently safe places (dangerous strangers admitted to one's private life via social media); clueless parents not up to protecting their children. The moral is found in many contemporary legends: you just can't be too careful in our dangerous modern world.

Thirty years ago, this contemporary legend would probably have spread by word of mouth. Fifteen years ago, it more likely would have been disseminated via e-mail, as people who received the message forwarded it to all of their contacts. Today, social media allow the tale to travel even faster, to even more people.

Americans, for instance, warn that particular companies have connections to racist groups (for example, that a fried chicken franchise is owned by the Ku Klux Klan); or report that a popular clothing designer appeared on a TV talk show and stated that he (or she—the story is told about different designers) did not want black people wearing the designer's clothes, so he (or she) deliberately designed clothing lines that would not fit blacks (Fine & Turner, 2001). Such stories share an underlying theme that African Americans have a subordinate place in a largely white-controlled economy. Not surprisingly, whites do not have many such tales about black-controlled firms (although they have circulated warnings that some businesses are controlled by other conspiratorial elements, such as satanists).

Other contemporary legends explore gender conflict. For example, women pass along warnings about methods that gang members, rapists, and other criminals use to prey on women, just as men share stories about seductive women who intend to harm males. Any social fault line—between ethnic groups, the sexes, bosses and employees, students and professors, and so on—can inspire rumors or legends.

Other social changes also inspire contemporary legends. For instance, numerous legends warn about the risks of AIDS, including the widespread story of a person who awakens after a sexual encounter to discover the message "Welcome to the World of AIDS" written on the bathroom mirror, and warnings that AIDS-infected IV-drug users leave used needles in the coin return slots of pay phones (Goldstein, 2004). Similarly, stories of organ thefts—that is, of stolen eyes, kidneys, and other human organs—have global popularity (Campion-Vincent, 2005). In less industrialized countries, these stories warn about westerners who only pretend to adopt children but actually harvest their organs to be used for transplants in the United States; Americans and Europeans tell one another about people awakening after sexual encounters only to discover that a kidney has been removed. The morals of these stories—warnings about imperialistic exploitation or the risks of casual sex—reflect issues that are themselves the subject of claimsmaking.

As these examples illustrate, the larger significance of rumors and contemporary legends is that they are, in a sense, ripped from the headlines. They translate topics of claimsmakers' concern—racial and ethnic tensions, the impact of immigration, the spread of AIDS, and so on—into melodramatic, disturbing stories, however unlikely, that people tell one another, assuring their listeners that the tales are really true, that the events happened nearby, to someone who knows someone they know. To be sure, many of those who pass along these stories do not think of themselves as participating in the social problems process. Rather, they consider these merely memorable stories, troubling and worth repeating. They probably don't view themselves as claimsmakers, or these stories about social problems as claims.

Note, however, that many rumors and contemporary legends do share a worldview. They generally warn that the world is a dangerous place, bedeviled by dangerous villains, and that one can't be too careful. Ordinary activities, such as driving in a car, visiting the shopping mall, and striking up a conversation with a stranger turn out to be portals into a world of violence and victimization. Thus, there is a sort of conservatism underlying most contemporary legends, a worldview characterized by the suspicion that change is dangerous and needs to be approached with great caution.

Joke Cycles

A second form of contemporary folklore that builds on social problems claimsmaking is the **joke cycle**. Joke cycles are sets of jokes that share a form ("knock knock" jokes) or a topic (jokes about blondes); a cycle often becomes quite popular for a time, before losing favor. Some folklorists seek to explain the emergence of particular joke cycles as reactions to awareness of social problems; Dundes (1987) argued that the popularity of elephant jokes in the 1960s reflected public attitudes toward the civil rights movement, and the dead-baby joke cycle of the 1970s was a reaction to concern about abortion and contraception.

At first glance, these interpretations may seem peculiar, but Dundes noted that elephant jokes (for instance, "Why do elephants paint their toenails red? To hide in cherry trees") often ridicule the elephant's efforts to fit into a particular setting, and they often portray elephants as sexually dangerous. The timing of this joke cycle—it emerged in the 1960s, when the civil rights movement was at its height—suggests that this may have been an indirect means of expressing resistance to the cause of integration.

Similarly, the dead-baby joke cycle (for example, "What's red and sits in a corner? A baby chewing razor blades") presented various disturbing images and emerged during the early 1970s, shortly after the contraceptive pill became widespread and around the time that abortion was being legalized. It is not impossibly far-fetched to view joking about dead babies as linked to ambivalence about these changes. Although not everyone finds them convincing, such interpretations suggest that even the silliest-seeming joke cycles may be part of the social problems process.

Many joke cycles pose much less difficult interpretive problems. There is a long tradition of joke cycles that play on and reinforce racial, religious, or ethnic stereotypes (Dundes, 1987). Similarly, other joke cycles are grounded in stereotypes regarding gender or sexual orientation. Various joke cycles depict different target groups as being lazy, stupid, dirty, sexually promiscuous, or having other undesirable qualities. Repeating such jokes can be seen as a sort of claim about different sorts of people; of course, it is always possible for those telling the jokes to deny this, to insist that they're just joking.

The links between joking and claimsmaking are especially apparent with joke cycles inspired by dramatic current events—such as the explosion of the space shuttle *Challenger* in 1986; or the terrorist attacks on the World Trade Center on September 11, 2001 (Ellis, 2003; Oring, 1987). One important quality of such **topical joke cycles** is that we know the date they started spreading. Obviously there were no *Challenger* jokes before January 28, 1986 (the day the explosion occurred).

Studies of topical joke cycles reveal that such jokes spread widely and very rapidly through informal channels. Media commentators, for instance, noted the existence of jokes about the *Challenger* within a few days following the catastrophe, although the jokes themselves were not circulated by the media (which viewed the jokes as in very bad taste and therefore unrepeatable). In such cases, both the number of jokes told and the number of people who report having heard them increased rapidly in the days and weeks following the event that inspired the jokes (Ellis, 1991). Of course, after a few weeks people stopped telling these jokes, presumably because those who might have enjoyed them had, by that time, already heard them, but also because the subject no longer seemed topical.

Box 6.6 How Jokes Spread

Once upon a time, jokes spread mostly by word of mouth, but the Internet enables jokes—like all other sorts of information—to instantaneously travel around the globe. Of course, a joke in English needs to be translated if it is to reach non-English speakers, and this happens surprisingly often.

Shifman, Levy, and Thelwall (2014) searched for translations of 100 popular English-language jokes in nine other languages; some were "global hits" that were translated into almost all languages, while others turned out to be "translation-resistant"—rarely or never translated. Jokes that failed to spread to other cultures depended on a good deal of familiarity with American culture (such as a joke that incorporated stereotypes about differences between people who live in New Jersey versus Alabama), or they emphasized the frustrations of capitalism (such as jokes about unhappy employees or exploitative corporations). However, other jokes, about men and women having different concerns, or about the importance of shopping and consumption in contemporary society, spread widely.

These findings suggest that jokes that speak to social problems may—but need not—spread widely, depending on how their claims are framed. Perhaps people in all cultures find their work frustrating, but the particular frustrations depicted in an English-language joke may not resonate with people in other cultures. On the other hand, frustrations with gender differences or the consumer economy may be more easily translated. A joke that successfully constructs a social problem in one culture may not seem as funny in other places.

Topical jokes tend to spread where they have relevance (see Box 6.6). Local scandals may become the subject of local joke cycles, but they are unlikely to spread beyond that locality. For example, the on-camera suicide of Pennsylvania's state treasurer in 1987 inspired a joke cycle in that state, but those jokes did not spread widely beyond the area where he was a familiar figure (Bronner, 1988). In much the same way, the 1986 Chernobyl nuclear reactor disaster—which released radiation—did not become the subject of extensive joking in the United States (which seemed geographically far removed from the danger), but it did become the subject of a substantial joke cycle in Europe (where people worried about their exposure to radioactive contamination) (Kurti, 1988).

Why do people tell jokes about disasters? It is easy to argue that there is nothing funny about these events, and that such jokes are inappropriate. The most popular explanations are psychological—either that such jokes are symptoms of a "sick" society, or that telling jokes is cathartic and eases people's psychological strain. Sociologists might argue, however, that topical jokes, like contemporary legends that address subjects of current claimsmaking, offer an indirect way of expressing public attitudes toward troubling social conditions. Jokes often reveal skepticism of media constructions of events (Oring, 1987).

Here it is worth noting one other form of folk humor: the photocopies of jokes, cartoons, mock memos, and such that are posted in offices and other workplaces (Dundes & Pagter, 2000). This "office folklore" has become much easier to reproduce and disseminate, thanks to improved technologies, such as photocopiers, fax machines, e-mail, computer software, and smartphones, which allow people to create, modify, store, and transmit photos and other graphics very easily (Ellis, 2003). Often these bits of folklore suggest considerable skepticism about the workings of bureaucracies and the abilities of their leaders. Like legends and joke cycles, such office humor often addresses ethnicity, class, gender, and other familiar bases for social conflict. The fact that they are widespread suggests that their subversive reconstructions of different social problems are relatively popular, although—as is the case with all other types of folklore—it is always possible to shrug off objections by insisting that these postings aren't serious commentary, that they are just in fun. Still, such folklore remains one way in which ordinary people can express their thoughts and respond to more visible claimsmakers.

THE PUBLIC'S ROLE IN THE SOCIAL PROBLEMS PROCESS

Although opinion polls, focus groups, social media, and contemporary folklore all offer ways of understanding something about how the general public responds to constructions of social problems made by claimsmakers and the media, none of these methods can hope to tell the whole story. After all, the general public is very large and very diverse. It includes people who virtually ignore social problems claims, but also people who follow claimsmaking with enthusiasm. It includes people from a wide range of social groupings—different occupations, different ethnicities, different social classes, different genders and sexual orientations, different political ideologies, and on and on. These various groups have, if not different values, at least different interpretations of which values are most important and how they ought to be realized. There are, then, all sorts of differences that can affect how people in the general public will respond to particular social problems claims.

Moreover, even people who seem to respond in the same way—who, for example, give the same response to a survey question—may, in fact, be quite different. Some people may be energized by particular claims—they may become committed, inspired to join the cause, to devote their time, money, and energy to bringing about change. Others may become interested enough to follow the issue, read books and articles on the topic, watch TV coverage, and become well informed, although they may never actually enlist in the cause. Still others may be only dimly aware of the claims, knowing enough to tell a pollster that they think the problem is serious, but not moved to do anything more. In other words, what people mean when they respond to a survey question indicating their concern is not at all clear.

Similarly, people who hear and repeat contemporary legends or jokes may understand this folklore in very different ways. Some may indeed view themselves as participating in the social problems process, as expressing particular beliefs or attitudes; for example, probably many people who tell ethnic jokes understand that, in so doing, they are promoting particular stereotypes. But others may insist that this is just innocent fun, that it has no larger meaning.

Earlier chapters noted that claimsmakers often hope to affect public opinion, to make people aware of and concerned about a troubling condition, and that the media justify their own activities by referring to the importance of an informed public. Similarly, policymakers (discussed in Chapter 7) often argue that they are responsive to the "will of the people." Other actors in the social problems process, then, argue that public reactions play an important role. Claimsmakers, the media, and policymakers want to reach—and influence—the public, but those actors also pay attention to the public's reactions and try to adjust their own behavior in response (see Figure 6.1).

Figure 6.1 THE PUBLIC'S ROLE IN THE SOCIAL PROBLEMS PROCESS

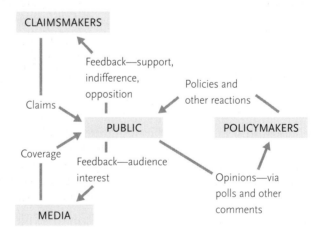

This book has emphasized the competitive nature of the social problems process: there are countless claims being promoted, and nearly as many media reports about troubling conditions. With all these bids for the public's attention, some claims inevitably must fail to attract the public's notice. This is why rhetoric—the way claims and media coverage are packaged—becomes important; the public is likely to ignore many claims and focus only on those that it finds particularly compelling.

This chapter has argued that all the ways in which social scientists measure public reactions, including public opinion surveys, focus groups, social media, and folklore, offer indirect, imprecise ways of interpreting what the public is thinking. We might wonder, then, whether we can hope to fully understand this stage in the social problems process.

However, there is other evidence of public reactions. Over time, we can also witness changes in people's behavior that reveal responses to claimsmaking. For instance, motorists have become more likely to use seat belts; some of this change is doubtless due to laws that subject people who fail to buckle up to fines, but it is also true that a growing proportion of the population now buckles up automatically, as a matter of habit. Over time, the proportion of the adult population that smokes has fallen—again, partly because of higher taxes and restrictions on where smoking is permitted, but also partly because a growing proportion of people sees smoking as risky behavior. Although our ways of measuring these changes are imperfect, the incidence of child abuse and other family violence has probably fallen, people's willingness to express racist sentiments in surveys has dropped, and so on.

We can, in short, find evidence of actual changes in people's behavior that is motivated, at least in part, by the public's redefining what is wise, prudent, or appropriate. Although we cannot measure the public's reactions with precision, we can still recognize that the public is responsive to—and an active part of—the larger social problems process.

MAKING CONNECTIONS

● *Claimsmakers study public reactions and reframe their claims on the basis of the feedback they receive from the public. See Chapters 2, 3, and 4 for more about the claimsmaking process.*

● *Public opinion polls that measure the reaction to claims about a social problem also help determine which issues garner attention from policymakers. In the next chapter, you will learn more about the policymaking process.*

● *Public reactions to social problems change over time. Chapter 10 discusses how reactions to social problems have evolved throughout history.*

CASE STUDY
PUBLIC REACTIONS TO EPIDEMICS

Epidemic diseases can create major societal crises: the Black Death of the fourteenth century is thought to have killed nearly half of Europe's population; the influenza epidemic following World War I killed tens of millions of people worldwide (and at least 500,000 in the United States). In recent decades, there have been several flu epidemics, as well as concerns about HIV/AIDS, West Nile virus, SARS (severe acute respiratory syndrome), and MERS (Middle East respiratory syndrome). These tend to be constructed as major—or at least potentially major—social problems, with extensive media coverage and doctors and officials acting as expert claimsmakers. The Ebola crisis of 2014 is one recent example, although it is quite possible that, by the time you read this, claims about some other epidemic will be circulating.

Ebola is a very serious, contagious disease; it is often fatal. It was first discovered in 1976, and soon became the subject of a bestselling novel and other claims warning that it had the potential to become a devastating global plague (Preston, 1994). In 2014, there was an Ebola outbreak in Liberia, Guinea, and Sierra Leone. These are relatively poor countries in West Africa, with health systems that lack the resources to handle a severe epidemic. Western nations began to send health workers and supplies to help fight the outbreak, but between March 2014 and early 2015, the number of infected people and the death toll continued to rise, although new cases were becoming much rarer. By June 2015, a total of some 27,000 cases had been reported (BBC, 2015).

The news media treated Ebola as a major story, and much of their coverage was alarming, with the emphasis on the danger that the disease could spread worldwide. When Ebola reached the United States (a traveler who had visited Liberia flew to Texas, was diagnosed, and died after infecting two of the nurses treating him), coverage became even more intense. There were predictions that the worldwide death toll from Ebola would reach one million, and although Ebola cases diagnosed in the United States could be counted on the fingers of one hand (in a couple of other cases, infected American health care workers were brought to the United States for treatment), some commentators called for drastic restrictions on travel, not just from the relatively small area in West Africa where Ebola was a problem, but from anywhere on the African continent.

To try and counteract these fears, government officials tried to assure the world that, while more resources were needed to address the disease where it was epidemic, procedures were in place to prevent the disease from spreading in other locations, such as the United States. As with other epidemics, claims about Ebola were attracting lots of attention.

How did the public respond to these claims? Polls showed that about a quarter of the population was quite concerned: Gallup polls found that 24 percent of Americans reported that they personally worried about getting Ebola; only 52 percent reported that they were at least somewhat confident of the federal government's ability to handle the outbreak; and Ebola was ranked as the third most serious health care problem facing the United States (Newport, 2014; Saad, 2014). These results resembled earlier patterns of concern during the flu epidemics of 2005 and 2009; news reports of epidemics do worry substantial minorities of people. Confidence in the nation's leadership makes a difference: the Ebola outbreak occurred during Barack Obama's presidency, and Republicans expressed less confidence in the government's ability to address the problem, whereas when the 2005 bird flu outbreak happened during George W. Bush's administration, it was Democrats who expressed more doubts.

Public reactions to the spread of Ebola also took the form of rumors and contemporary legends. Consider, for example, a pre-Thanksgiving report that 250,000 turkeys in Texas had been infected with Ebola; this story originated with *Daily Buzz Live* (an online news website with a track record of presenting dubious claims), but then was picked up and spread via social media. There were any number of analogous claims: that various celebrities had contracted Ebola; that Ebola-infected workers in factories had contaminated chocolate, corn chips, or cell phones; that Ebola outbreaks had occurred in assorted American cities; that a "ghost ship" filled with Ebola-infected rats was heading toward the United States; that people who had died from Ebola had returned to life as zombies; and so on. Some of these tales had a political edge, such as warnings that the Centers for Disease Control and Prevention was instituting a mandatory program of Ebola vaccinations; the Obama administration had a large stockpile of plastic coffins, or it was allowing infected illegal immigrants into the country; or a Republican governor had cancelled trick-or-treating (all of these stories and more can be found on the Snopes.com website). Many of these reports were variants of stories that had circulated during earlier epidemics; all, of course, expressed worries that Ebola could spread widely.

Other stories, circulating in Africa, expressed skepticism about Western authorities' claims about Ebola. Such stories claimed: Ebola had been created by the CIA or some other agency in the federal government; people came down with Ebola only after receiving shots from the Red Cross; or Ebola was part of a larger plot to exploit Africa's natural resources. Again, these stories paralleled earlier tales that blamed Westerners for HIV/AIDS and other diseases and warned that Western health workers conspired to harm Africans (White, 2000). News reports that American aid workers who became infected with Ebola and were evacuated to the United States, where they were given expensive, experimental treatments, were viewed with suspicion: had the Americans developed an Ebola cure intended to save only whites?

And, as might be expected, Ebola also inspired a range of jokes, including humorous graphics (a poster of a politician or celebrity with a tagline about Ebola—for example, President Obama shown in a biohazards protective suit announcing, "My fellow Americans, there is absolutely no reason to panic"). Many of these circulated via social media; several paralleled jokes that had circulated during previous epidemics.

By the spring of 2015, the public health campaign to control the Ebola outbreak in West Africa had succeeded. The total death toll was estimated to have been about 11,000—a substantial number, but well short of a million. Only one person had died in the United States; another handful were treated successfully in the United States (and a couple dozen who had been quarantined for three weeks after having been exposed to the disease turned out not to have been infected). This parallels the course of other recent disease outbreaks: intense media coverage warns of the potentially catastrophic consequences if the disease spreads. Although officials strive to explain the measures that are being taken to address the problem, the public becomes alarmed—in particular those already unsympathetic with the current administration express doubts, and rumors and jokes spread. Then, once the disease is brought under control, the threat is forgotten—until the next epidemic comes along.

Questions

1. Media coverage and public reactions of newly announced epidemics tend to be especially alarming and, in retrospect, exaggerated. Why?

2. What sorts of cultural resources can the public draw on to reconstruct warnings about new epidemics and other health threats?

3. By the time you read this, the 2014 Ebola outbreak is likely to have faded in our memories. Does this scare resemble other, more recent concerns?

7

▦

Policymaking

▦

Most claimsmakers hope to do more than simply draw attention to a troubling condition; they also want to change things, to improve social arrangements so that the problem can be, if not eliminated, at least made better. Toward this end, claimsmakers seek to change social policies, to alter how the society deals with the troubling condition; and this means that their claims must reach those who have the power to make policy changes—the **policymakers**. The most obvious way to change policy is through the law. Laws define what is and is not legitimate within a particular jurisdiction; they specify what is required, what is permissible, and what is forbidden. So the study of policymaking turns first to the study of legislative bodies—Congress, state legislatures, city councils, and so on—that not only pass laws but also allocate funds and issue guidelines to the various official agencies that administer those laws.

We are used to seeing media coverage about legislative debates over proposed new laws; such debates can be a high-visibility arena for policymaking. Votes on controversial legislation—to fund or cancel a program, to criminalize or decriminalize a behavior, and so on—are dramatic, visible policymaking moments. But much

199

policymaking is less visible. Many new laws attract little attention, and once passed by legislators, those laws must be implemented, which creates further opportunities for behind-the-scenes policymaking. All manner of government agencies enforce and implement laws. Though our thoughts may turn first to law enforcement agencies (such as the FBI or local police forces), we must recognize that all sorts of administrative agencies oversee how particular laws are applied (for example, the Environmental Protection Agency is charged with administering many federal environmental policies). Even local governments have specialized officials responsible for enforcing health ordinances and other local laws. And because laws usually cannot spell out how they should be applied in every possible circumstance, much of the work of interpreting how the law should be applied falls to such agencies, which therefore find themselves making policy.

In addition, in the United States, court rulings have the power to shape the law. Appellate courts, for example, can rule that legislators have exceeded their authority by passing laws that are unconstitutional, or they can rule that the way a particular law is being applied or enforced is not legal. In dramatic cases (such as the *Roe v. Wade* ruling, which dictated that states could not restrict a woman's access to abortion during the first trimester of pregnancy), Supreme Court rulings can shift fundamental perceptions of what is considered legal. Thus, sometimes government agencies and courts also act as policymakers.

However, we should not equate policy with law. A wide range of organized nongovernmental bodies—think of corporations, churches, professions, charities, and so on—set their own rules or policies. When a homeless shelter announces rules regarding who is qualified to seek admission or how people must behave if they are to be allowed to remain in the shelter, this, too, is a form of policymaking. Although this chapter will tend to concentrate on how legislatures and other government bodies establish laws, we should not forget that policymaking occurs in many different settings.

POLICY DOMAINS

One way sociologists think about how legislators and other poli-cymakers organize policymaking revolves around the concept of **policy domains** (Burstein, 1991). A policy domain is that part of the political system that focuses on a particular social issue, such as family problems, criminal justice, or health policy. A given domain includes many people who are especially concerned with the issue addressed by that domain, including legislators, other officials, and people outside the government. For example, Congress has committees that deal with health issues; various federal agencies, such as the Centers for Disease Control and Prevention and the National Institutes of Health, address those issues; and outside the government, there are interest groups, think tanks, medical profes-sionals, and other experts especially concerned with health policy. In general, health policy is likely to be formulated by those who belong to that policy domain; after all, these are the people most knowledgeable about—and most willing to devote time and energy to—health policy issues. Although Congress as a whole must vote on health-related legislation, the legislation itself is shaped within the health policy domain.

The concept of a policy domain is akin to but not the same as the concept of an arena (see Chapter 5). An *arena* is a setting where claims can be presented (a congressional committee's hear-ings might be an example). A *policy domain* is a network of people who share an interest in a particular policy issue; those people may oversee several arenas in which claims about that issue can be presented (such as different committees' hearings, specialized newsletters, and so on).

We can begin thinking about policy domains by considering the social circumstances of legislators. Although analysts usually focus on the federal Congress, we can assume that similar consid-erations affect state and local legislative bodies. Imagine a social problems claim that has been attracting attention: the media have been covering the story, public opinion polls may indicate that people are expressing concern about this troubling condition, and claimsmakers and constituents may contact legislators and ask them to take action. These circumstances might lead to a new law—to policymaking—but then again, they might not.

A new policy is by no means an automatic outcome. After all, there are lots of people who want legislators to do lots of different things, and legislators cannot possibly respond to all of these demands; there are simply too many calls for action. It would cost too much to implement them all, and many of them call for legislators to take contradictory actions. Moreover, legislators may have their own ideas about what ought to be done. Although some claims about valence issues enjoy nearly unanimous agreement (see Chapter 2), people disagree about many position issues, so there may be both people who favor and people who oppose passing a particular law. How can legislators sort out all of these demands (see Box 7.1)?

Recall that Chapter 5 spoke of the media's role in agenda setting. It helps to think of legislators as having an agenda—a prioritized list of things they want to address. The list of demands they face is impossibly long; legislators don't have enough time or enough money to do everything that they are asked to do, so they need to establish priorities, to decide which things really need to be addressed now.

Once again, we see the competitive nature of claimsmaking. Just as claimsmakers must compete for media coverage and public attention, they also must compete for places on legislators' agendas. During this process, claimsmakers may wait years until they finally get legislators to address their concerns. Because laws touch on virtually all aspects of social life, there is terrific competition for legislators' attention among people calling for new laws or changes in existing laws. One result is the establishment of lobbyists, professionals responsible for knowing the ins and outs of the legislative process, who maintain networks of contacts with

Box 7.1 What Influences Congress

Congress is a policymaking body that often comes under criticism for failing to be responsive to the will of the people. Burstein (2014) examined a sample of sixty proposals before the 101st Congress (1989–1990). His research considers three potential influences on the policymaking process:

- *Public opinion.* Thousands of bills are introduced in each Congress, but pollsters only ask questions about a few. When survey data are available, members of Congress are likely aware of what the public wants, and this may influence their behavior, but in most cases there are no polls to guide them.

- *Advocacy.* Both insider and outsider claimsmakers try to influence Congress. However, while a few bills tend to attract heavy attention from advocates, most bills attract little or none. Looking at the full range of proposals before Congress suggests that advocacy does not have much effect on whether legislation is passed.

- *Information.* If public opinion and advocacy have limited effects, what does influence Congress? Some proposals become the subjects of hearings, where congressional committees hear testimony. There is evidence that some sorts of testimony—particularly claims about the likely impact of the legislation—have some influence.

It is easy to adopt a simplistic explanation for policymakers' actions, but the evidence suggests that policymaking is in fact subject to lots of different influences.

legislators and their staff members, and who understand how to effectively package claims so as to attract legislators' interest and support. Most industries, professions, and other well-established interest groups maintain permanent lobbying operations to try to influence lawmaking.

Recall the discussion of ownership in Chapter 3—how some claimsmakers become the established authorities on an issue, and how other people turn to those claimsmakers when questions arise regarding their issues. One way to maintain ownership of an issue is to establish a lobbying operation so that someone is always ready to convey your views to those assembling legislation.

Attempting to influence policymaking can require patience. The political scientist John W. Kingdon (1984) offers one model for understanding how particular policies arrive at the top of Congress's legislative agenda. He describes three streams: (1) the problem recognition stream, (2) the policy proposal stream, and (3) the political stream. Each stream is constantly flowing, but the three streams often have minimal contact with one another. On occasion, however, they seem to converge, and when they do, Congress is more likely to act. While Kingdon's focus was Congress, his three-stream model has implications for other policymakers.

The Problem Recognition Stream

What Kingdon calls the **problem recognition stream** is already familiar; it has been the focus of the preceding chapters. In the process of problem recognition, claimsmakers identify troubling conditions, name those conditions, devise compelling rhetoric to persuade others to become concerned about those conditions, and campaign to bring those conditions to the notice of the press, the public, and policymakers. These claimsmakers' efforts can receive a boost from current events—an attention-grabbing news story about a terrible crime or a natural disaster can catapult an issue into prominence. But most claimsmakers who hope to influence policy need to work to keep their constructions visible, interesting, fresh, and compelling so that they can maintain continual pressure for policymakers to act; thus, the claimsmakers' particular views are readily accessible, should the policymakers' attention begin to turn toward their issues.

The Policy Proposal Stream

Kingdon's second stream—the **policy proposal stream**—consists of more specialized constructions, those that offer specific proposals for new legislation. Such proposals may be fairly general, in that they sketch broad ideological approaches toward a new policy; for example, at any given time, there are probably advocates calling for the government to create new programs to help the poor, as well as other advocates arguing that existing antipoverty programs are misguided and ought to be cut back. Other policy proposals may be quite elaborate and specific; advocates may design detailed plans for action or even draft suggested legislation for consideration.

All sorts of people work at devising policy proposals: in addition to the various experts, think tanks, and officials discussed in Chapter 4 who may develop proposals as part of their claimsmaking, there are lobbyists, as well as legislators and their staff members. Whereas outsider claimsmakers tend to concentrate their activities in the problem recognition stream, the policy proposal stream features far more insiders, those members of the polity who populate particular policy domains. Just as claims compete for public recognition, policy proposals compete for policymakers' attention. Again, patience is required: policy advocates must continually test the waters, constantly revise and repackage their proposals, and wait for a moment when those proposals can get a hearing (see Box 7.2).

The Political Stream

Finally, what Kingdon calls the **political stream** refers to what we might think of as the current political situation. Who has been elected, what ideologies do they hold, and what interests do they tend to represent? A new president or a new Congress may favor particular approaches to government (such as being relatively sympathetic or unsympathetic toward government regulation). Any legislature's activities reflect its composition: Does one party have a

Box 7.2 Waiting for the Next Policy Wave

The political scientist John W. Kingdon (1984) quotes an analyst for a Washington interest group:

> When you lobby for something, what you have to do is put together your coalition, you have to gear up, you have to get your political forces in line, and then you sit there and wait for the fortuitous event. For example, people who were trying to do something about regulation of railroads tried to ride the environment for a while, but that wave didn't wash them in to shore. So they grabbed their surfboards and they tried to ride something else, but that didn't do the job. The Penn Central collapse was the big wave that brought them in. As I see it, people who are trying to advocate change are like surfers waiting for the big wave. You get out there, you have to be ready to go, you have to be ready to paddle. If you're not ready to paddle when the big wave comes along, you're not going to ride it in. (p. 173)

The competition for space on policymakers' agendas is intense, and not all claims can succeed. This quote suggests that advocates need to be persistent, prepared, and flexible enough to take advantage of shifts in the policymaking environment. There may be various ways to frame an issue in order to advance the desired policies.

dominant majority? Do the legislature and the chief executive come from the same party? What other issues are competing for the politicians' attention? Is the economy fairly robust, or are budgets tight? Such factors shape the degree to which legislators believe they have a free hand. Politicians also track public opinion, and they may respond to perceived shifts in what the public favors. The political situation is constantly evolving, affecting what legislation might receive consideration—let alone pass—at any given time.

The Policy Stream Model:
Convergence of the Three Streams

Kingdon's policy stream model (Figure 7.1) illustrates how these three streams come together and assumes that, at any given moment, people are actively promoting the recognition of different problems, the adoption of different policies, and assorted political opportunities. All of these people are competing for attention and influence over the policymaking process. This intense competition ensures that most of these efforts will fail; it is just too hard to gain a place near the top of the agenda. However, sometimes the streams converge, with each reinforcing the others' influences. Sometimes a particular construction of a troubling condition complements a particular policy proposal that, in turn, coincides with the current political alignments. In those cases, proposals for new policies stand a much better chance of being enacted.

The competitive world of policymaking, with its cacophony of diverse claims demanding attention, helps explain why policy domains are so important. Policymakers cannot hope to master all of the issues, to stay on top of every topic. Instead, people specialize; they become familiar with one or two domains. Legislatures, for example, assign their members to committees (and often those committees are divided into more specialized subcommittees) charged with overseeing particular sorts of legislative proposals, and many committees can be seen as belonging to particular policy domains. These committees are much smaller than the larger legislative body, and they offer individual legislators opportunities to become relatively familiar with the issues within a specific policy domain. Policy domains bring knowledgeable people together: lobbyists, officials from related agencies, and legislative staff members often specialize in particular policy domains, and they focus their attention on the committees most concerned with that domain. This greater familiarity with a domain's issues translates into influence; committees' recommendations often influence the larger legislative body. After

Figure 7.1 KINGDON'S POLICY STREAM MODEL

Problem Recognition Stream

(Claimsmakers' constructions of problems, media coverage of claims, and public response to claimsmaking draw attention to different issues.)

Policy Proposal Stream

(Policy community [officials, interest groups, think tanks, experts, etc.] devises various proposals for policy changes.)

Political Stream

(Party affiliations of officials, political alliances, and public opinion regarding satisfaction with government create the current political environment.)

Confluence

(When streams merge, opportunities are greatest to actually change social policies.)

Source: Kingdon, 1984, pp. 92–94.

all, these committee members are the people most knowledgeable about the issue.

In advancing policies, legislators can draw on a repertoire of tactics. Once they decide to emphasize particular issues (rather than any of the multitude of other possible issues they might promote) and choose to endorse specific policy proposals (among the broad array of available choices), legislators can adopt a public posture to promote their chosen policies: they can make speeches, publish their thoughts, appear on television programs, and generally seek to draw attention to their proposals. Others work backstage. Whether their efforts are public or relatively private, legislators must try to muster allies among their colleagues; they must find others who share their concerns and are willing to join the cause.

Legislators' committee positions serve as an important resource; legislators can use their committee positions to hold hearings to draw attention to the issue they're promoting. They can invite people to testify at these hearings, to present their views. Note that the power to control these invitations, to decide who will speak at these hearings, allows legislators to ensure that the hearings will highlight particular positions or proposals. Again, hearings vary in the degree to which they seek publicity. Sometimes witnesses are chosen for their ability to draw media coverage; hearings featuring show business celebrities, sympathetic victims who can recount their sufferings, or figures who have been implicated in scandalous events are more likely to become subjects of media reporting. Well-orchestrated hearings—that is, those that attract heavy media coverage and involve dramatic presentations by witnesses—can help increase an issue's visibility and can give a cause the momentum needed to get legislation passed.

Sometimes this process results in what seems to be a significant, sudden policy change: the passage of a pathbreaking law. However, when we step back from the legislature's final vote and examine the streams leading up to the shift, we may recognize that the legislators' change of heart was preceded by social changes, particularly in problem recognition—in how claimsmakers, the media, and the public constructed the troubling conditions. There also may have been a long series of policy proposals appearing to be headed nowhere, before someone devised what proved to be a winning package. And often the political situation will have changed as well, making available the necessary votes. In other words, dramatic new legislation tends to emerge only when the three policy streams converge. For example, although earlier laws treated adolescent runaways as delinquents, subject to incarceration in juvenile facilities, by the 1970s Congress had shifted to a new policy affirming that running away was not a criminal matter and funding shelters to protect—not detain or return—runaways (Staller, 2006).

More often, however, legislative reform is incremental rather than sudden. A first bill may create a tentative, exploratory program, with advocates settling for a modest compromise measure that can be implemented. They hope this new policy will be a foot in the door—that once they have gained this initial level of acceptance, it will be possible to press for further policy measures. Passage of a first, relatively minor law may be followed by a series of additional laws over the next few years that expand and further institutionalize the policy shift. For example, the initial federal hate crime law was the Hate Crimes Statistics Act (1990), which merely required that the FBI begin keeping records of reported hate crimes (Jenness & Grattet, 2001). The Hate Crimes Sentencing Enhancement Act, which followed in 1994, allowed federal judges to impose harsher sentences on those convicted of some hate crimes. In the meantime, most state legislatures passed their own hate crime statutes, and in many cases they passed additional laws that expanded the definition of hate crimes or increased the penalties for those convicted. Over time, then, the domain of hate crime policy expanded.

Although policymaking is obviously a key stage in the social problems process, it has largely been taken for granted by sociologists (political scientists have tended to be the social scientists most interested in policy formation). The remainder of this chapter will try to suggest some sociological dimensions for analyzing the policymaking process; it will look at social organization and the pressures on policymakers before turning to policies as social constructions, to the rhetoric of policymaking.

PRESSURES ON POLICYMAKERS

We have already noted that policymakers operate under constraints. Lots of people insist that they take action, yet policymakers have limited resources at their disposal. Hence, they must set priorities and establish an agenda. But the effect of these constraints varies among policymakers—and among the issues they are asked to resolve.

We tend to think first of the most visible, most contentious policy issues. For example, consider abortion: This issue can be easily understood by most people; it leads different people to have sharply opposing views about what policy ought to be, so policymakers cannot possibly satisfy everyone; and those conflicting opinions sometimes are expressed with great passion. Topics related to abortion policy—legislative action, court decisions, and so on— receive considerable media coverage, and however policymakers act regarding abortion is likely to become widely known and is sure to anger at least some people.

However, hot-button issues like abortion are atypical. Much policymaking is almost invisible. We can presume that an agency in the federal government sets standards for, say, the composition of the concrete used in federal highways. This is basically a technical matter: most of us don't know anything about the chemical and physical properties of concrete. We probably prefer that the government build the best-quality highways (so that the roads won't deteriorate quickly) at the lowest possible cost, but we have no idea what sort of concrete composition is required, and we expect somebody else—presumably experts in that agency—to handle the matter. On the other hand, we might imagine that the people who manufacture concrete—who doubtless view the federal government as a major customer—will have strong opinions about concrete policy: they probably want to encourage concrete consumption, but they don't want those policies to cut into their profits. Probably the industry employs lobbyists to work with legislators and officials in the various agencies that determine concrete-related policies. This sort of insider claimsmaking leads to policies being made almost entirely out of the public view.

This is why policy domains are so important. Each domain contains the people who are most interested in—and most knowledgeable about—a particular set of issues. Although we might agree that, as taxpayers, we all have an interest in whether the government buys the best concrete at the lowest possible price, few taxpayers have the time or energy to pay attention to that policy domain, let alone to play an active part in that policymaking process. This means that, within some domains, policymakers have a relatively free hand: they aren't closely watched, and they aren't subjected to strong, competing pressures.

Policymakers respond to this freedom in different ways. At least sometimes, policymakers adopt relatively activist stances to take advantage of their powers. For example, when Congress passed the Rehabilitation Act of 1973, the law contained a section prohibiting discrimination against "handicapped" persons (Scotch, 2001). This was a minor provision in a much larger, apparently routine bill designed to renew a federal vocational rehabilitation program; the antidiscrimination section attracted little notice while the bill was being considered in Congress.

However, officials at the Department of Health, Education, and Welfare's Office of Civil Rights (OCR) took an active role in interpreting the new law's provisions very broadly. They argued that the law's antidiscrimination section required altering a wide range of social arrangements previously taken for granted, such as modifying curbs and other physical barriers to wheelchair access. The OCR found allies in the emerging disability rights movement, and the agency's broad interpretation led to far-reaching changes, such as requirements that public buildings be refurbished to be accessible to the disabled. It is quite possible that without the OCR's decision to promote an expansive interpretation of the new law, disability policy would not have changed as dramatically or as quickly as it did. In contrast, we can imagine occasions when agencies might choose to turn away from potential policymaking opportunities and decide simply to continue administering ongoing policies.

Of course, there is always the possibility that officials will suddenly find that what in most years would be routine, virtually invisible decisions are suddenly subjected to the glare of publicity. How a state's wildlife agency manages, say, its river otter population, is not ordinarily a major public issue, but under the right circumstances, it can become a contentious topic, with people who enjoy fishing arguing that otters are pests and need to be eliminated, while environmentalists demand that otters be protected (Goedeke, 2005). In such cases, policies that usually might be shaped by insider claimsmaking may be subjected to countervailing demands by all sorts of insiders and outsiders, the policymaking process now made visible through media coverage (see Box 7.3).

It is also not certain how policymakers will respond to such conflicting demands. Although at first glance it might seem obvious that officials are influenced by lobbying efforts, the evidence on this score is relatively weak and, perhaps contrary to popular belief, a fair amount of evidence suggests that legislators are responsive to public opinion. We might suspect that insider claimsmaking is most likely to be effective when policymaking is not especially visible. This does not mean that policies are necessarily made in secret or that the process is always corrupt, but simply that much policymaking occurs outside the spotlight of media coverage. When policymaking attracts more media attention, policymakers probably become more responsive to public opinion (Burstein, 2014).

Box 7.3 Influencing How Medical Research Is Funded

Congress allocates money to the National Institutes of Health (NIH) to fund medical research. Before the 1990s, the NIH awarded funds to researchers based largely on the scientific merits of the proposals; research that was thought to be relevant to helping cure many diseases tended to be favored in this process. There also was pressure to ensure that funds would flow to geographically dispersed researchers—members of Congress being more likely to support NIH allocations if some of the dollars supported research in their districts.

Beginning with the 1980s campaign to make HIV/AIDS a research priority, advocates began calling for research targeted toward curing breast cancer and other particular diseases. Typically, these campaigns had support from patients and their friends and families. Often they argued that research for their cause was underfunded: they might, for instance, divide their disease's research budget by the number of deaths caused by that disease; if the resulting figure was lower than comparable numbers for other diseases, they could claim that the disease wasn't being treated as seriously as others. Advocates' rhetoric might also highlight the innocence of the people afflicted by their disease by portraying them as having become ill through no fault of their own, while calling into question funding for diseases such as lung cancer (often brought on by individuals' decisions to smoke). The advocates' efforts did redirect policymaking; in recent decades, funding has shifted to provide more support for diseases that have been the subjects of prominent advocacy campaigns.

Source: R. Best, 2012.

Note, too, that policymaking on an issue can occur in multiple arenas. More than one congressional committee may be involved with legislation related to a particular policy domain; proponents can launch proposals before each committee and then, depending on how the different committees respond, choose to concentrate their efforts in those arenas that seem to offer the best prospects. In addition, policymaking arenas may be found at both the state and federal levels. Advocates can press for new policies at both levels: success at the federal level can provide momentum for further state-level campaigns; on the other hand, a successful state campaign or two may help persuade federal officials that they need to act. Similarly, those dissatisfied with the laws that are passed can press agency officials for interpretations that will shape policy implementation in particular directions; or if the agencies aren't responsive, it may be possible to appeal either the law's content or its implementation through various courts. Many doors offer openings to policymaking, so there are multiple opportunities for modest beginnings that get an issue's foot in the door and might lead to greater policy changes.

Although we tend to equate policymakers with government officials, remember that policymaking also can occur in the private sector. Corporations, churches, or other organizations can devise their own responses to claims about troubling conditions. Unlike government officials, who may be subject to countervailing pressures, private policymakers are less accountable to those outside their organizations. Foundations, for example, may donate money to encourage certain social policies (Silver, 2006).

As private entities, foundations have considerable latitude in choosing which projects to support; and they are flexible, able to make decisions and even shift their priorities relatively quickly. In earlier decades, major foundations sometimes worked in partnership with the federal government: foundations funded experimental social programs, and then evidence that those programs had been effective was used to justify establishing federal social policies based on similar models, much as examples of successful state or local government programs can be used to promote federal legislation (Silver, 2006). In recent years, however, the federal government has tried to reduce its involvement in social programs by arguing that private, "faith-based" (that is, church-sponsored) programs can provide social services more efficiently or effectively than government agencies can. Thus, today's private efforts seem less likely to inspire larger public programs.

As we have seen, myriad organizational considerations can shape the direction of policymaking. Particular instances of policymaking will depend on the constellation of parties—claimsmakers, legislative committees, interest groups, official agencies, and so on—who are willing to weigh in on a particular issue. These actors become elements in Kingdon's (1984) policy proposal and political streams. But we should never forget that policymaking also depends on the problem recognition stream, on how social problems and their proposed policy solutions are constructed.

SYMBOLIC POLITICS AND THE RHETORIC OF POLICYMAKING

Policymakers must explain and justify their actions; that is, they must convince others that their policies are wise and appropriate. Such persuasion necessarily involves rhetoric—efforts to convince others that the new policies are the best courses of action (see Box 7.4). Why is this policy needed? What problem is it intended to solve? Why is this particular policy the most appropriate means for addressing the problem? To the degree that policymaking is a public act, policymakers need to anticipate and address such questions. This task requires yet another reconstruction, one that highlights certain aspects of the troubling condition and explains how and why a particular policy will solve the problem.

The political scientist Deborah A. Stone (1989) argues that policymaking involves the construction of **causal stories**. After all, a policy solution is most likely to be effective in solving a problem if it reflects an understanding of what causes that problem. Causal stories classify troubling conditions into familiar categories according to the nature of their causes. Different categories of causes invite different policy remedies. For example, a troubling condition might be depicted as having an accidental cause (which is to say that neither the events leading to the troubling condition nor their

---

Box 7.4 Shifting the Rhetoric for Children's Policies

In American culture, children are easily portrayed as sympathetic figures, vulnerable and deserving protection. Therefore, it is not surprising that Gormley (2012) found that, during the 1960s, debates about policies aimed at children often invoked moralistic rhetoric. These claims argued that policymakers had a moral obligation to lend a helping hand to children and others who were weak and vulnerable, and to ensure that all citizens had equal opportunities.

In more recent decades, children's advocates have advanced moralistic claims less often; instead, policy debates tend to feature economic arguments. These claims emphasize that the benefits of the proposed policy will outweigh its costs, that the costs of prevention are less than the costs of fixing what could have been prevented, or that investing in children is wise.

The shift from moralistic to economic rhetoric is apparent in claims addressed to policymakers, for example, in testimony before congressional committees. And the same rhetorical choices are made by the policymakers in their own statements about children's policies. The change is apparent not just at the federal level, but in discussions about children's policy in state legislatures.

What accounts for this rhetorical shift? Perhaps, as society becomes more diverse, it may be harder to make what policymakers consider compelling moral arguments about the worth of all children. Perhaps claimsmakers have access to more social scientific data, so they find it easier to offer numeric measures of costs and benefits. Whatever the reason, the rhetoric surrounding policymaking changes over time.

---

consequences were intentional). Put simply, accidents cannot be helped, so no one is blamed for them.

Other causal stories have other implications. Another popular explanation depicts social situations as caused by intentional action; this is, for example, how we think of most crimes—that people know they are supposed to obey the law, but sometimes they deliberately break laws. A third causal story emphasizes inadvertent causes: people do things intentionally, but their actions have unintended consequences.

It is possible to devise competing constructions of the same troubling condition using all three types of causal stories. Consider Hurricane Katrina, in 2005, which broke the levees in New Orleans and resulted in catastrophic flood damage. It is possible to construct the effects of the hurricane as an accident (the storm just happened to strike the city); or as a product of inadvertent causes (officials built the city's flood control system to withstand less severe storms because strong levees would have been much more costly, and it seemed unlikely that such a powerful storm would directly strike the city); or even as intentional (such stories might involve human intent [politicians willingly constructed levees that left the city's poorest districts at grave risk] or divine will [God was deliberately punishing New Orleans for its sinful ways]). Different causal stories carry different policy implications: Should the city be rebuilt? If so, who should pay for the rebuilding? Should anyone be blamed for the disaster?

Note that the choice of a causal story also affects the characterization of the people affected by the troubling condition—the policy's **target population**—in very different ways (Schneider & Ingram, 1993, 2005). Some causal stories depict troubling conditions as affecting vulnerable but morally worthy people—victims who deserve the policymakers' help and support. At the other extreme, stories can characterize target populations as villains—individuals who embody the troubling condition, and whose bad behavior needs to be controlled through the new policy's implementation. Note that different causal stories can construct the same target population in various ways, so, for example, drug addicts might be depicted either as villains (people who knowingly break the law) or as victims (whose hopeless lives lead to despair that causes them to turn to drugs).

Target populations can be relatively powerful (that is, politically influential), or relatively weak, and their status shapes policymakers' constructions. Contrast the differences in the ways politicians talk about Social Security (a program that benefits older citizens—one of the population segments most likely to vote) and welfare programs (which benefit poorer people, who vote less often): whereas Social Security recipients are generally described as having a right to expect that their benefits will be protected, when it comes to welfare some politicians express skepticism that welfare recipients actually need—or deserve to receive—their benefits.

It is important to appreciate that there is nothing inevitable about these constructions; the same troubling condition could lead policymakers to devise very different causal stories and characterize the target population in very different ways. A causal story that is widely accepted and is taken for granted at one time may fall out of favor, pushed aside by a rival construction that might have once been unthinkable but now has wide acceptance.

When new constructions take hold, people throughout the social problems process may begin to rework their positions to fit the new story. Prior to the environmental movement's rise, for instance, pesticide manufacturers marketed products under tough, militaristic brand names, such as Arsenal or Torpedo (Kiel & Nownes, 1994). However, once policymakers began to respond to claims about the dangers posed by pesticides and the need for tighter regulation of the industry, the companies began describing their products as "crop protection chemicals," and devised less threatening brand names, such as Accord or Green Mountain. The rise of a new causal story can force many parties to adapt.

Not all causal stories and their associated policies are equally attractive, equally compelling. Ideally a causal story needs to be easily understood. That is, a good causal story should be easy to tell, simple enough to be conveyed by the media (which—as described in Chapter 5—prefer stories that can be converted into relatively straightforward secondary claims), and easy for audiences to follow. It also helps if the problem can be presented as having a straightforward, easily understood solution, and if that solution can be promised to be economical. Policymakers would prefer to construct their policies as effective and inexpensive: "this should solve the problem once and for all." Of course, such policy claims create expectations among the policymakers' audiences.

Policymakers typically emphasize the *instrumental* purposes of their policies. That is, they claim that the policy is intended to make a difference, to correct or improve a particular troubling condition in society. Of course, such claims make sense. The content of policymakers' claims—the causal stories, the definitions of the target populations, and so on—depict the troubling condition as having particular sorts of features, and also present the policy as the appropriate measure needed to address the troubling condition's causes, the target population's needs, and other aspects of the policymakers' constructions.

However, analysts often argue that policies can serve *symbolic* purposes as well. That is, policies embody values, serving to promote particular constructions of the world. Consider drug laws. The historical record is filled with examples of efforts to ban the distribution and use of illegal drugs, and most of those efforts have failed. The classic example is the United States' experiment with Prohibition, the period when alcohol was treated as an illegal drug. During Prohibition, an illegal trade in alcohol flourished; it created new opportunities for organized crime and led to considerable corruption. After about a dozen years, policymakers reversed course, legalized alcohol, and sought to regulate drinking through various liquor control laws limiting the conditions under which alcohol could be sold and consumed. Of course, alcohol problems did not disappear; alcoholism remains a major health problem and drunk drivers continue to kill people, but most policymakers consider the problems associated with legalized alcohol to be less troubling than those that might emerge if alcohol again became a target of prohibition.

It is easy to make parallel arguments about the problems associated with laws against other illegal drugs (MacCoun & Reuter, 2001). However, many policymakers insist that legalizing drugs is unthinkable. Legalization might be interpreted as constituting approval of drug use; it would "send the wrong message"—that is, it would seem to endorse the wrong values. Maintaining a strong commitment to the prohibition of drugs may not have particularly positive instrumental effects; experts disagree, but it is at least possible to argue that the effects of legalizing drugs would be no worse than the consequences of our current prohibitionist policy. However, antidrug laws also serve important symbolic purposes: they affirm society's commitment to sobriety and other moral principles.

Symbolic considerations are important, particularly when policymakers are elected officials. Topics that become contentious public issues—alcohol in the decades leading to Prohibition, or such contemporary topics as abortion, drugs, and welfare—encourage policymakers to adopt positions that play well as symbolic politics. Such policies affirm that one is standing up for the right values, and policymakers can assert that, at least in principle, these policies should work (even when their track record suggests that, in practice, such policies do not work as anticipated).

The notion of symbolic politics reminds us that policymaking is also a form of rhetoric, that it can be intended to persuade audiences—a category that can include the media, the public, and even claimsmakers (whom the policymakers may hope to placate, so they will stop calling for further policy changes)—that the policymakers have done the right things for the right reasons. We need to be alert to the dramatic nature of policymaking, to watch for the ways that policymakers—particularly elected officials—put policymaking to symbolic uses (see Box 7.5).

The competition for policymakers' attention and the policymakers' own desire to get favorable publicity for their activities encourages dramatizing the creation of new policies. Thus, policymakers often announce new policies with considerable fanfare; for instance,

Box 7.5 Figuring Out How to Talk about Torture

The photographs showing American soldiers mistreating prisoners at the Abu Ghraib prison during the Iraq War created a sensation. During wartime, governments often insist that their troops' conduct during military operations is legal, necessary, and appropriate; often it takes years, even decades, for criticism to surface. But the pictures from Abu Ghraib were impossible to ignore.

Still, Del Rosso (2015) argues, the photographs had to be interpreted: what was the meaning of what they showed? What did they reveal about the war, the American government, and the military? Several congressional committees investigated and, over time, interpretations emerged. Clearly, the low-ranking soldiers shown in the picture were implicated, and some of them were punished. But the military denied that their actions were anything more than the aberrant acts of a few individuals; one former defense secretary charged with investigating the incident described it as "*Animal House* on the night shift." To be sure, the military revealed documents listing officially approved methods of interrogation, including some harsh methods that required approval from superiors. However, these were defended as forms of "enhanced interrogation" (a more neutral term that suggested captives' treatment was under control) rather than "torture" (a word with only negative associations).

Although the Abu Ghraib photos drew attention and inspired some debate, the government found ways to talk about them that did not seem to challenge the war effort. The war's defenders constructed the scandal as a regrettable incident, rather than a revelation of a fundamental problem with the entire war effort.

the new policy may be given a distinctive name in order to convey the sense that this policy represents a dramatic change from past practices. For example, American political leaders have a fondness for "declaring war" on social problems; there have been heavily publicized wars on poverty, cancer, drugs, and most recently, of course, terrorism (J. Best, 1999). War rhetoric conveys a sense of widespread commitment to eradicating a social problem; calling a particular policy a "war" serves symbolic, not instrumental, ends. The problem with this sort of war rhetoric is that it creates very high expectations. Americans tend to think of wars as relatively brief struggles that are supposed to end in total victory (for example, U.S. involvement in World War II lasted less than four years, and the Axis powers all surrendered). Our history is characterized by a series of short, generally successful wars; it is not marked by a Thirty Years' War or a Hundred Years' War. In fact, military conflicts that seem unlikely to be resolved quickly—Vietnam is the most obvious example—quickly become unpopular.

Of course, social problems are not clearly identifiable enemies that can be defeated and driven to public surrender. There isn't one form of cancer; there are dozens. Curing cancer would actually require many different cures. Similarly, people are poor for lots of different reasons, and no single policy is likely to address all of those causes; eliminating poverty is likely to require attacking many different causes over a long period. Solving social problems usually takes time and often occurs piecemeal (see Box 7.6).

Because successful policies often proceed gradually, their contributions may go almost unnoticed, although they can transform society's face over time. Consider the impact of childhood vaccination programs, stricter fire codes, or mandatory educational requirements—all policies that we take for granted. Such policies do not result in dramatic year-to-year changes, but over decades they can produce profound transformations. A look back in time can produce surprising revelations: in 1900, measles was one of the ten leading fatal diseases (U.S. Census Bureau, 1975, p. 58); today, of course, measles has virtually been eliminated. It is a shock to realize that this disease—now easily managed through childhood vaccinations—was once a serious threat to life. The policy's success is simply taken for granted.

Box 7.6 The Undeclared War on Traffic Fatalities

In 1966, 50,894 Americans died in traffic accidents; in 2013, there were only 32,719 such deaths. In fact, the decline has been much more dramatic than those numbers suggest: Deaths fell even as the population grew by almost 65 percent, the number of drivers more than doubled, and the miles driven more than tripled. The number of traffic fatalities per 100 million miles driven dropped from 5.5 in 1966 to 1.1 in 2013 (National Highway Traffic Safety Administration, 2014).

Numerous apparently mundane policy changes account for this improvement, including the following:

- **Better cars.** Various safety features (such as seat belts, padded dashboards, electric turn signals, and air bags) became mandatory.

- **Better roads.** Various road improvements were made, including additional lanes, controlled-access highways, broader shoulders, and better signs.

- **Better drivers.** Tougher limits were imposed on alcohol consumption, and licensing was both delayed and made a graduated process for beginning drivers.

No one declared war on traffic fatalities, and no single policy change can account for the declining death toll. Rather, lots of minor policy changes nibbled away at the problem, but the cumulative effect is impressive.

This example serves as a reminder that often social policies are effective because of the combined effect of many small improvements, rather than dramatic policy pronouncements—such as heavily promoted wars on social problems—designed to get politicians favorable headlines.

Compare such quietly effective policies with the noisy announcements heralding many new policies. The announcement of a new war on a particular social problem raises expectations and thereby creates opportunities for prospective critics. After four or five years— roughly as long, remember, as Americans expect a war should last— it will be possible for critics to point to evidence that poverty or drug use or whatever the current pressing issue is continues to exist, and to argue that the new policy has failed. In other words, policies enacted with an eye toward symbolic politics are often vulnerable to critiques that are themselves grounded in symbolic arguments.

In summary, policymaking has important sociological dimensions (see Figure 7.2). Policies emerge only under favorable social conditions, and they involve yet another reconstruction of the troubling conditions—this time by policymakers who must devise a plausible causal story, depict a suitable target population, and so on. Nor is this the end of the matter. We have already noted that the tendency to herald new policies in dramatic terms, as the means

Figure 7.2 POLICYMAKING IN THE SOCIAL PROBLEMS PROCESS

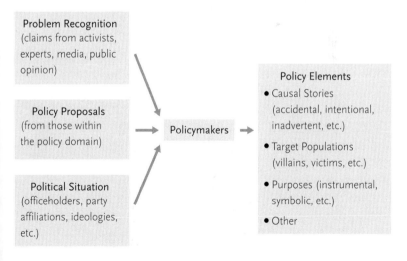

Problem Recognition
(claims from activists, experts, media, public opinion)

Policy Proposals
(from those within the policy domain)

Political Situation
(officeholders, party affiliations, ideologies, etc.)

Policymakers

Policy Elements
• Causal Stories
  (accidental, intentional, inadvertent, etc.)
• Target Populations
  (villains, victims, etc.)
• Purposes (instrumental, symbolic, etc.)
• Other

by which a troubling condition can be defeated or eliminated, sets the stage for future critics. We will have more to say about the process of evaluating social policies in Chapter 9. Before examining the construction of those critiques, however, we need to explore how policies are implemented through social problems work—the topic of the next chapter.

MAKING CONNECTIONS

- *Activists compete for attention from policymakers. Chapter 3 describes how these outsider claimsmakers try to influence the policymaking process.*

- *Policy changes frequently result from a shift in how the public or the media construct a troubling condition. See Chapter 6 for more on the role of public reactions in the social problems process.*

- *After policymakers ratify a new policy, it still must be implemented. The next chapter explores how social problems workers put a policy into action.*

CASE STUDY
Legalizing Marijuana and Same-Sex Marriage

Policy changes regarding marijuana and same-sex marriage have been much in the news in recent years, but legislative bodies (a frequent arena for policymaking) have not played a prominent role in these developments.

Beginning in the mid-1960s, marijuana use began to spread to college students and middle-class youth generally; before that time, marijuana had a much lower profile—it was thought to be smoked primarily by jazz musicians, ethnic minorities, and others on the periphery of American society. By 1977, more than half of Americans under thirty years of age reported having smoked marijuana; usage among young adults fell off a bit in later years, but a 2013 Gallup poll estimated that 38 percent of adult Americans had tried marijuana (Saad, 2013).

Since the 1960s, marijuana has been the subject of extensive claimsmaking arguing that it is no more dangerous than alcohol, that Prohibition had failed, and that criminal laws against marijuana also should be abolished. The 1970s saw several campaigns to reduce penalties for marijuana use in various states, and advocates believed that time was on their side. If most people under thirty had smoked marijuana in 1977, then by, say, 2007, that would be true for most people under age sixty. Surely, as a growing percentage of voters had had firsthand experience with the drug, opposition to legalization would wither.

At roughly the same time, attitudes toward homosexuality also underwent considerable change. The gay rights movement became widely visible in the early 1970s. At that time, polls showed considerable opposition to homosexuality. A 1977 Gallup poll found that 39 percent of Americans thought that gay or lesbian relations between consenting adults should be illegal, and that rose to 57 percent in 1986 (when fear of AIDS was near its peak), before falling to only 28 percent in 2015 (Gallup, 2015). Approval of marriages between same-sex couples rose from 27 percent in 1996 (the first year the question was asked) to 60 percent in 2015. Younger adults were consistently more tolerant of gay and lesbian rights than were older adults.

Both marijuana and same-sex marriage have been the subjects of policy changes in recent years. In 2012, Colorado and Washington passed statewide referenda ending their laws against selling, possessing, or using marijuana, and established systems making it possible to purchase the drug for recreational use. In 2014, Alaska, Oregon, and the District of Columbia followed suit. These changes had been preceded by laws legalizing medical marijuana in twenty-three states. (This was the situation when this book was being revised; there may have been further changes by the time you read this.)

A 2004 court ruling striking down the Massachusetts law against same-sex marriage made it the first state to issue marriage licenses to gay and lesbian couples. By early 2015, thirty-seven states had legalized same-sex marriages through court decisions in twenty-six states, legislative action in eight states, or popular referenda in three states. Then, in June of that year, the Supreme Court ruled that same-sex marriages were legal across the country.

Notice that marijuana and same-sex marriage typically did not become legal through legislative action. Although most state laws are the result of the state legislature's deliberations, many lawmakers were not eager to vote in favor of legalizing either marijuana or same-sex marriage. These were likely to be contentious issues; while both causes certainly had advocates campaigning on their behalf, there would have been substantial numbers of voters opposed to the legalization of marijuana or same-sex marriage. In contemporary American politics, election campaigns rely heavily on short television ads, and negative ads that attack one's opponent are especially common (and effective). Thus, an ad stating that "My opponent voted in favor of legalizing marijuana [or same-sex marriage]!" might be effective in turning out the vote, and might also overshadow any other issues in a race. It is easy to understand why many legislators would have been reluctant to provide their opponents with that sort of ammunition.

Advocates for changing these laws therefore began to look for alternative routes to policy changes. In the case of same-sex marriage, they favored a legal argument that laws prohibiting gay marriage violated the equal-protection clause in the Constitution. It is important to appreciate that marriage has three sorts of meaning for Americans: emotional (that is, we tend to think of marriage as something that happens when two people fall in love with one another); religious (in that large numbers of weddings are religious ceremonies); but also legal (married individuals have all sorts of rights and privileges under the law, such as taxes generally being lower for people who file as married couples). Thus, advocates of same-sex marriage argued that, by being excluded from the rights available to married people, they were not receiving their constitutionally guaranteed equal protection under the law. In state after state, courts accepted those claims, and struck down state laws forbidding same-sex marriage.

The campaigns for legalized marijuana took a different path. In most states, advocates campaigned to get the legislature to legalize the medical use of marijuana. Often this would involve having patients and doctors testify that marijuana did more to help some patients than other available treatments. This construction circumvented concerns about drug abuse—only people who had a legitimate medical need for marijuana (such as alleviating nausea caused by chemotherapy) would have access to the drug. Legalizing medical marijuana was a humanitarian policy change in that it would reduce the suffering of people who were sick through no fault of their own; moreover, these proposals had the support of medical authorities.

Opponents of medical marijuana warned that it was a foot in the door, a first step down what would surely become a slippery slope toward legalizing the drug. In practice, some states, including California and Colorado, passed medical marijuana laws that made it relatively easy for anyone who could locate a sympathetic physician to get a prescription for marijuana (O'Brien, 2013). An infrastructure to provide the new medication emerged: there were growers licensed to grow marijuana for medical use, and dispensaries where individuals with prescriptions could go to buy the drug. In Colorado, the marijuana industry indeed supported the campaign to decriminalize recreational marijuana. However, a 2010 referendum in California failed in large part because the growers who supplied the medical marijuana market opposed broader legalization, which they feared might increase competition and cut their profits (Doherty, 2011).

There is, in short, no automatic series of stages that states follow; local conditions affect policymaking.

Still, the relatively rapid acceptance of same-sex marriages—and what seems likely to be a growing number of states legalizing marijuana use—reveals that, particularly regarding controversial social issues, claimsmakers may find it easier to circumvent legislatures that are reluctant to act without prior evidence that the courts and public opinion will support policy changes.

QUESTIONS

1. To what degree does public opinion seem to have influenced policy changes toward marijuana and same-sex marriage?

2. Under what circumstances can landmark court decisions, such as the Supreme Court rulings on school desegregation and abortion, become key to policymaking?

3. Under what circumstances are legislative bodies likely to take the lead in policymaking?

8

▓

Social Problems Work

▓

The previous chapters explored the initial stages of the social problems process: claimsmaking, media coverage, public reaction, and policymaking. At each of these stages, people construct and reconstruct social problems: claimsmakers first draw attention to troubling conditions; the media then transform the claimsmakers' primary claims into secondary claims; next the public adds its own interpretations; and finally policymakers reframe issues in ways that can be addressed by new social policies.

This chapter concerns social problems work—the next stage in the social problems process. In this stage, too, people reconstruct the meaning of the troubling condition—but with a difference. The earlier constructions—during the stages from claimsmaking through policymaking—tended to characterize social problems in fairly abstract, general terms as widespread, even society-wide, problems. For instance, claimsmaking about the problem of poor people without medical insurance is likely to discuss the numbers of the uninsured poor, whether those numbers are rising or falling, how much caring for the uninsured costs, and so on. These claims may feature a typifying example or two, but the focus tends to be broad—on the implications of the troubling condition for the larger society. That is, claimsmaking, media coverage, and policymaking tend to take what sociologists call a **macrosociological** approach. In social problems work, the focus narrows. *Social problems work* consists of applying constructions of social problems or social policies to their immediate, practical situations (Holstein & Miller, 2003; Miller & Holstein, 1997). Instead of discussing, say, crime, in the abstract, people doing social problems work construct specific events as instances of crime, even as they conclude that other events should not be treated as crimes. Social problems work is how people apply constructions of social problems in their everyday lives.

Most obviously, people engage in social problems work when their jobs require that they implement social policies. For example, medical professionals such as doctors and nurses will encounter sick people who don't have medical insurance, and they must decide what to do in such cases—whether to provide care or turn the ill away. Such social problems work is where "the rubber meets the road"—occasions when general, theoretical constructions about social problems or social policies must be applied to real-world situations. Although some sociologists define social problems work more broadly, to encompass any occasion when people apply their constructions of social problems (for instance, in everyday conversations), this chapter will emphasize the social problems work done by "street-level bureaucrats" (Lipsky, 1980): people who work as police officers, teachers, social workers, doctors and nurses, counselors, and so on—those who have to implement whatever policies have been devised for dealing with troubling conditions.

Social problems work often occurs in face-to-face interactions—for example, when a doctor examines a patient, a teacher instructs a student, or a police officer questions a suspect. To describe the participants in these interacting pairs, we will refer to **social problems workers** (that is, the doctors, teachers, and others whose jobs involve carrying out social policies) and their **subjects** (the people—variously called *addicts, clients, defendants, offenders, patients, suspects,* *victims*, and so on—who in some way embody a socially constructed social problem). Therefore, parts of this chapter will adopt a more **microsociological** perspective, focusing on the dynamics of these interactions between individual social problems workers and particular subjects. To understand these face-to-face encounters, however, we must also consider the larger social context within which these interactions develop. This chapter will begin by considering this context and, in particular, the nature of the jobs that social problems workers do. Then, after exploring the nature of interactions between social problems workers and their subjects, we will expand our focus to consider the sorts of social problems work that occur in everyday life.

ON THE JOB

Social problems workers find themselves squeezed between great expectations and mundane reality. The expectations travel from the top down; they are imposed on social problems workers by the larger society, by policymakers, and particularly by those who directly supervise what social problems workers do. At the grandest level, these expectations come from the larger culture's understanding of social problems work. In general, we expect doctors to heal the sick, teachers to help their students learn, police to fight crime by enforcing the law, and so on. These expectations are reaffirmed by popular culture. Think of all those television series featuring dedicated doctors and nurses, cops and prosecutors, teachers, and so on. In general, these heroic figures confront and solve instances of social problems in each episode: patients are healed, criminals are brought to justice, or whatever. Because most of us have fairly limited real-world contacts with social problems workers, these idealized images may shape how we think of social problems work; we may imagine that social problems work is as straightforward and effective as these melodramas imply.

Further, social problems workers operate within broad-based institutions—such as medicine or the legal system—that state both general principles and specific rules that should govern the social problems workers' actions. Police, for example, enforce the criminal laws that define not just the nature of various crimes, but also boundaries for legal police conduct. The activities of different social problems workers are governed by various institutional sets of rules—professional codes of conduct, standards for appropriate behavior, and so on. These rules provide another layer of expectations that constrain how social problems workers should act.

Finally, most social problems workers belong to particular organizations—a police force, hospital, or welfare agency—that have bureaucratic hierarchies, including supervisory personnel who have their own expectations for their subordinates. Organizations vary in the importance they place on implementing particular policies; for instance, some police departments assign a much higher priority to enforcing hate crime laws than other departments do (Jenness & Grattet, 2005). A police chief may decide that traffic offenses are becoming a problem in the community and order the department's officers to be especially vigilant about ticketing traffic offenses, or a hospital administrator may discourage medical personnel from ordering expensive tests. In these examples, officers who fail to issue tickets and doctors who continue to require lots of tests may become targets of their supervisors' disapproval. Obviously such organizational expectations act as further constraints on social problems workers.

The combination of cultural, institutional, and organizational expectations may be thought of as pressing social problems workers from above; these are all ways in which the larger society tries to shape how social problems work is conducted (see Figure 8.1). At the same time, social problems workers find themselves confronting the realities of the particular people and situations they encounter. Police officers observe minor traffic violations, or see a group of youths congregating on a street corner or an intoxicated person

Figure 8.1 SOCIAL PROBLEMS WORKERS IN THE MIDDLE

Organizations employ social problems workers and supervise their performance.

Institutions (such as law or medicine) frame expectations for different sorts of social problems work.

Policymakers set policies that must be carried out by social problems workers.

Social Problems Workers

Media depict idealized versions of social problems workers and report on actual social problems work.

Observers witness social problems workers' performance.

Subjects demand the attention of social problems workers, often in interactions marked by tension.

shambling down the sidewalk, or answer a call about a domestic dispute. These are all occasions when the officers face choices: Should they ignore what they see? Should they investigate further by speaking to the individuals involved? Or should they take official action, such as issuing a ticket or making an arrest? During any day on the job in social problems work, lots of decisions of this sort will need to be made.

All this means that most social problems workers have considerable discretion. Their supervisors cannot oversee all of their actions, and on many occasions a social problems worker may conclude that "going by the book"—following the institutional and organizational rules—isn't the wisest, or best, course. Society tends to idealize social problems work, but social problems workers recognize that what they do must be practical. They may have reservations about the wisdom of the policies that they are expected to execute—those policies may seem too idealistic to fit the gritty, practical world that the social problems workers confront—and they may choose when to invoke, and when to ignore, particular policies (Åkerström, 2006). In short, they must draw on their own experiences, as well as their conversations with other social problems workers about how best to do their jobs, in order to decide what to do in any given instance.

Social problems workers vary in the amount of decision-making discretion they have; the lone police officer on patrol is harder to supervise than a social welfare caseworker whose supervisor's desk is only a few feet away. In general, the historical trend has been for institutions and organizations to try to reduce the independence of individual social problems workers in the name of ensuring a higher standard of performance. For example, it used to be common for new police officers to learn on the job by being partnered for a time with an experienced officer who could show the ropes to the newcomer; increasingly, this sort of informal apprenticeship has been replaced by academies where officers-in-training receive weeks of classroom training on criminal law and police procedure.

Similarly, medicine changed during the early twentieth century: medical schools began being accredited, states established procedures for licensing physicians, and there were other formal developments designed to ensure that all doctors would have at least a minimum set of qualifications and be able to provide at least a minimum standard of care (Starr, 1982). In much the same way, recent efforts by the federal government to use standardized testing to measure the performance of students in the nation's schools are an effort to improve the caliber of instruction in individual classrooms. In other words, the discretion of social problems workers can itself be constructed as a social problem in that it can lead to inconsistent work that may be, among other things, corrupt or incompetent. Therefore, reformers devise policies to press social problems workers to be more consistent and to meet higher standards of performance. Such reforms emphasize professionalism; they encourage social problems workers to think of themselves as having special training and qualifications, and to aspire to meet their professions' high standards (Freidson, 1986). These reforms often require paperwork: social problems workers are required to provide records of their actions, or even to apply for approval to proceed—measures intended to give supervisors more control over the individual social problems worker's performance. Still, there is an inherent problem: grand principles, whether they are laws or professional standards, must be translated into practical actions. The social problems worker remains the front-line figure, the person who has to have some discretion to assess particular situations involving particular subjects and decide what ought to be done (see Box 8.1).

The tendency toward the professionalization of social problems work has other consequences. Our discussion of claimsmakers (particularly in Chapter 3) noted that claimsmaking campaigns often originate with activists who may have personal experiences with a particular troubling condition, or who may hold ideologies that help them frame critiques of existing social arrangements. Such activists invest time and energy in claimsmaking because they feel strongly that this issue is important and must be addressed. In some cases, activists may even engage in private policymaking by establishing their own grassroots programs to address troubling conditions. For example, after some members of the hippie community became concerned about the vulnerability of adolescent runaways, they established shelters to provide runaways with food, shelter, and

Box 8.1 Policing with Big Data

Social problems work can be changed by new technologies. Police agencies are beginning to use big data—examining records of large numbers of reported crimes and other records to identify patterns in criminal activity. These patterns might be difficult, if not impossible, for police to identify in their daily patrols. In dramatic cases, it may be possible to recognize links among serious crimes that have been committed in different jurisdictions, so that police may realize that a serial killer or serial rapist has been at work, and perhaps even discover that a particular individual has been near each of the crime scenes. While not proof of that person's guilt, such information can suggest directions for future inquiry. More routine uses of big data allow police to allocate their resources to times and places where they are most likely to be needed so that police can be more efficient, less reactive, and better able to anticipate trouble.

Of course, big data is simply a tool. The constructions that emerge from the data analysis come from the police. Based on their experiences and the priorities of their agencies, they choose the sorts of patterns for which they search. And, of course, it is very easy to forget this, to begin to say, in effect, that "the computer tells us to do _____." But it is—as is the case in all social problems work—the police who must do the interpretive work by figuring out what to look for in the big data, and constructing meanings for whatever it is those data show. Technology can aid the police, but it cannot replace their assigning meanings to their work.

Source: Sanders, Christensen, & Weston, 2015.

other basic necessities (Staller, 2006); similarly, early feminists created centers for rape counseling and shelters for battered women.

Such grassroots operations tend to be staffed by volunteers and equipped through donations, but it is difficult to maintain them on that basis. The need for stable funding—to cover salaries and other costs—eventually leads these agencies to request government support. But this support usually comes at a cost; the agency may be expected to demonstrate that it is a professional operation, staffed by social problems workers who hold the appropriate credentials (rather than sharing the ideological positions of those who started the grassroots operation) and who can be counted on to abide by whatever legal constraints come with government funding.

There are exceptions to this pattern of professionalization. The obvious example is Alcoholics Anonymous (and the other twelve-step programs modeled on AA) that consist solely of people "in recovery." AA is an all-volunteer organization that refuses to acknowledge the relevance of professional credentials; its members turn to one another for support because AA's ideology insists that only those who have experienced alcoholism and recovery are qualified to guide those with drinking problems toward sobriety (Rudy, 1986). Even here, however, the emergence of health insurance provisions to cover alcohol and drug rehabilitation treatment has led to the creation of careers in alcohol and drug counseling, in which individuals who have themselves passed through the recovery process can become "professional ex-s" employed by rehabilitation centers to lead AA-like groups (J. D. Brown, 1991). Thus, the practical problems of maintaining the funding needed to support a stable program of social problems work tend to foster at least a sort of professionalism among social problems workers.

All this means that social problems workers have difficulty maintaining the ideological and emotional edge that helps motivate primary claimsmakers. At earlier stages in the social problems process, troubling conditions have been constructed and reconstructed, often in melodramatic terms, to make claims as persuasive as possible. In the construction of new crime problems, the crimes tend to be depicted as terribly harmful, and the criminals who commit those crimes tend to be characterized as callous, brutal, terrible people. Similarly, other troubling conditions, such as poverty, tend to be characterized as grave threats that inflict harm on innocent, good victims. Most claimsmaking portrays a melodramatic world populated by evil villains and innocent victims. In contrast, the people whom social problems workers actually meet on the job present more variety, complexity, and ambiguity than most social problems constructions promise. Police officers find themselves dealing with lawbreakers who may be hurt, frustrated, angry, sick, drunk, desperate, and so on—in other words, very different sorts of people from the melodramatic evildoers who must be brought to justice by, or the sympathetic victims who require the protection of, television's heroic cops. Similarly, other social problems workers meet people who are less admirable, less noble, and less innocent than the victims portrayed in many claims. Social problems work is not so clear-cut, so unambiguous, as claimsmakers and policymakers imply it will be.

CONSTRUCTING CASES

Typically, social problems work entails dealing with a series of individuals, subjects who require attention. On a given shift, a police officer encounters any number of people; the officer may stop some of them, others may hail the officer, or the dispatcher may send the officer to a place where someone thinks the police are needed. Similarly, a physician deals with a series of patients who feel sick, a social worker meets with various clients who may need assistance, and so on.

Each contact with a subject requires the social problems worker to assess the nature of the encounter: the police officer needs to decide whether a law has been broken and, if so, what the specific violation was (this was a robbery, that was an illegal turn); the doctor needs to decide whether the patient is actually ill, what the illness might be, and how best to treat it; and so on. Note that social problems workers may decide that there is really nothing wrong, or at least that there isn't anything wrong enough to require official action: the police officer may simply warn the person to stay out of trouble; the doctor may decide that further treatment is unnecessary.

A central theme in social problems work is the construction of **cases**; that is, social problems workers must decide whether particular subjects represent *instances* of a previously constructed troubling condition that requires attention through the application of an appropriate policy. Thanks to institutional and organizational expectations, social problems workers have an array of categories or labels that they might apply to the subjects who become their cases, as well as procedures for dealing with those cases (Chambliss, 1996). But first, subjects must be classified as cases; that is, individual people's practical problems must be translated into the categories (crimes, diseases, and so on) used by the social problems workers. Studies of social problems workers find that they consider a wide range of factors in making these assessments, asking questions such as:

• *What seems to be the problem?* Most obviously, social problems workers must label their subjects by categorizing their troubles. Such assessment involves yet another process of social construction. Consider a physician. Doctors are trained to recognize different diseases; a doctor who meets a new patient will ask questions designed to identify a familiar pattern of symptoms, such that the doctor can, with some confidence, declare that the patient suffers from a particular disease. Labeling the patient's disease will, in turn, allow the doctor to prescribe the appropriate treatment for that illness. Just as doctors construct individual patients as having particular maladies, other social problems workers classify their subjects into familiar categories: police officers must decide whether a crime has been committed (and if so, which crime) and whether there is sufficient evidence to make an arrest; educators must determine which students are having trouble learning, and then seek to identify the source of the difficulty (perhaps by diagnosing a particular learning disability); and so on.

Often a social problems worker is able to conclude that a particular subject does not meet the standards to become a case, or that the subject represents a sort of case that a different kind of social problems worker handles. Such rejections or referrals may frustrate both subjects and social problems workers. If a physician proves unable to classify a patient's symptoms, the patient is likely to be dissatisfied with the doctor (and the doctor may conclude that there is nothing really wrong—that the patient is just a hypochondriac, someone who complains without a valid medical reason).

• *Which aspects of the case are relevant?* The need to classify each case into a familiar category leads social problems workers to focus on those features of the cases that are relevant for purposes of classification or treatment. For example, a doctor trying to diagnose an illness will be interested in particular symptoms that can help distinguish among different possible diagnoses, but may be uninterested in hearing about other symptoms that can't help with the diagnosis. These narrowly focused concerns may produce tension between the social problems worker and the subject: the social problems worker may dismiss some of the subject's concerns as irrelevant (which may frustrate the subject), and the social problems worker may in turn be frustrated by the subject's failure to grasp which information needs to be reported.

• *Does this seem to be a serious matter?* (For example, has someone been seriously injured?) Obviously, the more serious the problem, the more likely it is to be pursued—and to be assigned a higher priority—by the social problems worker. Differences regarding these judgments also can lead to tension between subjects and social problems workers. People may try to convince police officers, for example, that a fight was just a minor misunderstanding, that everyone has calmed down and that there's no need to make an arrest; on other hand, patients may insist that their symptoms are serious, and that the doctor needs to take action.

- *What is the nature of the subject?* Social problems workers may classify subjects by race, gender, social class, age, education, or any of the other status categories commonly used to locate individuals within their larger social context. Often, cultural expectations dictate that different kinds of people should be treated differently—most people would doubtless agree that a police officer ought to treat a child of six differently from someone who is sixteen, or sixty-six for that matter. In other instances, subjects may suspect that the social problems worker is unjustly focusing on race or class; for example, an African American motorist who has been stopped may suspect that the police officer has engaged in racial profiling. Subjects and social problems workers may disagree about the relevance of the subject's characteristics for doing social problems work; for instance, subjects may complain that people of their status receive more—or less—attention from social problems workers than the circumstances of their cases warrant.

  Social problems workers often are more concerned with other, nondemographic aspects of their subjects. For instance, an individual's demeanor may affect the social problems worker's actions. Is the person calm or upset? Is the social problems worker being treated respectfully? Those who challenge the authority of police officers are more likely to wind up arrested than those who remain calm and respectful. Another consideration is the individual's career as a subject. Some subjects come to the attention of social problems workers again and again; they become the equivalents of students repeatedly sent to the vice principal's office. Social problems workers often become frustrated with such repeaters, particularly if those subjects seem to have ignored earlier advice or admonitions.

- *Are other people watching?* The knowledge that there is an audience observing the social problems worker's interactions with a subject can make things more complicated for both parties. During a conversation between a police officer and a teenager, the presence of other youths may make it harder for either party to back down. In particular, audiences may make social problems workers more careful, so as to avoid criticism of their conduct. Here, too, both parties may become frustrated because the other is, in a sense, playing to the gallery.

● *Are there work-related considerations?* Is the social problems worker's shift about to end? No one is eager to spend after-hours time filling out paperwork. Has the social problems worker's boss encouraged—or discouraged—particular practices? All manner of organizational and individual considerations can shape social problems work.

In particular, a social problems worker's job is often complicated by a heavy caseload. For example, doctors may be expected to deal with many different patients, just as social workers or public defenders are assigned many clients. There may be a constant influx of new cases—new patients, new arrests, and so on—that need to be addressed by social problems workers. A social problems worker can ill afford to devote too much time to any one case, lest the flow of new cases creates an unmanageable backlog, a queue of other people needing that worker's services. This pressure to deal with cases in an efficient, expeditious manner encourages social problems workers to focus on just the professionally relevant features of each case. But, of course, this narrowing of focus creates yet another source of tension: subjects may feel that their cases are not receiving the careful, individualized attention they deserve.

In short, social problems work is complicated; many factors can influence how social problems workers decide to deal with particular cases. At the same time, they usually find themselves under pressure to be efficient, to deal with cases as quickly as possible, so as not to get backlogged. Social problems workers typically resolve this dilemma by devising *routines*, standard practices that allow them to sort through cases, classify them, do what needs to be done, and then move on to the next case. For example, both prosecutors and defense attorneys learn to deal with their heavy criminal court caseloads by negotiating guilty pleas (so that many

Box 8.2 Dealing with Atypical Cases

The campaign against interpersonal sexual violence has generated programs to address both the victims of violence (for instance, by providing them shelter) and the victimizers (who may be required to undergo group counseling). When the campaign began, interpersonal violence was typified as something men did to women. But what about cases in which one woman assaults another?

According to Malinen (2014), the social problems workers who deal with sexual violence have, over time, divided into somewhat different schools of thought. She argues that there is a "Violence Against Women Subworld," with origins in the women's movement, that constructs the problem as gendered so that sexual violence is seen as one way men use their historically greater power against women. Social problems workers who adopt this perspective have a difficult time knowing how to respond to complaints about women assaulting women.

In contrast, other social problems workers are part of an "Anti-Violence Project Subworld," with origins in the gay and lesbian rights movement, that is focused on attacks on gays, lesbians, and other sexual minorities. Rather than focusing on male domination, it sees sexual violence as rooted in a culture of "heteronormativity." These social problems workers find it much easier to address complaints about women attacking women.

Every form of social problems work is likely to feature different schools of thought that offer distinctive interpretations for causes of the problems they address, as well as different ways of doing the work itself.

cases can be handled in a relatively short amount of time). Lawyers on both sides must review the record to identify the key relevant features of each case; this evaluation allows them to classify these cases not just in terms of which law was violated, but also in terms of the seriousness of the defendant's particular offense, which in turn enables them to figure out reasonable terms for negotiating an appropriate guilty plea (see Box 8.2).

In the course of dealing with many cases, social problems workers may become aware of deficiencies in the policies they are charged with implementing. Perhaps a policy's language is ambiguous; perhaps it fails to address particular sorts of cases; perhaps social problems workers realize that the policy isn't producing the desired results—there are all sorts of possible problems. As the people with the most firsthand experience with these issues, social problems workers may devise practices that modify the policy in hopes of making their work more effective, so the boundary between policy implementation and policymaking may blur.

THE SUBJECT'S VIEW

As the preceding discussion has made clear, social problems workers are encouraged to view the people they deal with as cases, as instances of a particular disease, crime, or other troubling condition, rather than as unique individuals. But, of course, the people who constitute those cases—those who, depending on the particular kind of social problems work, are termed *patients, complainants, defendants, students, clients,* and so on—do not see things that way. These subjects tend to view their experiences as special, unique. They want to discuss their particular symptoms, the reasons they had for making particular choices or taking particular actions, the specific series of events that led them to the social problems worker.

A person who feels sick and goes to the doctor experiences illness as a personal, unique series of events and wants the doctor to return his or her body to good health. People's perspectives as subjects within the medical system—or with any other form of social problems work—are personal, individualistic. We would prefer not to be treated as "just another case." It can therefore be shocking to discover that, among themselves, social problems workers may refer to their subjects not as individuals but as types of cases. For example, hospital personnel may speak of "that stomach ulcer in

Room 313"; such depersonalization violates the subject's expectations for individualized social problems work (Chambliss, 1996). We have already noted that tensions may arise because social problems workers and their subjects are likely to view their interaction in very different ways. The differences in the perspectives of the social problems worker who needs to classify subjects into cases of familiar categories, and the subjects who want to have social problems workers acknowledge them as individuals with unique problems create another, familiar tension. Subjects often criticize social problems workers for being uncaring or insensitive, even as social problems workers complain that subjects expect individualized treatment for what, in the social problems workers' view, are common, routine problems (see Box 8.3).

Often, then, social problems work requires guiding subjects to redefine both their selves and their problems. An individual whose drinking has led to difficulties at work or at home is likely to explain those difficulties in idiosyncratic terms: if only my boss weren't so unreasonable, if only my spouse were more understanding, if only people could recognize that sometimes I need a drink; oh, maybe sometimes I drink a little too much, but it doesn't really hurt anyone else; and so on. The individual subject is likely to present a unique, autobiographical account of the circumstances that brought him or her to the social problems worker's attention: if only people would try to understand my point of view, they would recognize that what I did was reasonable.

The social problems worker's task is to help the subject rework that idiosyncratic account into a more general construction. The subject needs to reinterpret whatever unique combination of events led to the encounter with the social problems worker, to learn to construct those events as instances of a larger troubling condition— excessive drinking, family violence, criminal activity, or whatever. Ideally, the subject will adopt the new identity offered by the social problems worker: "I am an alcoholic"; "I am a battered wife, and my husband is an abuser"; and so on.

Box 8.3 Veterinary Death Work

When a sick man or woman consults a physician, the patient (the person who needs the doctor's help) and the client (the one who will pay for the service) are one and the same. This is not true for all medical professions: pediatricians, for instance, treat the child but expect to be paid by the parent. Veterinarians face a similar situation: they treat animals, but work for those animals' owners. This can create tensions, particularly involving decisions about whether to treat or euthanize a pet.

In some cases, veterinarians may feel that an animal should be treated: perhaps it may be possible to cure the pet, or at least to prolong its life. But some pet owners/clients may be unwilling to follow these recommendations: perhaps the treatment will be expensive, with costs projected at thousands of dollars; perhaps the result will be imperfect, for instance, the animal will be unable to control its bladder. In such cases, clients may reject the proposed treatment and request euthanasia. Veterinarians may be frustrated by these reactions, by the clients' refusal to remain committed to the animal. In other cases, a client may insist on keeping an animal alive, even after the veterinarian believes that euthanasia is warranted. If the animal's condition will only deteriorate, and treatments can only prolong and perhaps increase its pain, the veterinarian may consider the client's refusal to euthanize the pet as wrong.

In both sorts of cases, veterinarians find themselves negotiating with clients, trying to convince them that the appropriate course is to delay death, or to hasten it.

Source: Morris, 2012.

Twelve-step programs, for example, demand that subjects undertake this sort of redefinition of self: Alcoholics Anonymous meetings begin with participants identifying themselves as alcoholics, and the program's first step is to admit to being powerless over alcohol. In other words, subjects are urged to identify themselves as instances of a general type of problem (so that they say, in effect,

"I am an alcoholic, and my personal troubles are just one instance of the larger problem of alcoholism"). The subjects are helped to understand that what once seemed to them to be their personal, unique circumstances can be understood—and are understood by the social problems workers and others—as just another case of a general problem.

Social problems workers not only find it necessary to convert individual subjects into cases in order to do their jobs effectively, but they also may believe that subjects need to identify themselves as cases if they are to benefit from the process. Some social problems work is based on force, or *coercion*: people who are arrested by police, brought to trial by prosecutors before judges, and sentenced to prison or probation are usually reluctant participants in the process; most would prefer to avoid the social problems workers' attentions. Even so, coercive social problems workers try to gain their subjects' cooperation using a combination of sticks ("You don't want to make this any harder on yourself") and carrots ("Be cooperative, and you may get a break"). Subjects who constantly offer maximum resistance make the social problems worker's job difficult; it is usually preferable to convince subjects to go along with the process, at least to the extent of accepting being defined and treated as a case (see Box 8.4).

Of course, not all social problems work is coercive; many social problems workers offer desired *services* to subjects who seek them out, providing different sorts of aid, assistance, or therapy. For example, physicians, social welfare workers, drug counselors, and so on see themselves—and are probably seen by their subjects—as helping the subjects deal with their difficulties. Yet again, a key to these services is persuading the subject to accept the social problems worker's construction of the case, first to concede that the social problems worker has correctly defined the problem and to adopt the suggested identity ("Okay, you're right, I'm an alcoholic"); and second, to follow the social problems worker's recommendations for addressing the problem. Following the prescribed program often involves adopting the social problems worker's construction of the

Box 8.4 Who's Empowered?

The movement to establish shelters for battered women had its roots in a feminist ideology that these women were fleeing relationships in which they had been dominated, so shelters needed to help their clients become empowered. But how should shelters address their clients' powerlessness? Gengler (2012) observed a shelter where workers offered women choices as a way of making them feel empowered. Women had five "points" they could "choose" to "spend"; thus, missing a support group meeting meant spending a point. Once they spent all their points, they could be asked to leave the shelter. The language of "spending points" implied empowerment, but many women saw the points as punishments levied by the staff members who controlled their lives in the shelter.

The shelter expected the women to attend group meetings that were intended to empower women by teaching valuable skills they could use to improve their parenting and other aspects of their lives. The women often resisted this agenda: they would redirect the group meetings by telling stories about their experiences; they would question the qualifications of staff members (who were often younger and without children) to teach them about life and parenting; or they might even leave the group—all tactics that could be interpreted as empowered choices. In turn, staff members sought to maintain the shelter's rules; they reminded the women that the rules were necessary and that it was important not to disrupt the groups—responses that laid the responsibility for any problems on their empowered clients. This example shows how the rhetoric adopted by social problems workers can be a tool to maintain control—even when it seems to promote freedom and empowerment.

situation, so subjects ideally acquire a new view that is supposed to help reduce or even solve their personal difficulties.

This process of subjects accepting the social problems workers' constructions is not always smooth. The social problems workers' redefinitions may be resisted by some subjects who insist on alternative interpretations. In general, subjects who have more resources (more money, more education, more social support, and so on) find it easier to resist whatever pressures the social problems workers apply, but even subjects with limited resources may be able to resist. A homeless person may insist on living on the street and refuse to enter a shelter, or someone arrested for violence against an abortion clinic may insist that it was a moral act in accordance with God's law (a view that even many abortion opponents would reject).

Note that these subjects' acts of resistance may have different degrees of social support: on the one hand, for example, a homeless person may be unable to explain the decision to live on the streets in terms that make sense to anyone else; on the other, some abortion opponents may endorse the morality of antiabortion violence.

Much resistance, though, is less active, less visible. Doctors advise countless patients to eat less, stop smoking, drink in moderation, and get more exercise. To the doctors' frustration, many patients fail to follow this sensible advice and continue to suffer deteriorating health. Most forms of social problems work have these sorts of repeat subjects: most people who go through drug treatment programs return to drug use, most inmates released from prisons wind up back in prison, and so on. Often, of course, it is possible to construct these repeaters in sympathetic terms, as victims of larger social forces (for example, not only do ex-inmates retain the disadvantages [such as limited education and job prospects] that initially encouraged their involvement in crime, but having been imprisoned usually further reduces their options, making recidivism more likely). Still, many social problems workers place much of the blame on the subjects, arguing that if only the subjects had been sincere, determined, and otherwise virtuous, they might have avoided becoming repeaters.

In general, social problems workers prefer their subjects to be compliant, willing to adopt the workers' constructions, so that their interaction with the subjects can be cooperative and the social problems work effective. However, at least some social problems workers anticipate resistance and noncooperation; the police, for example, have the power to arrest and restrain suspects, regardless of whether those subjects acknowledge the officers' authority. Other subjects may choose to go through the motions, viewing temporary submission to the social problems workers' authority as a necessary annoyance. Social problems workers, in turn, may watch for—and insist on—evidence of the subject's genuine cooperation. For instance, a drug court that offers clients the possibility of avoiding imprisonment by participating in therapeutic programs may expel clients who fail to participate fully in the program, sending them back into the penal system. Because so many tensions are built into the relationships between social problems workers and their subjects, the social problems workers are often disappointed, and it is not surprising that they may develop a certain cynicism about their work.

LOOKING OVER THEIR SHOULDERS

Social problems workers face an additional consideration: they know that they may be held accountable for their performance. Figure 8.1 illustrated how social problems workers find themselves in the middle, experiencing pressures from many directions. In particular, individual workers have supervisors, bosses who oversee how social problems work is done. These supervisors have expectations: they probably expect social problems workers to be productive (that is, to deal with their cases quickly and efficiently so that the agency's work doesn't back up); they may assign priorities, telling their workers to treat some cases as more important, deserving more careful attention than others; they want their workers to avoid mistakes or other actions that might result in critical attention being focused on the agency; and so on. Most social problems workers understand their supervisors' expectations, and they usually try to avoid displeasing their bosses.

Similarly, supervisors have others looking over their shoulders, and not just their own superiors within their organization's hierarchy (very large agencies may have several levels of authority between the agency head and the lowly, street-level social problems workers who actually deal directly with the agency's subjects). But agencies operate within a larger environment: most depend on a legislative body or other outsiders for their funding; there may be professional bodies that oversee professionals' conduct (such as state boards that license physicians); and an agency may become the subject of media coverage, or even a target of claimsmakers' criticisms. It is very easy for attention to turn to criticism, and for criticism to lead policymakers to begin interfering with an agency's operations.

Therefore, everyone involved at all levels of social problems work—for example, from the police chief to the cop on the beat—must consider not just how best to deal with the subjects of social problems work, but also how those dealings might be regarded by others. The responses of social problems workers to these considerations revolve around two central principles.

First, social problems workers try to control the flow of information about their activities. They generally prefer that others learn about the work they do directly from them. Thus, agencies issue formal reports summarizing their activities, and they may employ public relations specialists to help guide media coverage of the agency's activities. Having control over information means that social problems workers may try to choose what they report; they may even try to cover up some information, to keep it secret. Not surprisingly, social problems workers may seek to release information that portrays their activities in the best possible light, even if doing so requires distorting what they report. This sets the stage for an ongoing struggle between various levels of supervisors who want to know what social problems workers do so that they can be held accountable, and the social problems workers who seek to manage what others learn about their work.

The second principle is that social problems workers try to limit outsiders' authority over their activities. Here, their argument is that only social problems workers can truly understand the nature of their work and the pressures under which they operate. To the degree possible, they want their performance judged by others who share their views of the job—that is, colleagues, fellow social problems workers who can be expected to sympathize with their position and endorse their actions. For example, teachers' unions often object to outsiders' proposals to award teachers merit pay on the basis of their students' test performance (the teachers argue that test results reflect too many things the teachers can't control), just as police often resist reforms that would create review boards with civilian (nonpolice) members overseeing complaints of police misconduct (on the grounds that outsiders cannot understand the real-world pressures that police face). Social problems workers object to such proposals because they give outsiders a measure of power over social problems work (see Box 8.5).

Social problems workers vary in their ability to control information and ward off outsider interference with their activities. In general, the more resources the subjects of social problems work command, the more likely it is that social problems workers will be scrutinized by outsiders and the more carefully they need to monitor any behavior that might be observed. For example, whereas police in an upper-middle-class suburb may view themselves as providing services to the community's residents and strive to maintain good relations with the local press and with the community generally, police in lower-class urban neighborhoods may have a freer hand because their work tends to be more hidden from public view.

When social problems work—such as health care, teaching, or policing—is directed toward subjects who are relatively poor and powerless, what happens is far less likely to attract public attention and concern than when comparable services for wealthier subjects are seen as failing. Moreover, poorer populations tend to have more problems that require more services, so social problems workers who deal with poorer subjects often find themselves swamped with work compared with those working with better off, less needy

Box 8.5 Disciplining Doctors

People entrust physicians with their well-being, presuming that doctors have special knowledge and will do their best to help them. But sometimes doctors make mistakes or otherwise behave badly. The task of overseeing and disciplining doctors falls to state medical boards. Initially, the members of these boards were physicians, who were the only ones judged qualified to review complaints about other doctors and, in the most serious cases, take away a fellow professional's license to practice medicine.

Having only doctors on these boards eventually attracted criticism on the grounds that the board members might find it easier to identify with doctors than with their patients, and therefore be reluctant to levy punishments, even when others might think this was warranted. Many states began to add people chosen from the general public to also sit on the boards, to provide viewpoints that were not from within the medical profession. Horowitz (2013) is a sociologist who has firsthand experience serving as a public member on such boards, and has also done research on other boards. She argues that while the public members can raise questions in some cases, the members of the board who are physicians are able to draw on their professional knowledge to frame what is at issue in most cases. Inevitably, a board's decisions attempt to balance their physician-members' medical expertise (as well as their determination to protect their profession's independence from excessive regulation by officials) and the public members' efforts to ensure that the medical profession is providing enough self-regulation to protect the interests of patients and the general public.

subjects. At the same time, policymakers tend to be more responsive to middle-class demands for improved social problems work, so resources tend to flow to those social problems workers who need them relatively less. All this ensures that the quality of social problems work suffers—particularly work directed at less advantaged subjects—so social problems workers feel an even greater need to manage information. The result is a cycle of disappointment and fresh complaints about failing schools, unprofessional policing, and so on.

EVERYDAY SOCIAL PROBLEMS WORK

This chapter has focused on police, social workers, and other people who do social problems work for a living, carrying out the formal policies enacted to address claimsmaking about troubling conditions. However, we should recognize that we all sometimes become amateur social problems workers. Chapter 6 noted that the public reconstructs social problems claims in their everyday conversations. Similarly, ordinary individuals become aware of shifting constructions of troubling conditions, particularly via media coverage of claimsmaking and policymaking, and they find countless occasions to apply these constructions in their everyday lives.

Consider, for example, changing expectations regarding race and gender. The everyday world has become less segregated. Discrimination can take many forms; the southern states' legalized systems of racial segregation that were the targets of the civil rights movement (that is, laws that segregated everything from schools and hospitals to drinking fountains) are only the most obvious example; other forms are less blatant. For instance, prior to the emergence of the women's movement, women made up only a small minority of admissions to medical schools and law schools. Things have changed; most careers—like most neighborhoods, most schools, and most other settings—are more open to people of different races and both sexes. This is not to imply that there is absolute equality everywhere we turn. There is not. But expectations—and complaints—have shifted; for example, where activists once campaigned to open business schools to women students, they now complain that women in business confront a "glass ceiling" that makes it hard for women to move into the upper reaches of corporate leadership.

Everyday life is filled with occasions when people's behavior reflects changes in the larger culture, such as increasingly widespread assumptions about racial and sexual etiquette—the growing sense, for example, that blacks or women deserve to be treated with respect. Such changing manners, regarding how people respond to all sorts of differences—homosexuality, disabilities, unmarried couples cohabitating, and on and on—may be seen as one of the most common forms of social problems work, even if much of it has come to be taken for granted as simply the way people think they ought to act. Of course, managing such reactions may be quite conscious, as when women having abortions must decide how to think—and feel—about their experience.

One form of everyday social problems work, then, is to smooth over what once might have been awkward occasions. Close personal relationships—ties between friends or family members—may offer the most extreme examples. Here, people know one another well; each person is understood to be a unique individual, with his or her own character and patterns of behavior. Such relationships can be seen as the opposite of the efforts of professional social problems workers to classify their subjects into cases belonging to particular categories (see Box 8.6).

A consequence of such highly personalized understanding of one another is that families and friends are often slow to construct those they know well as instances of larger troubling conditions. Cousin Joe may get drunk a lot and even hit his wife, and Jane next door may often get moody, but it is possible for those who know Joe and Jane to tell themselves that these are just personal quirks: "Joe's under a lot of strain"; "That's just how Jane is." It often takes time for friends and family to begin to use the larger culture's vocabulary of social problems—to speak of alcoholism, or domestic violence, or depression.

The media offer guidance for such everyday social problems work: many television talk show episodes are designed to help viewers reinterpret interpersonal problems as instances of larger

Box 8.6 We All Do Social Problems Work

It is easy to identify people who do social problems work as a full-time job—police officers, psychiatrists, and the like. It is perhaps more difficult to recognize the parallel sorts of work we all do in our day-to-day lives.

We all encounter everyday troubles, occasions when the smooth flow of everyday life is disrupted (Emerson, 2015). We face minor misunderstandings, frustrations, even disputes, and we need to make sense of these troubles, to construct meanings for them. This may be a unilateral process, which we accomplish on our own, choosing to leave what is troubling unstated, perhaps as a way to avoid conflict (think of not mentioning your partner's annoying habits). Other troubles lead to bilateral interaction—prompts, discussions, even arguments—intended to raise and hopefully address concerns (as when you and your partner air your differences). In still other cases, some third party is told about the dispute—perhaps just a friend, or perhaps some sort of professional social problems worker (such as someone who does couples counseling). It is easy to recognize what the counselor does as social problems work, but all of the other efforts to deal with trouble also can be seen as informal social problems work.

In very serious instances—as when professionals inform parents that they need to recognize that their child is a case of some established social problem—individuals can find themselves continually interpreting events in everyday family life in terms of some standard social problem (Francis, 2015).

social problems, and to offer advice—where to seek help, and so on. For example, friends, family members, and coworkers may be urged to stage an "intervention" to pressure an individual to acknowledge and do something about his or her drinking problem. In this way, ordinary people are encouraged to think that they, too, can assist professional social problems work, that they can recognize things that happen as instances of troubling conditions and respond appropriately, by guiding the subject toward professional social problems workers.

Social problems work, then, is a key stage in the social problems process because it connects general discussions of macrosociological social problems with the practical realities of individuals' lives. At one time or another, all of us experience troubling conditions, either personally or through our contacts with other people, and we all come into at least occasional contact with professional social problems workers. On these occasions, the currently available constructions of troubling conditions can affect us in many ways—through media messages, through the policies interpreted by social problems workers, and so on. What happens to us, what happens to those around us, and how we understand what's happening when we become involved with social problems work are all part of the social problems process. And, in turn, people's experiences with social problems work can lead to various reactions, which will be addressed in the next chapter.

MAKING CONNECTIONS

• *Through their jobs, social problems workers transform the meaning of a social problem from an abstract, general condition to a specific or immediate situation.*

• *The measurement of social problems workers' success will be discussed in the next chapter, on policy outcomes.*

• *Social problems workers frequently become targets themselves of claims by activists and experts and are subjected to new policies to address repackaged social problems. Chapters 3 and 4 explain how claimsmakers frame troubling conditions.*

CASE STUDY
Responding to Police Violence

Questions about violence by police officers are not new. Often, the cases that receive the most attention involve African American men killed by white police officers. In 2014–15, high-profile cases in New York, Maryland, Missouri, and South Carolina attracted substantial media attention, but there have been other celebrated cases during the half century that followed the "long, hot summers" of the 1960s, when rioting occurred in black neighborhoods in hundreds of U.S. cities. These outbreaks often began with outrage over police behavior during traffic stops or other routine arrests. Some recent cases have achieved notoriety because police officers' actions have been captured on cell-phone videos, but there is nothing new about video evidence: the 1991 arrest of Rodney King received international attention precisely because a bystander with a video camera recorded King being beaten by several Los Angeles police officers.

These cases often lead to debates over the nature of police work. Press coverage in the immediate aftermath of the violent incidents is often quite critical of the officers' behavior. The officers in question may have their actions formally reviewed by their departments; in some cases, they have been tried on criminal charges, or for federal civil rights violations. Yet, very often, critics of the officers' behavior are disappointed by the outcome of these proceedings, as the officers typically are acquitted of wrongdoing.

These cases reveal complex attitudes regarding police work. On the one hand, police officers are supposed to embody ideals of justice and the rule of law; on the other, popular culture often celebrates tough cops who bend or even break the rules. Police are praised as the "thin blue line"—the protectors who stand between an orderly society and the breakdown of civilization, even as they are criticized for being an alien, "occupying force."

These competing claims usually focus on policing in African American and Hispanic neighborhoods. Although many police departments work to diversify their forces, urban police departments tend to have a larger share of white officers than the cities that they police. Often officers are not part of the communities they police; instead, many police in central cities have their homes in the surrounding suburbs. And, while there are many advocates for community policing, few officers walk beats enough to become familiar figures to the residents in particular neighborhoods—rather, many officers remain insulated in their patrol cars. Critics argue that this fosters a police culture that dehumanizes the population being policed as being different from the officers.

Incidents of police violence—and especially occasions when officers fire their weapons—are supposed to be investigated, but these investigations are usually internal, that is, they are conducted by the officer's superiors within the police department, as are other instances of alleged corruption or other police misconduct. For decades, critics have questioned the validity of such procedures, worrying that members of a department will be reluctant to find fault with the behavior of fellow officers, so that even serious lapses of judgment may be exonerated or given minor punishments. These critics have called for civilian review boards, in which nonpolice representatives on the board participate to ensure that interests other than just those of the police department are taken into consideration.

In general, police have resisted calls for civilian review boards. They argue that policing is especially difficult work, and that outsiders are incapable of understanding the complex situations officers face, the need to make decisions quickly. In particular, police argue that their work is dangerous, that they must confront and protect themselves from people who may pose serious threats. If police are a thin blue line, then they are continually, at least potentially, at risk. In their view, officers do what they feel they must to protect themselves. How can nonpolice officers possibly understand the situations in which police find themselves? How can civilians, with plenty of time to review what happened in some incident, be allowed to second-guess an officer's choices? Such arguments frame police opposition to civilian review boards.

Civilian review boards take various forms. Some are conducted by independent agencies outside the police department; others have a mix of civilian and police members; some hear appeals only after the department's review has rendered a decision; and so on (Ferdik, Rojek, & Alpert, 2013). Regardless of how the process is structured, police tend to oppose the boards, even as citizens who have experience with the boards frequently complain that the process favors the police. This widespread dissatisfaction explains why cities may use civilian review for a time, only to eventually abandon the process.

In rare cases, incidents of police violence attract widespread public attention because the incident has been captured on video, or because there were witnesses, or because the police injured a citizen with no history of criminal involvement. Perhaps the case received extensive media coverage. Perhaps there were organized protests demanding action. In rare instances, the incident may trigger rioting. Such cases push police work into the spotlight, and criminal charges may be brought against the officer.

When such complaints lead to a trial, the officer's defense almost invariably invokes the thin-blue-line rhetoric. The emphasis is on the dangerous nature of police work and the need for officers to make quick decisions under difficult circumstances (Kindy & Kelly, 2015; Smith & Pollack, 2003). Juries tend to find such arguments persuasive. Like review boards (regardless of whether they have civilian members), juries rarely punish officers for violent actions. Critics may argue that the thin-blue-line rhetoric exaggerates the dangerousness of police work, but there is general acknowledgment that policing is a risky form of social problems work. And, of course, everyone is exposed to popular cultural depictions that portray police work as highly dramatic, requiring exceptional bravery to thwart terrible villainy. Relatively few incidents of police violence attract public attention, but even highly publicized cases rarely result in punishments for the officers. There is tremendous reluctance to second-guess social problems workers.

At present, there are calls for police to wear body cameras so that there will be a video record of incidents from the officer's point of view. Knowing that their actions are being recorded might lead some officers to be more cautious before taking action. But a video record of an incident—like the recollections of those involved—can be made meaningful only through the constructions of the people who view it.

QUESTIONS

1. Compare efforts to discipline police and parallel methods of controlling some other category of social problems workers. To what degree do they resemble each other, or differ?

2. How important is popular culture in shaping how people think about various forms of social problems work?

3. To what degree is having a video record of social problems work likely to affect what happens?

9

■

Policy Outcomes

■

The social problems process can be lengthy. In its typical form, as described in earlier chapters, claims lead to media coverage, public reaction, and policymaking, and the resulting policies shape social problems work. At each stage in this process, actors reconstruct the troubling condition: just as media workers repackage the primary claims of activists and experts into secondary claims that fit the media's requirements for suitable news or entertainment, social problems workers must figure out how to bring the idealized generalities that inspired the social policies to bear on the gritty, practical situations they confront. At every stage in the social problems process, there are likely to be shifts in how the troubling condition is understood, as it is constructed and reconstructed by different people.

This chapter concerns what we can view as the final stage in the process: its *policy outcomes*, reactions to the way that social problems workers have implemented policies. There is a broad range of possible outcomes. At one extreme, we can imagine everyone agreeing that a particular policy solves the problem; perhaps all interested parties smile, dust off their hands, and turn their attention to something else. The Nineteenth Amendment to the Constitution, which granted women the vote throughout the United States, might be an example; women's right to vote became a part of the political landscape that is now simply taken for granted. However, this sort of complete satisfaction with social policy is probably rare. At the other extreme, a policy may be completely rejected, perhaps because it is seen as having failed to work, or even as having made things worse. For instance, the Eighteenth Amendment, which established prohibition of alcohol as the law of the land, was quickly found unsatisfactory and repealed (via the Twenty-First Amendment). Most policies fall between these extremes and are seen as flawed—satisfactory in some respects, but unsatisfactory in others.

In most cases, policies fail to make the troubling conditions that they are intended to address vanish. This should not come as a surprise. Crime, racism, poverty, and most other troubling conditions are unlikely to disappear simply because a particular policy has been implemented. These conditions tend to have multiple causes—consider all of the various things that might lead someone to commit a crime—and it is unlikely that any one policy can address them all. It is almost certain that more will remain to be done. This helps explain why so few social policies are regarded as completely successful.

It is significant that our culture speaks of social *problems*. The very term implies that there must be a solution; after all, schoolchildren learn to *solve* arithmetic *problems*. We might use other terms to characterize society's troubling conditions. We might call them **social conditions**, an expression that does not seem to imply the same confidence that there must be a solution; or **social issues**, a term that draws attention to disagreements or debates without necessarily raising expectations that they can be resolved. But because we think in terms of social *problems*, people often judge social policies as falling short if they don't solve everything; they tend to criticize policies that don't work, construct interpretations for those policies' shortcomings, and make recommendations regarding what ought to be done differently.

This chapter will focus on such critiques—what we will call *policy outcomes*. As we will see, the range of such outcomes is very broad (see Box 9.1). Even when people agree that a policy is flawed, they may have very different interpretations about what the flaws are, what causes those flaws, and how the flaws might be repaired. This chapter cannot possibly explore all of the many ways that people respond to social policies; it can only sketch some key features about policy outcomes. The discussion will begin by considering how policy outcomes can evolve into new claims, and then turn to the types of people who participate in constructing policy outcomes, as well as the rhetoric they tend to favor.

NEW CLAIMS BASED ON POLICY EVALUATION

As suggested already, general acceptance of a social policy's success may be relatively rare. Certainly our attention is drawn to cases of vocal critical reactions, in which people charge that the policy is somehow imperfect. These reactions can be viewed as new claims, claims that the flawed social policy itself now constitutes a troubling condition that needs to be addressed. Although such claims about policies' flaws can take many forms, we can identify three general types of critiques about social policies.

Critique #1: The Policy Is Insufficient

The first critique is that the policy is *insufficient*. Here, critics argue that the policy was a step in the right direction, but that it doesn't do enough and, as a result, has fallen short of what is needed to eliminate the troubling condition that it was intended to address. For example, critics might argue that an antipoverty program, although it may help some poor people, is insufficient to end poverty; or that a civil rights law does not do enough to eradicate the legacy of racism. An insufficient policy, according to its critics, does too little.

Box 9.1 Aid Is in the Eye of the Beholder

The same policy can inspire very different assessments from people in different situations. Letukas (2013) examined newspaper coverage of U.S. relief efforts following the 2004 Indian Ocean tsunami, which killed about a quarter-million people in twelve South Asian countries. In response, the United States and other countries around the world sent significant aid to the areas affected by the disaster:

- Press coverage in the United States tended to be self-congratulatory, celebrating the generosity and importance of American aid.

- In contrast, newspapers in India viewed the American aid program as excessive. The Indian press tended to emphasize that as the world's largest democratic nation, India was perfectly capable of addressing its own needs, and did not need assistance from other countries.

- However, in Indonesia (not only the country hardest hit by the tsunami, but one plagued by corruption and ineffective government agencies), newspapers complained that the disaster aid was insufficient, that additional help was needed to facilitate recovery.

- Newspapers in Thailand had yet another reaction: the aid was misplaced. The tsunami struck the coastal regions that are a major destination for tourism, which is a vital part of the country's economy. The Thai press was less concerned with receiving aid donations than with encouraging Western tourists to return.

In other words, policy outcome reactions to tsunami aid programs varied widely among the nations affected by the disaster.

The critique of insufficiency is often promoted by those who supported the original claims that led to implementation of the social policy. Having identified a particular troubling condition and having successfully urged policymakers to act, they now claim that the policy just isn't enough, that the policy needs to be extended or expanded to better deal with the troubling condition. Often these new claims are part of a broader strategy. After all, when claimsmakers first draw attention to a troubling condition, they may anticipate considerable resistance from the press, public, and policymakers who find the claims too unfamiliar or the claimsmakers' proposals too radical. Although they may privately think that eliminating the troubling condition will require extensive—and expensive—policy changes, claimsmakers may fear that it will be impossible—at least at first—to convince the public and policymakers to buy into such far-reaching changes. It's better to call for specific, narrower—and cheaper—policies; that is, it's better to ask for something that others might be willing to give. And, as discussed in Chapter 7, policymakers may adopt a similar approach, settling for a modest initial program in hopes that it will be a foot in the door. Once many people accept the need to do something about the troubling condition, it may be possible to mount a new campaign, arguing that the original policy is insufficient and that more needs to be done.

Critique #2: The Policy Is Excessive

The second critique, which is the opposite of the first, states that the policy is *excessive*. The argument is that the policy goes too far, that it does too much and needs to be rolled back. For example, some critics argue that laws protecting endangered species are too broad (in that they block economic progress in order to protect minor, unimportant species), too cumbersome (in that there are too many bureaucratic steps required to demonstrate compliance with the laws), and not in society's best interest (in that the requirement to protect endangered species impedes society from achieving other important goals). These, too, are claims—claims that policies have an inappropriate, damaging impact.

Those who present claims about excessive policies are likely to have resisted those policies in the first place. They may have seen the proposed policy as threatening their interests or their values, yet failed to block the policymaking process. Now they have returned to argue that the policy has, in fact, proved to be excessive, and they may seek to cut it back. In particular, they may try to convince media workers, members of the public, and policymakers who supported the initial policy that they made a mistake, that it is time to backtrack and undo the damage.

Critique #3: The Policy Is Misguided

Finally, policies may be critiqued as *misguided*. Once again, these evaluations are claims that the policy has led to a troubling condition, but in this case the claim is not so much that the policy goes too far or not far enough, but that it heads in the wrong direction. There are various bases for making such claims. For example, the critics can argue that the *construction of the troubling condition* that led to the original policy was mistaken, that the problem needs to be understood in completely different terms (see Box 9.2).

Such claims often offer alternative definitions of the troubling condition that are grounded in a different underlying ideology. For example, concerns about the spread of sexually transmitted diseases among adolescents and about teenage pregnancy have led liberals to advocate policies for sex education and for providing youths better access to contraception and abortion (Irvine, 2002). In effect, such programs of reproductive health services define the troubling condition as caused by society's failure to deal effectively with the reality of widespread adolescent sexual behavior. These programs had long met resistance from—and were sometimes blocked by—conservatives who worried that sex education and reproductive health services might promote adolescent sexual activity.

However, the emergence of HIV/AIDS as a major health risk led many schools and communities to adopt expanded new programs. After the programs were in place, some conservatives presented an alternative construction of the troubling condition by arguing

Box 9.2 The Difficulties of Devising a Policy
toward Trans Fat

When medical researchers and consumer activists began to warn
that dietary fat was linked to heart disease, they chose to focus on
the dangers of saturated fat. Their campaign eventually resulted in
the Nutrition Labeling and Education Act of 1990, which required
food manufacturers to show the amounts of total fat, saturated fat,
and cholesterol in their products. Consumers were urged to seek
out foods that used nonsaturated fat, including trans fat.

However, other researchers were beginning to demonstrate that
trans fat was dangerous; they would eventually argue that trans fat
posed an even greater risk to health than saturated fat. However, this
research failed to capture much media coverage, nor did it inspire activists to pick up the cause. Instead, trans fat became a focus for insider
claimsmakers, federal officials who pointed out that trans fat was implicated in thousands of cases of heart disease and deaths. This led to a
2003 change in food labeling, requiring that trans fat be listed; more
recently, there have been calls to ban trans fat from the food supply.

The case of trans fat offers a reminder that particular constructions can take hold during policymaking. Claiming that saturated fat
was the culprit gave claimsmakers a villain to campaign against. It
was only in retrospect that critics argued that the anti–saturated fat
movement had failed to notice an even more harmful food ingredient, one that required policy modifications.

Source: Bacon, 2013.

that it was the liberals' policies that were promoting sexual activity
among the young; the conservatives' counterclaims argued instead
for abstinence-based programs designed to discourage premarital
sexual behavior. There are many similar examples, cases in which
critics argue that the assumptions behind social policies—such as
those dealing with poverty or homelessness—are mistaken, and
that only by reinterpreting the nature and causes of the troubling
condition can effective policies be designed and implemented.

Other critiques may generally accept the initial construction of the troubling condition, yet argue that the *policies* that emerged were in some way misguided. For example, Lipsky and Smith (1989) argue that constructing social problems as emergencies often wastes resources. Emergencies are defined as short-term challenges for which policymakers tend to adopt short-term solutions, but it often might make more sense to establish long-term arrangements to deal with such conditions. For instance, instead of viewing homelessness as an emergency that requires short-term shelter and other assistance, it might be less costly and more helpful in the long run to establish programs to make stable, low-cost housing available for longer periods. Just because people agree about the nature of a social problem doesn't mean they won't disagree about how best to deal with it.

One important theme in critiques about misguided policies is that the policies actually make things worse, that they exacerbate the troubling conditions they are designed to eliminate. That is, these claims often describe policies as having *ironic* consequences. For instance, critics argue that antidrug policies actually encourage the spread of illicit drugs (for example, they might argue that arresting drug dealers increases the risks of dealing and reduces the supply of drugs, leading to higher drug prices, which in turn attract more people to the now even more lucrative business of drug dealing), or that programs designed to lift people out of poverty actually increase the numbers of poor people (here the argument might be that the more generous social welfare programs become, the more likely it is that people will choose to remain dependent on welfare rather than working) (MacCoun & Reuter, 2001; Murray, 1994). Note that the former critique tends to be favored by liberals, while the latter usually is presented by conservatives; claims that policies have ironic consequences are not limited to particular ideologies. Such claims often describe a vicious cycle: a troubling condition leads to a policy that makes the condition worse; in response, the policy is expanded (because that's how people have agreed to address this issue), which in turn causes the condition to get even worse, and so on. Critics insist that the only way to break this cycle is to devise completely different policies that approach the problem from a fresh direction. A somewhat different critique of misguided policies argues that the implementation of the policy—the *social problems work*—violates the policy's true intent or purpose. Here, critics claim that the initial construction of the problem and policy—perhaps what was intended by its advocates to be a supportive, generous plan to help the afflicted—is being subverted by social problems workers. Such critiques may contrast the public face of a policy with its hidden workings, arguing that, for example, job training programs usually do not help their clients find good jobs so much as steer them into low-paying, dead-end jobs (Lafer, 2002). Alternatively, the critics may argue that the social problems workers are abusing their positions, wasting resources, or paying too little attention to the needs of those the policy is meant to help. Claims about police brutality or police corruption, for instance, are less about flawed laws than about problems with the ways the laws are enforced.

In short, there are various ways to construct the workings of social policies as imperfect—as troubling conditions in their own right. The social problems process does not usually come to an end after a particular social policy has been implemented. Rather, new social policies often provide the raw material for launching yet another social problems process, one in which critics construct claims that the policy is doing too little, too much, or the wrong thing; that this in itself is a troubling condition; and that something ought to be done about it. In fact, dissatisfaction with the operation of current social policy is an element in most claimsmakers' rhetoric. A glance back at the examples in earlier chapters will reveal that many of the claimsmaking campaigns we have discussed throughout this book have focused, at least to some degree, on the deficiencies of existing social policies. This means that social problems processes can be linked through time: when one runs its course, it often inspires one or more new claimsmaking campaigns, as illustrated in Figure 9.1.

Figure 9.1 ONE SOCIAL PROBLEMS PROCESS CAN INSPIRE OTHERS

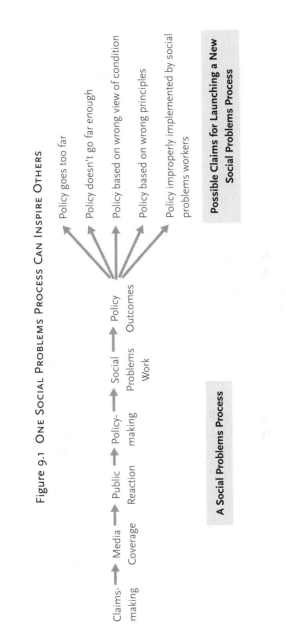

ACTORS, EVIDENCE, AND EVALUATION

The previous section described several ways to criticize the workings of social policies. But who presents these critiques? And what sorts of rhetoric do they use to make their claims convincing? This section considers some of the actors who play prominent roles in constructing outcomes to the social problems process, as well as the sorts of evidence that they are likely to feature in their claims.

Most obviously, *social problems workers* can become critics. As noted in Chapter 8, it is not unusual for social problems workers to be ambivalent about the policies that they must implement. Moreover, they have a good sense of what is—and isn't—working. Social problems workers often have to report to their supervisors about what they have been doing. Because most social problems workers keep records, they have two important advantages in debates over social policy outcomes: they understand how social problems work is actually practiced, and they have access to those records. Again, Chapter 8 noted that social problems workers seek to control information about their work, and this desire shapes their claims. They have an interest in convincing other people that they're doing a good job and, perhaps, that they would be able to do an even better job if only they had more resources—more personnel, a bigger budget, and so on. Thus, social problems workers may be reluctant to challenge either the basic policies that they are supposed to implement, or the manner in which they actually implement those policies, unless they can, in the process, advocate receiving additional resources for their agencies.

Because they control their agencies' records, social problems workers are particularly likely to support their claims with evidence of organizational activity—that is, measures of how much work they do. It is relatively easy for them to compile this information: police departments can tally the number of arrests made during the previous year, hospitals can count the number of patients, and so on. Social problems workers can use these data to demonstrate that they have been busy doing what they are supposed to do, and they often argue that the fact that they are busy is evidence that they need bigger budgets and additional personnel to handle the demand for their services. In other words, social problems workers are particularly likely to use measures of organizational activity to support claims that existing policies are insufficient, and that they need to be expanded to give social problems workers more resources.

Sometimes the social problems workers' *subjects*—the people whose lives constitute the troubling condition that the policy is supposed to address—offer their own evaluations. For example, poor people may criticize antipoverty programs for not doing enough to help poor people, just as both people who have been arrested and crime victims may complain about mistreatment at the hands of the criminal justice system. Again, as noted in Chapter 8, subjects often are frustrated in their dealings with social problems workers, and they may be dissatisfied with the actual implementation of social policies.

Like social problems workers, subjects have the advantage of firsthand experience with how policies work, and they are most likely to draw on these experiences for evidence to support their claims. Thus, they tend to favor anecdotal accounts—this is how the policy failed to work in our particular cases, or in the cases of people we know—which then serve as typifying examples for what are constructed as larger policy failings. (Recall a lesson from Chapter 2: typifying examples are rarely typical; they are chosen because they offer compelling illustrations of claims.)

Whereas social problems workers usually argue that policies are insufficient, subjects' critiques can be more varied. Subjects, too, may claim that the policy is insufficient; for example, they might argue that there are long waiting lines and other delays because there aren't enough social problems workers to aid the subjects who need services. Or they may warn that policies are excessive; for instance, they may charge that people who commit minor criminal offenses may suffer unreasonably harsh, life-damaging penalties. Or subjects may insist that the policies are misguided; for example, they may claim that social problems workers ought to help their subjects, rather than coerce them. Properly chosen typifying examples can support any of these critiques.

Compared with social problems workers, subjects tend to have significant disadvantages when critiquing policies. To the degree that subjects draw on their own personal experiences to document the policy's shortcomings, audiences may dismiss the subjects' claims as self-interested. High-status subjects' claims may receive careful attention. But the subjects of many kinds of social problems work have relatively few resources (that is, they have limited money, education, and social status), and the very fact that they are subjects can be stigmatizing (in that they may have been labeled as criminals, mentally ill, and so on). Although it is not impossible for low-status or stigmatized subjects to devise claims criticizing how a particular social policy operates, these disadvantages can make it much harder to get the media, policymakers, and other audiences to attend to the subjects' claims.

The prospects are better for a third set of critics, those whose claims launched the initial social problems process—the *original activists and experts* who first drew attention to the troubling condition and the need to do something about it. These people may already have the advantage of ownership; that is, the media and policymakers may be used to listening to what these claimsmakers have to say about this troubling condition. In particular, experts' critiques may seem more credible because they have professional credentials, and these experts may be seen as offering authoritative assessments. Claimsmakers' criticisms that the policy they promoted has somehow failed to deal effectively with the problem, then, stand a somewhat better chance of being heard than do critiques from other people.

In fact, such dissatisfaction from claimsmakers may be expected. As noted in Chapter 7, policymakers may have altered the claimsmakers' original proposals; social policies often are products of

Box 9.3 On the Third Hand

Successful claimsmakers must find ways to keep the press, the public, and policymakers focused on their issues. One way to do this is to advocate for expanding policies. The antitobacco movement has attempted to do this by drawing attention to *thirdhand smoke*.

The initial campaign against tobacco focused on the increased health risks to smokers, which resulted in policies such as placing warning labels on cigarette packages. By the 1980s, the movement began to emphasize the risks of secondhand smoke, arguing that by breathing in smoke from others' cigarettes, nonsmokers also faced increased health risks. This reconstruction accounts for campaigns to restrict places where people are allowed to smoke.

Claims about thirdhand smoke seek to extend the argument an additional step, by arguing that residue from smoking may contain harmful chemicals. While there is little scientific evidence to support these claims, advocates insist that babies and children may be especially vulnerable to these harms. Bell (2014) argues that the plausibility of these claims is enhanced by people's ability to recognize odors left by smoking. Many nonsmokers find these smells annoying, and it is easy for them to imagine that they may identify potentially harmful conditions.

There are serious practical obstacles to scientifically demonstrating the effects of thirdhand smoke—presumably all people have some exposure to smoke's residue. Still, claimsmakers view this as a possible tactic for calling for further restrictions of tobacco use—a way of making a familiar issue fresh.

compromise, as policymakers try to placate both claimsmakers who are calling for action and opponents who want to do nothing, or as little as possible, or perhaps something very different. To the degree that a policy was a compromise measure, everyone may anticipate that the initial claimsmakers will still be dissatisfied and want more, that they are likely to argue that the policy was insufficient and call for further reforms (see Box 9.3).

Activist and expert claimsmakers alike may draw on both anec-
dotes and measures of social problems workers' activity to document their claims that policies are insufficient. Like subjects, they
can use typifying examples to show that the policy doesn't do
enough to help those affected by the troubling condition. Expanding the policy may require nothing more than increasing resources
(bigger budget allocations and so on), but it may also involve
domain expansion (see Chapter 2). Here the claimsmakers argue
that the policy defines the troubling condition too narrowly, that a
broader definition is needed so that a larger share of those affected
can be helped.

Alternatively, like social problems workers, claimsmakers can
point to statistical evidence (perhaps collected by social problems
workers) to demonstrate that there is a growing problem requiring further action. After social policies are established to deal with
previously neglected troubling conditions, social problems workers' statistics often display a marked jump. For example, the campaign to draw attention to child abuse led to laws requiring that
doctors, teachers, and others report instances of suspected abuse;
not surprisingly, the number of reported cases increased dramatically. But child abuse claimsmakers could then use these statistics
to argue that the increased numbers of reports proved that child
abuse was a growing problem, that current policy responses were
insufficient, and that additional resources were needed to fight
child abuse.

Policies may be critiqued not only by the claimsmakers whose
efforts led to policymaking, but also by *rival activists and experts.*
These are people who opposed the original claims and the resulting
policy, whose counterclaims proved unsuccessful during the social
problems process. They are, of course, predisposed to be critical;
and they are particularly likely to argue either that the policy is
excessive, or that it is misguided. In their view, the policy was
a failed experiment: it didn't work, and it may even have made
things worse. These rival claimsmakers call on policymakers to

undo the damage, and they warn that expanding the policy will only exacerbate matters.

These rival claimsmakers also can draw on both anecdotal and statistical evidence. Their typifying examples point to subjects whose lives have been harmed by their contacts with social problems workers implementing the policy (for instance, a nice middle-class college student who suddenly faces felony charges for possessing a small amount of drugs, or a welfare recipient who is discouraged from finding work by a system of benefits that encourages dependency). Similarly, they can interpret the available statistical evidence as showing that the policy is having negative effects (that, say, the war on drugs has imprisoned large numbers of people, and a disproportionate share of these are African Americans; or that people are remaining welfare recipients for longer periods of time than under the preceding policy). Note that just as initial claimsmaking campaigns can be mounted by either liberals or conservatives, these critiques by rival claimsmakers who opposed those campaigns are not restricted to one ideology: both liberal and conservative claimsmakers can frame parallel critiques of policies that each opposed (see Box 9.4).

Thus far, we have examined policy critiques by four different groups: (1) social problems workers, (2) subjects, (3) the initial claimsmakers whose activities led to the policies, and (4) opposition claimsmakers who stood opposed to the original claims. Each group tends to favor particular arguments and to rely on particular sorts of evidence. Although some successful policies can lead to social problems work that attracts minimal criticism, other, more contentious issues inspire prolonged, visible debates. Topics such as abortion, gun control, drug law enforcement, environmental regulation, health care, and welfare policy are widely known to be issues about which people have disagreed in the past, disagree at the present, and in all probability will continue to disagree in the future. Such contentious policies attract many critics—sometimes from all four groups—but often their critiques tend to be discounted because

Box 9.4 Using Alarmist Rhetoric to Attack an Immigration Policy

In 1999, Utah passed a law enabling undocumented immigrants to obtain a driver's license: the law's proponents argued this would enable immigrants to obtain automobile insurance, open bank accounts, and so on. They acknowledged that undocumented workers had become important to the state's economy, and advocated dealing with the reality of the immigrants' presence. In their view the new policy was effective: nearly 100,000 people would eventually get state-issued driver's identification, and the great majority went on to get car insurance; whereas the alternative was to have larger numbers of unlicensed, uninsured drivers on the road.

However, this policy soon came under attack, and it would be repealed in 2008, as Utah passed several laws targeting undocumented immigrants. The policy's opponents adopted dramatic, emotional rhetoric, arguing that Utah had become a "sanctuary state," a "criminal portal" that was licensing criminals and terrorists. In the aftermath of 2001, rhetoric linking immigration to terrorism was, of course, especially alarming. In addition, opposition to immigration mounted during the new century's first decade, with claims about broken borders and demands for much tougher enforcement of immigration laws.

Stewart (2012) interprets the debate in Utah in terms of different narrative styles: The policy's proponents believed that they had the facts on their side, and their defense was low-key. In contrast, the policy's opponents' claims relied on arousing emotional outrage that, at least in this case, proved to be the more effective approach when debating the policy's merits.

each group is widely understood to have a vested interest in a by now predictable position in the debate, and therefore cannot be counted on to be an impartial judge of a policy's effectiveness. Is there no way to develop accurate, objective assessments of how social policies work?

THE SEARCH FOR IMPARTIAL EVALUATIONS

Doubts about whether interested parties can be trusted sometimes lead to efforts to solicit impartial evaluations of how well policies work. The most obvious of such efforts take the form of **evaluation research** (Rossi, Lipsey, & Freeman, 2004). Evaluation research usually involves some sort of social scientific assessment of a policy's effectiveness; the hallmarks of such research are efforts to create objective measures of a policy's costs, benefits, and outcomes. Often the evaluators are outsiders, chosen because they do not come from within the ranks of social problems workers, although such evaluations also can be done by insiders. The real issue is not who does the evaluation, but whether the methods used to produce the evaluation can lead to information that others will find convincing.

In theory, the most compelling evidence would come from careful experiments to assess the policy's effectiveness. At a minimum, two matched groups of subjects would be compared: social problems workers would apply the policy to the experimental, or treatment, group; and the control group would experience something else (usually whatever social problems workers did before the policy was implemented). In practice, experimental designs are often more elaborate: there may be several treatment and control groups that undergo slightly different conditions. Well-designed experiments can provide fairly convincing evidence regarding whether a policy works better than whatever preceded it.

There are, however, significant problems with experiments. One problem is that experimental research tends to be time-consuming, in part because designing the research, carrying it out, and then analyzing the results can take a long time. But experiments also take time because the evaluators may want to wait to follow up with the subjects who experience the policy. It may take time for the policy's effects to be felt, or a policy's early effects on the subjects' lives may wear off over time; since it takes a while for either of those consequences to become apparent, researchers may prefer to make their final measurements years after the subjects' contacts with social problems workers end. In addition, experimental designs, because they can be elaborate and take years to complete, are often costly. As a practical matter, people engaged in policy debates are often too impatient to wait for experimental results that may not be available for years, as well as unwilling to pay for such expensive research.

Therefore, evaluation research usually winds up using less compelling, nonexperimental methods to study policy effectiveness. Often such studies consist of two sorts of comparisons. The first is across time: the evaluators compare a particular measure of the old and new policies' effectiveness (for instance, under our old policing policy the crime rate was X, whereas under our new policy it is Y). Second, evaluators may compare different places (other cities, states, or countries) to see whether our policy seems to be more effective than those used elsewhere.

The evidence produced through such comparisons is weaker than the findings of experiments because the differences between the old and new policies may actually have been caused by another factor (such as the economy booming or declining), or perhaps the other places used for comparison aren't really comparable (for instance, City A's agencies are known to be corrupt, City B has a very different ethnic composition, and so on). Such comparisons pose complicated problems for researchers: both the troubling conditions that the policies are designed to address and the policies themselves are likely to vary from time to time and place to place; in addition, policymakers, social problems workers, and others may insist that they already know whether and why a policy works, so the evaluators' findings may not be welcome.

There is another problem: to hold down costs, nonexperimental research often winds up measuring policy effectiveness using whatever data have already been collected. In practice, this usually means using the records kept by the social problems workers—the measures of organizational activity discussed earlier, such as the number of arrests or the average amount of time that clients continue to receive welfare benefits. This information may be suggestive, but it often doesn't answer the key questions: Do lots of arrests mean that crime is under—or out of—control? Do clients stop receiving welfare benefits because they have been helped out of poverty, or because they have become frustrated with the policy and have given up?

Since it is difficult to produce high-quality, inexpensive data quickly, evaluation research rarely provides the last word in assessing policies' effectiveness. Too many questions remain. Typically, such research depends on the records compiled by social problems workers, and those records have limitations. Imagine an effort to evaluate a new antidrug policy. Evaluation researchers might try to compare available measures of organizational activity, such as the number of drug arrests or the value of the drugs seized before and after the policy's introduction. But note that this approach raises various questions: Are those records accurate? (How, for example, is the value of the drugs seized calculated?) Were the records kept in the same way before and after the policy was introduced (or was there perhaps a more systematic effort to count every case once the policy went into effect)? And, after all, what do such measures mean? Do more drug arrests and more drugs seized mean that the policy is working (because, presumably, drug dealers and drugs are being taken out of circulation), or do they suggest that the policy is failing (because there seem to be more dealers to arrest and drugs to capture)?

In short, evaluation research tends to rely on imperfect, ambiguous data, and the correct interpretation of its results is often unclear. Depending on the assumptions that evaluators bring to their work and the choices that they make in deciding how to measure the policy outcomes, it is often possible for evaluators to come to very different conclusions. And although evaluation research is theoretically impartial, evaluators can be "hired guns," brought in to buttress a particular tale. A policy's advocates may commission research that allows them to point with pride at evidence of their policy's success, while the policy's opponents may present their own research suggesting the policy's shortcomings. Not surprisingly, then, evaluation research often fails to gain acceptance as the authoritative, impartial, last word on a policy's impact.

The knowledge that evaluators may design research that seems to affirm their prejudices sometimes leads to efforts to devise special high-status, impartial bodies to evaluate policies and issue recommendations. At the highest level, the president or Congress often appoint national **commissions**; and state or local authorities may appoint similar bodies (Zegart, 2004). The commission members tend to be visible figures known for their integrity and chosen to represent a range of interest groups (for instance, leaders from business, labor, law, the media, and religion; members from both political parties; males as well as females; individuals from different regions and ethnic groups; and so on). In other words, the commissioners are meant to represent a broad range of those concerned with the policy. Such "blue ribbon" commissions may be appointed with great fanfare with the expectation that the commission's findings will also be well publicized, accepted as authoritative, and used to guide future policy.

Of course, selecting commissioners who already hold important positions and lead busy lives means that they will have difficulty devoting much time to the commission's work. The actual work tends to fall on the less well-known staff members, who assemble evidence about the policy's workings and guide the commissioners in making their recommendations. Moreover, a commission's recommendations may prove unpopular. Commissions tend to be appointed precisely because an issue is seen as divisive, so it is almost inevitable that whatever is recommended will prove controversial. Although commission recommendations sometimes receive considerable media coverage, they often fail to lead to the significant policy changes that the commission hoped to achieve (see Box 9.5).

Box 9.5 Commissions Explain Disasters

Dramatic disasters, such as the accidents that destroyed the space shuttles *Challenger* and *Columbia*, or the terrorist attacks of September 11, 2001, often lead to the appointment of special commissions to investigate the disaster's causes and make recommendations for policy changes that can prevent similar events from occurring in the future. These commissions' reports attract a good deal of attention, and are widely seen as authoritative verdicts regarding what went wrong and how policies should be changed.

Commissions, then, construct explanations. But this involves making choices, which, in turn, constrain commission findings. It turns out to be relatively easy for commissions to focus on individual decisions that, in retrospect, can be seen as mistakes (for example, overriding the advice of engineers who warned that cold weather might endanger the *Challenger*'s launch). It proves to be somewhat more difficult to criticize the organizations involved (thus, the 9/11 Commission noted that many agencies had failed to focus sufficient attention on the terrorist threat, but the commission did not blame them for what happened). Commissions tend to avoid institutional explanations (for instance, the commissions investigating the space shuttle accidents downplayed or ignored pressures from Congress and the White House for NASA [the National Aeronautics and Space Administration] to launch shuttles more regularly, although these pressures arguably encouraged the agency to treat risks as tolerable; while the 9/11 Commission did not ask how American foreign policies might have fostered the rise of terrorists). Having been appointed by high government officials, commissions tend to treat those officials carefully.

Source: Vaughan, 2006.

One other category of actors who play an important role in evaluating policy outcomes deserves attention: the *appellate courts* (see also Chapter 7). Policymaking often involves creating new laws, and social problems work often leads to legal actions. In turn, the people who find themselves targeted by new social policies can appeal their cases to higher courts. These appellate courts may rule on the constitutionality of the policies, affirming some, striking down others, and clarifying still others. In turn, *legal scholars* may try to influence courts' decisions by writing law review articles that criticize the legal basis for policies (Malloy, 2010). In the United States, a bill passed by legislators and signed into law by a president (in the case of federal legislation) or a governor (in the case of state legislation) may be modified—even ruled illegal—by appellate courts. Such court rulings may reject the policy itself, or the ways in which social problems workers implement that policy. This power makes courts important players in shaping policy outcomes.

Legislators are supposed to represent the popular will (recall Chapter 7's discussion of the various pressures they face), while courts are intended to provide a check on legislative enthusiasm. This means that even the most successful claimsmaking campaigns— those that elicit media coverage, mobilize public concern, and see their claims translated into new policies—may be constrained or rejected by the courts. For example, legislators often promote laws against burning the American flag, laws that have considerable vote-getting appeal (Welch, 2000). However, the courts have tended to recognize flag burning as protest, a form of political speech, protected under the First Amendment. Similarly, courts often constrain overly broad interpretations of new policies, restricting the grounds for defining, say, hate crimes (Jenness & Grattet, 2001) or sexual harassment (Saguy, 2003). The courts' rulings, in turn, may be denounced or constructed as new troubling conditions by assorted claimsmakers, media workers, policymakers, or social problems workers.

In sum, courts, like evaluation researchers and commissions, are often seen as failing to resolve debates over policy outcomes. However much we might like to imagine that an impartial interpretation will resolve people's differences in policy debates, such solutions prove elusive. People continue to disagree about which policies best address troubling conditions.

IDEOLOGICAL PREDISPOSITIONS

As we have seen in this chapter, there are many possible bases for criticizing how social policies are being implemented, as well as many types of people who might be moved to offer such critiques. From this we might conclude that all sorts of debates over policies are theoretically possible, but in fact, many policy discussions take fairly predictable forms.

Key to many policy debates is ideology. Within contemporary America, many people—including activists, experts, media workers, members of the general public, policymakers, and social problems workers—can locate themselves on a political spectrum that is understood to run from left to right—that is, from those who have relatively liberal views to those who hold relatively conservative views. Precisely how individuals construct this ideological spectrum varies: just as conservatives may lump together people who variously think of themselves as liberals, progressives, or radicals, and who recognize these as important distinctions, liberals may not appreciate the range of positions among those on the right.

In general, however, when discussing social problems, those on the left tend to emphasize the importance of equality and worry that society discriminates too much on the basis of race, class, and gender; they favor social policies that promote equality and discourage discrimination. And in general, those on the right emphasize the importance of liberty and social order; they worry that excessive social policies may constrain liberty and, in the process, damage overall societal well-being. Of course, these are questions of emphasis: few Americans would denounce either equality or liberty, yet they may disagree about their relative importance, or the best ways to achieve these values in particular situations.

This means that debates over social policies often break down into those favoring a more liberal position opposed to those favoring a more conservative stance. Each ideological side has its own activists in social movement organizations, think tanks filled with experts, media commentators, and policymaking politicians; the same people tend to find themselves allied over a range of policy debates. In fact, when individuals thought to be associated with a particular side break ranks on an issue and agree with those they usually oppose, the split is considered remarkable, something worth mentioning. Thus, when discussions about a particular policy outcome begin, it is often possible to predict who will line up on which side of the issue.

Not all ideologies fit neatly on the familiar liberal–conservative continuum. Think of libertarianism (usually viewed as a form of conservatism, but one that leads to what are typically thought of as liberal positions on issues related to drug use or sexual behavior), various religious doctrines (which can vary a great deal, depending on the theological interpretations being advanced), or feminism (which is centrally concerned with improving women's place in society). In addition, there are professional ideologies; professions have distinctive views of troubling conditions and how these conditions ought to be addressed. For example, recall Chapter 4's discussion of medicalization: medical authorities tend to favor constructing troubling conditions as medical problems that ought to be solved through medical solutions.

Ideologies are not unrelated to *interests*. Ideologies allow individuals to appeal to principles, such as equality, liberty, or women's rights, to argue that these values *should* guide how society responds to troubling conditions (for example, a liberal might criticize a particular social policy because it fails to alleviate the inequalities at the root of the troubling condition, and a conservative policy critique might focus on how the policy unreasonably constrains people's liberty). In other words, ideologies allow their adherents to construct principled arguments, to claim that this is the right thing to do because it is consistent with a particular value. At the same time, people frequently adopt ideologies that support their interests (for example, a large share of feminists are women whose interests the ideology advances, just as medical authorities often stand to benefit from medicalizing troubling conditions). The link between ideology and interest creates rhetorical opportunities for those who oppose a particular ideology: they can charge that proponents of a particular claim may be motivated less by a principled sense of what is right than by their self-interest, by the advantages they stand to gain if their claims succeed.

The tendency for ideological critiques to invoke values creates a range of questions that might be addressed in policy debates. On the one hand, critics can focus on practical questions: Is the policy effective? Does it do what we want it to do? Does it work better or cost less than alternative policies? On the other hand, critics can emphasize principles: Is this policy consistent with important values? Is it morally sound? Is it the sort of thing we ought to be doing? Policy debates often conflate these two approaches, so that opponents denounce one another's practical claims as being unprincipled, while rejecting the opposition's principled claims as impractical. Of course, an inability to agree on the questions that ought to be asked virtually guarantees that people will be unable to agree on the answers.

Ideologies, then, can be seen as predisposing how people may respond to policy outcomes. When people are allied with particular ideological stances—whether of a political, professional, or other nature—it is often possible to predict how these individuals will respond to a particular social policy. Those whose ideology led them to favor the policy in the first place are likely to claim that any shortcomings are due to the policy's being insufficient, and to argue for expanding or extending the policy to make up this shortfall. In contrast, those who stood ideologically opposed to the initial policy are more likely to claim that the policy is excessive or misguided, that it needs to be cut back or redirected. Although ideologies do not control how everyone approaches policy outcomes, they often shape the responses of at least some participants in the discussions (see Box 9.6).

Box 9.6 Ironic Consequences of the Civil Rights Movement

The civil rights movement set out to end the system of legal racial segregation in the South, and the passage of the Civil Rights Act of 1964 and the Voting Rights Act of 1965 can be seen as evidence that the movement succeeded. However, as McAdam (2015) observed, that success had ironic consequences that reshaped the American political landscape in ways that would affect future social policy debates.

For most of the century following the Civil War, the Republican Party was considered "the party of Lincoln"; this meant both that African Americans generally voted Republican (at least until Democrat Franklin Roosevelt brought them into his New Deal coalition in the 1930s) and that southern whites voted Democratic (which produced the "solid South" represented almost entirely by Democrats who supported maintaining legal segregation). However, the civil rights movement's successes during the Democratic administrations of John Kennedy and Lyndon Johnson reinforced blacks' ties to the Democratic Party.

Sensing an opportunity, the Republican Party began to appeal to white voters in the South, which led to a new political alignment: the South is once again solid—but it is solidly Republican (except in districts that are majority African American). This new arrangement is less overtly racist, but more ideological than in the past. Many of the southern Democrats had been populists; they favored policies that supported the poor—or at least poor whites. Their Republican successors tend to be more uniformly suspicious of spending on government programs to benefit the disadvantaged. Thus, the civil rights movement continues to shape partisan debates about social policy.

Once again we see the subjective nature of the social problems process. Just as claimsmakers must construct troubling conditions so that people become concerned enough to do something, and just as policymakers and social problems workers must construct practical responses to that concern, so, too, must critics devise interpretations of the workings of policies. They may decide that a policy is a great success (remember granting women the vote; no one now advocates disenfranchising women), or they may decide that it works pretty well and just needs a bit of fine-tuning (maybe we ought to install another traffic light at that dangerous intersection). Or, of course, some people may argue that the policy isn't working all that well and that we ought to do significantly more, or maybe a lot less, or perhaps something completely different. At the stage of policy outcomes, the social problems process comes to an end—unless it inspires an entirely new round of claimsmaking.

MAKING CONNECTIONS

- *Policy outcomes are reactions to policies after they have been implemented by social problems workers. However, as this chapter and Chapter 11 explain, the social problems process is cyclical, so policy outcomes become the basis for new claims.*

- *Social problems workers can become compelling critics of policies. As Chapter 8 explained, they understand how social problems work is actually practiced and see policy flaws firsthand.*

- *Both activists and experts frequently use typifying examples (discussed in Chapter 2) to make new claims that criticize policies.*

CASE STUDY
MODIFYING STUDENT LOANS

One hundred years ago, relatively few Americans graduated from high school, and less than 5 percent completed a college degree. Obviously, things have changed. Today more than 90 percent of twenty-five-year-olds have completed high school or its equivalent, and about a quarter have completed college. Higher education has always been costly, and young people from well-off families have always found it easier to afford college. Democratizing education—making more education available to more people—is widely seen as desirable, but policymakers have struggled with devising ways to help people pay the costs (J. Best and Best, 2014).

Federal student loans became part of the solution to this problem in 1958. Concerns that the Soviet Union's space program was ahead of its American counterpart led claimsmakers to argue that schools must be at fault (Bracey, 2007). Congress responded with the National Defense Education Act of 1958, which provided student loans to students in science and engineering. The program proved popular, and the Higher Education Act of 1965 made guaranteed student loans available to all bright young people who could not afford to pay for college—a policy intended to address what had been constructed as the problem of wasted brainpower.

By the 1970s, the student loan problem had been redefined as one of deadbeat students—people who took out loans but failed to repay them. Because the federal government was guaranteeing student loans, it was on the hook to make up the costs of loans that were not repaid. Congress began a series of investigations into the deadbeat problem, and passed a series of laws making it increasingly difficult for borrowers to avoid repayment.

Meanwhile, the percentage of young Americans going to college continued to rise, even as the cost of college increased. The availability of student loans affected this: more prospective students took out loans; colleges were less reluctant to raise tuition because they knew students could borrow; legislatures' support for state institutions did not keep up with rising college costs, so tuition paid by students accounted for a growing share of the budgets at those state schools; and the federal government's Pell Grant program (which provided grants—not loans—to students with the least financial resources) became less generous, so even the most impoverished students needed to take out loans. Inevitably, each year a larger percentage of students were taking out loans, and they were borrowing larger sums. However, these changes attracted relatively little attention as policymakers remained preoccupied with cracking down on deadbeat borrowers.

However, by the mid-1990s, the student loan problem began to be redefined yet again—as a problem of crushing debt. Young people who had borrowed tens of thousands of dollars were finding it hard to repay their loans and also launch their adult lives. How could they afford to marry, start families, or buy homes? The Great Recession that began in 2008 made these challenges even greater, because there were fewer jobs for new graduates. The recession also fostered yet another redefinition of the student loan problem, as critics began drawing attention to for-profit educational institutions that had been growing rapidly, and that depended almost entirely on their students receiving federal student loans. Roughly speaking, for-profits' students accounted for an eighth of all college students, a quarter of all student loan borrowing, and half of those who had difficulty repaying their loans.

In 2012, there were reports that total student loan debt exceeded total credit card debt, that it totaled a trillion dollars, and was increasing at a rate such that it might reach $2 trillion by around 2020. Student loan policy, which had been subject to policy outcome critiques for more than fifty years, now began to attract more attention in the news. The Obama administration advanced a number of policy changes; repayment plans that would limit student loan payments to 10 percent of an individual's disposable income, and after a period of years allow the remaining debt to be forgiven; as well as proposals to restrict access to student loans for colleges that failed to prepare students for graduation and careers.

In sum, there have been a series of narrowly constructed problems—wasted brainpower, deadbeat students, crushing debt, and the like—that inspired policy reforms designed to address those particular problems. But when policymakers focus closely on one aspect of student loans, other aspects tend to be ignored, allowing things to get worse, and setting the stage for the next reconstruction of the problem. For instance, while policymakers spent decades worrying about deadbeats, student borrowing was increasing markedly, which led to the redefinition of the problem as one of crushing debt.

It has proved far too easy for critics to focus on a series of narrowly defined issues. In the meantime, most observers ignore the big picture: college costs continue to rise much faster than the cost of living; a growing proportion of people are entering higher education; financial support from federal and state governments is not keeping pace with rising college costs; so, inevitably, ever more students are taking out loans for ever larger sums, which they then have more trouble repaying. A trillion dollars is an impressive amount of total student loan debt, and the figure continues to grow. When Congress gets caught up in debating, say, what interest rate should be charged on one type of federal loan during one particular year, all the other aspects of student loans get ignored.

Many social policies reveal similarly complex histories. Policy outcome claims criticize the workings of particular aspects of some large policy, such as deadbeat student borrowers or Medicare fraud. After these claims lead to adjustments in the policy designed to address the precise problem identified by the claimsmakers, a new set of claims focused on some different aspect of the problem emerges, only to have the cycle repeat itself. The danger—illustrated by the decades-long series of critiques of federal student loan policies—is that these narrow claims may fail to raise broader questions about the policy.

QUESTIONS

1. Over the years, critics of student loan policies have shifted focus from wasted brainpower, to deadbeat students, to crushing debt. Can you think of other policies that have attracted a series of different policy outcome critiques?

2. How can the press, the public, and policymakers decide whether a particular policy outcome critique deserves their attention?

3. What are some reasons why claimsmakers might choose to frame narrow—rather than broad—critiques of social policies?

10

Claims across Space and Time

The previous chapters have traced a six-stage social problems process from (1) the initial claimsmaking, through (2) media coverage, (3) public reaction, and (4) policymaking, and on to (5) the social problems work that implements the policy, followed by (6) policy outcomes. This sequence of stages should be seen as the natural history that a typical social problem might follow. To be sure, not every social problem fits the pattern exactly. Most important, many claims fail: they don't attract media attention, or they don't lead to public concern, or they don't lead to policy changes, or the policies are never implemented. The model of a six-stage sequence that has guided this book depicts a successful campaign to draw attention to a particular troubling condition and to get the larger society to try to do something about it. Other claims may follow different trajectories, but the model remains a useful framework for understanding the course taken by many of the claims that have the greatest impact.

There are, however, additional complexities that require some attention. Thus far, we have been thinking about social problems one at a time: here is how the U.S. Bureau of Narcotics constructed marijuana as a social problem in the 1930s, here is how today's authorities are constructing the crystal meth problem, and so on.

Such **case studies** are useful, but it seems obvious that the marijuana and crystal meth cases might have some important features in common, even though they occurred decades apart. After all, both cases involve claims that a particular drug is harmful and ought to be prohibited. This similarity raises important questions: Are such drug problems constructed completely independently; that is, does each set of claimsmakers start from scratch in assembling its claims, and do policymakers adopt a fresh approach each time they encounter claims about a new drug problem? Or are there underlying similarities in the way drug problems and drug policies are constructed, and if so, what are they, and why do they occur? Does the history of previous claims about drugs affect current claimsmaking? Do claims about similar troubling conditions always take the same form, or are they affected by the social circumstances in which they emerge?

This chapter explores some of these issues; in particular, it considers how claims vary from place to place, and from time to time. It begins with comparative research in which analysts compare what happens when claimsmakers raise claims about the same troubling condition in different places—in different cities, or in different countries. Then it examines diffusion, the way claims spread from one place to another. The third section of the chapter asks how claims evolve over time; it explores apparently cyclical claims—issues that attract considerable attention for a time, then fade from notice, only to be revived in a new wave of claimsmaking. The chapter concludes with a discussion of progress: claimsmakers often warn that things are getting worse, but is envisioning societal decay the best framework for thinking about social problems?

COMPARISON

Usually sociologists who study the construction of social problems conduct case studies (J. Best, 2015). That is, they examine one instance, one case of the social problems process—how and why a particular problem was constructed in a given place at a given time. In fact, many studies focus on specific aspects of a particular case, so different analyses of the same case might consider, for example, just how the claims' rhetoric was assembled to make a persuasive argument, who made those claims, or how the media covered the topic.

The main advantage of the case study is that it permits a careful, detailed analysis of how one particular instance of the social problems process developed. Most of the points raised in the earlier chapters of this book are the product of sociologists' case studies, and a large share of the sources cited in this volume's references present such case studies. But case studies have a major disadvantage: there is no way of knowing whether the case being studied is fairly typical or quite unusual. Throughout this book we have been discussing things that can happen during the construction of social problems. When we first diagrammed the social problems process in Figure 1.1, the picture seemed simple and straightforward. But later chapters featured more detailed, more complicated diagrams of the various stages in the social problems process. These complications reveal that not all social problems follow exactly the same trajectory; there are important differences in how social problems can develop, so the particular case being studied may not always be all that typical.

The simplest way to study such differences is to compare two cases that we might expect to be fairly similar. For example, Cynthia Bogard (2003) examined how the problem of homelessness was constructed in two major American cities—New York City and Washington, D.C.—during the early 1980s. She found important differences. In Washington, activists—a self-styled group of "Christian anarchists"—promoted homelessness as a moral issue; they devised clever protests designed to attract media attention (in a city filled with media workers), and they sought to involve nationally prominent politicians in the issue. While acknowledging that many homeless individuals were troubled by mental illness or substance abuse, the Washington activists constructed the homeless as rational figures who would stop living on the streets if only they had access to safe, nonintrusive shelters. In contrast, in New York City the issue of homelessness centered around a struggle between city and state officials over who ought to be held responsible for the condition—and pay the costs of fixing it. The state blamed the city for encouraging gentrification that had eliminated low-cost housing units and thereby had made their former residents homeless; the city, on the other hand, insisted that many of the homeless were seriously mentally ill individuals who now found themselves on the streets after the state had closed many of its mental hospitals. In New York, the homeless were typified as incapable of caring for themselves, and as a threat to public order. In short, the two cities featured different claimsmakers, with different interests, who constructed the homelessness problem in different ways.

Bogard's study shows that, even in dealing with the same problem during the same years, the social problems process can develop along different paths—with different claims made by different claimsmakers leading to different policies. There are all sorts of possible bases for making such comparisons:

- *Geography.* Bogard compared the social problems process in two cities, but it is possible to compare other geographic entities. Most obviously, analysts can compare how the same troubling condition is addressed in two or more countries (J. Best, 2001a).

- *Time.* Many social conditions have been around for a long time, so it is possible to compare two or more efforts to construct the same social problem in the same place during different times. For example, there have been a series of anticult campaigns in American history (Jenkins, 2000).

- *Similar conditions.* Some troubling conditions are understood to belong to the same category of social problems, so the basis for comparison seems obvious. For example, there are parallels in the ways that different drugs have been constructed as social problems (Reinarman, 1994).

● *Similar constructions.* Sometimes analysts compare problems that seem to be constructed with similar claimsmaking rhetoric. For instance, freeway shootings, stalking, and other crimes characterized as "random violence" can be compared, as can how claimsmakers construct different problems that involve "victimization" (J. Best, 1999).

● *Other bases for comparison.* Analysts might compare different campaigns by the same claimsmakers (for instance, examining how feminists—or medical authorities—construct various social problems), how different media construct the same problem, and so on. The bases for comparison are limited only by the analysts' imagination.

Figure 10.1 illustrates some of these forms of comparison among social problems processes. The top of the figure displays one six-stage social problems process (for a particular problem—call it Problem X). The same process is shown in reduced size at the center of the figure, where it is surrounded by other social problems processes that suggest various bases for comparison between the construction of Problem X and the construction of other social problems. Note that it is not necessary to compare the entire sequences of stages in two social problems processes; a sociologist might focus on comparing particular, even very narrowly defined topics (such as the use of statistics in two claimsmaking campaigns).

Comparison is a powerful method of analysis because it can help us discover both underlying similarities and unexpected differences. People involved in the social problems process sometimes assume that things have to be the way they are; they take it for granted that the problem pretty much has to be constructed in the terms with which they're familiar. One of the most important lessons from comparing social problems processes is that whatever we understand about social problems is a product of people's choices, that people—claimsmakers, media workers, policymakers, social problems workers, and so on—have chosen to highlight some aspects

Figure 10.1 BASES FOR COMPARISON AMONG SOCIAL
PROBLEMS PROCESSES

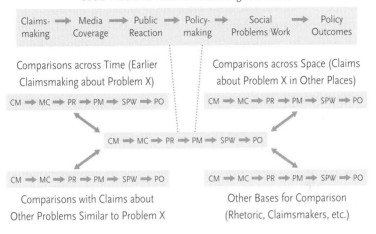

Social Problems Process Concerning Problem X

Claims-	→	Media	→	Public	→	Policy-	→	Social	→	Policy
making		Coverage		Reaction		making		Problems Work		Outcomes

Comparisons across Time (Earlier
Claimsmaking about Problem X)

Comparisons across Space (Claims
about Problem X in Other Places)

CM ➡ MC ➡ PR ➡ PM ➡ SPW ➡ PO   CM ➡ MC ➡ PR ➡ PM ➡ SPW ➡ PO

CM ➡ MC ➡ PR ➡ PM ➡ SPW ➡ PO

CM ➡ MC ➡ PR ➡ PM ➡ SPW ➡ PO   CM ➡ MC ➡ PR ➡ PM ➡ SPW ➡ PO

Comparisons with Claims about
Other Problems Similar to Problem X

Other Bases for Comparison
(Rhetoric, Claimsmakers, etc.)

of a troubling condition while downplaying others. It can be hard
to notice what those people have ignored, but comparisons often
can help us recognize that choices were made, and to ask how and
why those proved to be the favored choices.

Consider the issue of sexual harassment. Americans take it
for granted that sexual harassment is a type of gender discrimination, and that it should be defined broadly to encompass not
only demands for sexual favors but also inappropriate joking and
other behaviors that create a "hostile environment" (Saguy, 2003).
In France, however, sexual harassment has been defined not only
more narrowly (encompassing only demands for sex), but also very
differently (as sexual violence involving the abuse of hierarchical
authority). These different definitions evolved through different
processes: in the United States, court rulings gradually established
the domain of sexual harassment; in France, courts cannot establish
the law, so an act of Parliament was required—which was important because policymakers had to find a legislative consensus, and

there was not enough support for a broader definition of what constituted sexual harassment. Press coverage also differed in the two countries. The American press devoted a large share of its coverage to scandals—claims implicating prominent politicians in sexual harassment. In contrast, considerable French media coverage focused on the "excesses" of *Americans'* treatment of sexual harassment; commentators argued that France should avoid copying the Americans' example. In other words, there were numerous differences in how sexual harassment was constructed in the two nations.

Comparative studies often reveal such differences in how social problems are constructed, even when we might imagine that the issue would have to be constructed in the same way. If cell phones pose a threat of exposure to radioactivity, as some claimsmakers suggest, presumably the physical processes that produce those risks ought to be the same everywhere, exposing cell phone users throughout the world to the same dangers. Yet different countries construct health risks from cell phones in very different ways (Burgess, 2004). Comparative analyses, then, can expose the social processes that underpin the construction of even physical threats. Risks of radioactivity—usually thought of as understandable in terms of physics and biology—are socially constructed, as are all other social problems. Comparative research can help make such social processes visible.

DIFFUSION

Comparative studies reveal that the social problems process can lead to different outcomes in different places: two countries may construct a given problem in much the same way; or they may construct that problem in rather—sometimes dramatically—different terms; or one country may define the troubling condition as a big deal, while the other may dismiss it as unworthy of concern (see Box 10.1). However, it is especially interesting when a problem

Box 10.1 British Baby Boomers as a Social Problem

Birth rates rose after World War II ended, and people born between roughly 1946 and 1964 are called Baby Boomers—just one of the generations constructed by social commentators in recent years, a scheme that classifies those born between about 1965 and 1980 as Generation X, and those born after 1980 as Millennials. Generations are affected both by having experienced historical events such as war or economic crises at roughly the same points in their lives, and by their sheer numbers (members of large generations face more competition for jobs, and so on).

As the large numbers of Baby Boomers approach retirement, many commentators are worried about their countries' ability to cover the increased costs of having many more older people in retirement and health care programs. In Britain, these concerns have led to claims that the Baby Boomers are a social problem—that they have been the beneficiaries of generous social programs throughout their lives, and that they now selfishly expect Millennials—already hard-pressed by the Great Recession—to pay higher taxes to cover social programs to support the aging Boomers.

Bristow (2015) argues that these claims reflect the declining popularity of older interpretive schemes in British policy debates. Whereas earlier claims about social problems tended to emphasize social cleavages of class, sex, or race, or political clashes between the left and right, those frames have lost some of their rhetorical power. As a result, British claimsmakers construct generations with competing interests as a way of explaining society's problems. Obviously, such claims could be constructed in other countries, but so far such claims don't seem to have gained as much traction in the United States.

attracts attention in different places at about the same time. Although it is possible that the social problems processes in different countries are completely independent, unrelated to one another, another possibility is that claims have spread from one country to another, and we can study this process (J. Best, 2001a).

Diffusion is the term used by social scientists to describe the spread of innovations. New things—new ideas, new inventions, and so on—emerge in particular places, but then they spread from one group to another. If one group figures out a better way to, say, make arrowheads, that group's neighbors may copy or adopt the method for their own benefit. The process of diffusion involves sources, or **transmitters**, passing the innovation along to **adopters**. Successful innovations can spread across many societies and over thousands of miles.

Diffusion can occur in the case of social problems claims. A claim may originate in a particular town, region, or country but then spread to other places. Not all claims experience diffusion, and of those that do spread, some travel farther and more widely than others. What accounts for these differences?

All social problems claims argue that a particular condition exists and that it is troubling. Successful diffusion of a claim requires that adopters accept that these basic ideas apply to the adopters' setting—their community or nation. Certainly diffusion requires accepting the notion that the condition exists; a society whose members doubt the existence of a condition is unlikely to be receptive to claims about that problem. For instance, being worried about witches requires that people believe in witches; regardless of how worried about witches a society of believers may become, they will find it hard to spread their concern to a society of nonbelievers. Similarly, the condition must be seen as troubling: a society with a traditional aristocracy might view a decline in deference as quite troubling, but their claims probably would have little appeal for members of democratic societies, who might agree that the condition exists but view this as a cause for celebration rather than concern.

For a claim to spread from one society to another, then, potential adopters of the claim must come from cultures and social structures that allow them to recognize both that their society has the condition about which claims are being made, and that the condition is troubling. This means that claims are less likely to spread to societies very different from those in which the claims originated. In particular, adopters need to view their society as similar to the society where the claims originated (Strang & Meyer, 1993). When similarities are harder to recognize, diffusion becomes less likely.

For example, it is easier for social problems claims to spread among countries with a common language and interwoven histories. In recent decades, many successful claimsmaking campaigns have originated in the United States and then spread to England, Australia, and Canada (for instance, concerns about satanic ritual abuse traveled from the United States to all three other English-speaking countries). In addition, claims that originated in those countries have traveled to the United States (concern about both bullying and road rage, for example, spread from Britain to the United States) (J. Best, 2001a). On the other hand, American constructions of social problems often meet resistance in France; French media tend to criticize American policies and present alternative constructions for social issues such as sexual harassment, immigration, or obesity (Benson, 2013; Saguy, 2003, 2013).

Diffusion must occur through channels; that is, there need to be links, connections between potential transmitters and prospective adopters. Theorists of diffusion make an analytic distinction between **relational channels** involving interpersonal contact between transmitters and adopters, and **nonrelational channels**, such as mass media, that do not involve personal ties (McAdam & Rucht, 1993). In practice, the diffusion of claims usually combines both relational and nonrelational channels. Through informal ties (such as acquaintanceship) and more formal ties (such as memberships in the same professional organizations), people in different countries get to know one another well enough to establish relational channels: this person got to know foreigners while attending school abroad; these folks met at international conferences for police officers, or social workers, or whatever.

At the same time, information about social problems flows through nonrelational channels—through the press and entertainment media, through books and news broadcasts and the Internet. Relational and nonrelational channels are mutually reinforcing. Once again, it should be clear that a common language makes it easier for diffusion to occur through both sorts of channels. Translating claims into another tongue takes time; claims can travel faster when transmitters and adopters share a language.

All diffusion ultimately depends on the actors in the process—the transmitters and, especially, the adopters. Transmitters may make deliberate efforts to disseminate social problems claims to other countries. Drawing attention to troubling conditions is, of course, central to social problems claimsmaking, and some claimsmakers explicitly seek to spread their message to other nations. This is particularly true when claims depict large-scale, even global problems, such as population growth, ecological degradation, or economic globalization. Such claimsmakers become missionaries, seeking to spread their message abroad, through both relational and nonrelational channels. International social movements, for example, offer a way of spreading claims about troubling conditions to countries that might be expected to resist those claims.

In other cases, transmitters are more passive; their concern may be limited to their own country, even to a particular locality; they make no effort to promote the diffusion of their claims. Still, their claims may reach other countries, particularly via such nonrelational channels as media coverage, professional publications, and the like. Nonetheless, the key actors in diffusion are adopters. Prospective adopters must define conditions in their society as being sufficiently like those depicted in the transmitters' claims before they will join in spreading those claims.

Of course, societies have differences as well as similarities. There are likely to be both cultural differences (people in the transmitting society and those in the prospective adopting society are likely to construct the world in at least somewhat different terms), as well as differences in social arrangements (such as different legal or educational systems). Such differences are potential obstacles to diffusion; they make it easier for prospective adopters to conclude that a particular claim is not really applicable to their society. For example, tobacco smoking is much more common among males in Japan than in the United States or Western Europe (Ayukawa, 2001). Whereas other countries' governments have launched vigorous public health campaigns to reduce smoking, Japan has been slower to take such actions. Why? In Japan, the government controls tobacco distribution and derives considerable revenue from smokers. Also, it is hard to mobilize social movements in Japan to campaign against government interests. What is—and what is not—considered a social problem depends on a society's culture and social structure.

Therefore, diffusion is easier when claims are phrased in relatively abstract or theoretical language. **Theorization** is the presentation of claims that emphasize general, abstract principles and arguments: for instance, claimsmakers might describe sexism generally in terms of male, or patriarchal, domination rather than in terms of specific discriminatory practices; the former construction offers a general principle that might be detected at work in many different social settings, whereas the latter may seem applicable only in countries where those particular practices are common—and seen as troubling (Strang & Meyer, 1993). Theorization abstracts and simplifies. In the case of social problems claims, theorization smooths out the argument. It reduces specifics of limited, local relevance and rephrases the claim in broader, more general terms that make it more widely acceptable. The theoretical becomes significant; the practical, less important. Thus, a theorized claim is more easily spread to new societies, where it can be reformulated to take local culture and social structure into account.

As a result, claims about the same social problem often take somewhat different forms, depending on the social arrangements in different societies (see Box 10.2). In some cases, differences in social

---

Box 10.2 French Media on Immigration Issues

Immigration is a contentious social issue in France, just as it is in the United States, and the issue receives considerable attention from the news media in both countries. Benson (2013) notes similarities and differences in the coverage in the two countries.

Whereas U.S. news media basically operate as independent businesses in a marketplace competing for audiences and advertising dollars, the French government provides subsidies to support some news operations, particularly those that present diverse points of view. As a consequence, the French press draws more heavily from civil-society spokespersons (that is, from sources who are not government officials, but represent labor unions, religious organizations, universities, and so on), whereas American coverage tends to give more attention to comments by political figures or journalists. French stories are more likely to present serious debates about immigration policies, debates that focus on the social forces that draw North African immigrants to France; this is rather different from U.S. coverage, which emphasizes typifying examples of the plights of particular individuals affected by immigration.

It is easy to take a society's institutions for granted, to assume that news is gathered and presented in essentially the same ways in all countries. And there are lots of similarities. Still, the United States and France—two Western democracies—understand the role of the news media in somewhat different ways, and those different understandings have consequences. Immigration may be an important issue in both countries, but their media cover the issue in rather different ways.

---

arrangements may make it hard for claims to travel successfully. In recent years, for example, British claimsmakers have focused on various types of bullying—not just bullying in schools, but also bullying in other settings, including the workplace (Furedi, 2001). The British campaign against workplace bullying received considerable support from that country's powerful trade unions. In contrast, efforts to construct workplace bullying as a problem in the United States (where unions are less influential) have been markedly less successful. The abstract—and already familiar—problem of bullying (particularly among children) spread easily, but the more specific construction of workplace bullying did not. Similarly, the abortion issue evolved differently in the United States and Britain (Lee, 2003). British law has long regarded abortion as a medical matter, subject to physicians' authority, but Americans have come to view it as a question of rights.

Contemporary commentators argue that globalization has become a central concept for understanding the world. Countries are increasingly linked through trade, rapid transportation, and essentially instantaneous communications. Money and jobs—but also ideas—flow more freely across international borders. This means that the future is likely to feature even more diffusion of social problems claims (see Box 10.3). In part, this is because some claimsmakers seek to construct global issues such as climate change or terrorism. In part, it is because some troubling conditions, such as epidemic disease, may start in one corner of the world yet spread great distances. In addition to these considerations, however, improved communications (such as through the World Wide Web) give people around the world access to claims made in distant places, and at least some of those claims will be theorized in terms that make it easier for them to spread.

CYCLES IN CLAIMSMAKING

Early in the social problems process, it is very common for claimsmaking rhetoric to describe a troubling condition as new, or at least as deserving new concern because the condition is growing much worse. After the issue begins to attract more attention and people want to know more about it, there may be an effort to trace

Box 10.3 The Diffusion of Opposition to
Intimate Partner Violence

Ending intimate partner violence has been an important cause for the women's movement around the globe. International governmental and nongovernmental organizations have denounced violence against women as a violation of basic human rights. Since 1975, more than a hundred countries have responded by passing laws or otherwise changing policies to address intimate partner violence.

This campaign has led to cultural changes, to an altering of people's attitudes. Pierotti (2013) examined results from surveys of women in twenty-six low- and middle-income countries, such as Bolivia, India, and Uganda. In each country, two surveys were taken about five years apart, in which women were asked whether it was justifiable for a husband to strike his wife under several different circumstances (for example, if she argues with him, or she refuses to have sex with him). In every country, the percentage of women who rejected violence under all circumstances rose between the first and second survey.

These results suggest that there is an ongoing global cultural shift in attitudes toward violence against women. Obviously, changing cultural scripts about how men should treat women is a process—some men and women can be expected to get on board before others. In general, women who disapproved of violence were more likely to live in urban areas, and to have access to education and to the media, so they were more exposed to a range of messages about women's rights. And, of course, we can imagine that attitudes among men will lag behind those of women; but it is clear that claims opposing intimate partner violence have spread widely.

the troubling condition's history. For instance, claims about child abuse might include brief historical accounts stating that although adults have abused children for centuries, we now know better; or a history of poverty might argue that previous efforts to eliminate poverty have been misguided, and that a totally new approach is needed. Even the most unlikely topics, such as Columbus and noise, can have elaborate histories of claimsmaking (Kubal, 2008; Schwartz, 2011). Still, claimsmakers tend to focus most intensely on the troubling condition's current manifestations, rather than on its distant past. Most claims concentrate on the present situation and pay relatively little attention to the past; to the degree they do remember an issue's history, they may simplify it.

This narrow focus is unfortunate, because careful study of the history of a social issue can often place today's claims within an illuminating context. In particular, many troubling conditions are the focus of *cycles* of concern. That is, a troubling condition may become the focus of intense claimsmaking, then slip out of the spotlight for a while before returning as the focus of renewed attention.

A cycle of concern begins when a troubling condition that has been receiving little attention becomes the subject of claimsmaking (Downs, 1972). As a result, concern increases until it reaches a peak, then interest falls off once more, until the topic is again attracting little notice. This cycle is another way of thinking about the social problems process: attention increases as claimsmakers, the media, the public, policymakers, and social problems workers become involved. But why does interest decline? Why doesn't it remain high? Why are there cycles of concern?

Part of the answer is that the social problems process values novelty. Claims that seem new or fresh compete more easily in the social problems marketplace to attract attention from the media, the public, and policymakers. This is why claimsmakers who come to own particular issues find it necessary to constantly update and repackage their claims (as discussed in Chapter 3). But even when claimsmakers work to keep an issue visible, they find themselves at an increasing disadvantage because other, competing claims that seek to draw attention to topics that have been neglected are likely to seem more novel. The fact that a particular claim has been occupying center stage for a while begins to make other claims seem fresher, more interesting, particularly to the media, which depend so heavily on presenting novel material (see Chapter 5). In addition, as noted in Chapters 8 and 9, once the social problems process reaches the stage of social problems work, there is likely to be some disillusionment. Very often the policies touted as the solution to the problem haven't caused the problem to disappear; instead, the troubling condition endures, and people begin losing their enthusiasm for those policies.

All of this means that however successful claimsmakers have been in managing to raise concern about a particular troubling condition, that concern eventually is likely to decline, so the issue moves out of the limelight. However, that need not be the end of the matter; once enough time has passed, the previous wave of concern is likely to be forgotten, thanks to all of the competing claimsmaking campaigns that have captured the attention of the social problems marketplace in the meantime. Conditions may once more become ripe for drawing attention to what now again seems to be a neglected topic. Therefore, we should not be surprised to discover that the histories of many social problems display sequential waves of concern interspersed with periods when the topic receives relatively little attention.

For example, consider three waves of intense concern about delinquent gangs—youth gangs—in twentieth-century America. The first began in the 1920s, the second in the 1950s, and the third in the 1980s. Each period was marked by warnings that today's gangs were much worse—larger, better organized, more dangerous—than gangs in previous eras. Each wave featured claimsmaking by experts, such as sociologists, psychiatrists, and criminologists; each became the subject of both sensational news coverage and popular cultural depictions of gangs. Nor did these waves begin in the twentieth century; waves of concern about gangs date back to the 1840s in U.S. cities, and to the eighteenth century in London (Pearson, 1983).

We can spot similar sequential waves of concern regarding many other issues. The historian Philip Jenkins has described the oscillating attention given to the sexual exploitation of children (Jenkins, 1998) and to cults (Jenkins, 2000). The pattern turns up in surprising places; for example, Christian theologians periodically direct their attention to claims that there are "hidden gospels"— ancient manuscripts that were suppressed by religious authorities because they reveal that Christ's true message was antithetical to what the established church now endorses (Jenkins, 2001).

In each of these cases, a new set of claims attracts a great deal of attention for a time, but then concern begins to dissipate. When claimsmaking on the topic revives, usually people pay little attention to the previous wave of concern. The older set of claims— and the intense concern it generated—is often forgotten, as a new generation of claimsmakers reinvents the wheel. Even if the earlier claims are recalled, they tend to be dismissed: those people in the "good old days" may have thought they had a gang problem, but their gangs were nothing compared with ours.

What accounts for these waves of concern? One possibility, of course, is that the troubling conditions criticized by claimsmakers become more or less common over time, and claimsmaking merely tracks these shifts. Perhaps gang membership actually rises and falls in different historical periods. However, it is impossible to document such changes. There are probably always some gangs operating, but there is no long-term measure of such activity; in particular, in periods when gangs aren't a focus of attention, it is unlikely that anyone is charting gang involvement. When gangs attract concern, we have no way of being sure that the reason for the concern is that they have become more active.

Another possibility is that dramatic events attract media and public attention to particular social issues. For example, Jenkins (1998) notes waves of great concern over sexual crimes against children (as well as periods of much lower concern about these crimes). To be sure, during the waves of concern, heavily publicized news reports described terrible sex crimes against children; however, there were similar reports during the periods of low concern. During the waves of high concern, such crimes were depicted as *instances* of the larger problem of sexual violence against children—proof that something needed to be done. In contrast, during the periods of low concern, press coverage of such terrible crimes treated them as aberrant, exceptional behavior—not as representative of a larger phenomenon. It is difficult to make a strong case that claimsmaking activity simply rises and falls along with the increases and declines of a potentially troubling condition.

How, then, should we understand these waves of concern? One clue is that some of the same issues—gangs, cults, sexual crimes against children, even hidden gospels—appear again and again. Such recurrence might seem only sensible; it doesn't seem surprising that people would worry about these topics. But such wavelike patterns seem more striking when we realize that they occur in other societies and involve constructions that strike us as peculiar, such as waves of concern about vampires in East Africa (White, 2000). The variation in the types of concerns that are prevalent in different societies suggests that certain problems may be particularly easy to construct in particular societies—that some combination of cultural and social structural arrangements may foster such recurring claims (see Box 10.4).

It may help to think of societies as having the equivalent of fault lines—or "axes of variation" (Erikson, 1976). That is, social arrangements can create tensions between groups—between youths and older adults, between immigrants and the native-born, and on and on. Such tensions can flare into claimsmaking whenever self-identified groups find themselves competing for scarce resources, or whenever one group controls another's access to such resources. Claimsmaking is particularly likely to increase during periods of relative scarcity, when the competition between groups is more intense.

Such tensions can be expressed in lots of different ways. Probably most often, people complain about specific individuals or particular actions: "He shouldn't have done that!" But sometimes

BOX 10.4 THE NEW METHAMPHETAMINE PROBLEM—AGAIN

Emphasizing the chemical composition and biological effects of drugs ignores the social processes by which they come to be seen as problematic. Consider the history of methamphetamine and related synthetic stimulants (Parsons, 2014). Benzedrine arrived in the United States in the 1930s. It was seen as a useful stimulant, and was given to everyone from troops in World War II to enhance their performance, to tired housewives. Under various names, it would continue to be prescribed to individuals who needed to stay alert.

However, methamphetamine has also been the target of waves of claimsmaking. In the late 1960s and early 1970s, it was demonized as *speed* (as in the slogan "Speed Kills"). "Speed freaks" were often typified as hippies who had moved on from hallucinogens to more dangerous drugs. Then, in the 1980s (when concern about crack cocaine was also peaking), claimsmakers worried about ice, which they characterized as more dangerous than crack. If crack was viewed as concentrated in black neighborhoods, ice was portrayed as spreading among whites. More recently, in the late 1990s, attention turned to *crystal meth*. At first, "tweakers" were seen as primarily a rural problem, although by the year 2000 claims linking meth with Mexican immigrants helped portray the drug as a national emergency. In other words, the same drug was repeatedly revived, given a new name, and presented as affecting some new population of users.

The history of methamphetamine, then, offers an especially clear example of a social problem being repeatedly constructed within just a few decades.

tensions can be linked to larger claims so that particular actions are understood as instances of a more general, troubling condition. At any given moment we can imagine that tensions inspire countless grievances—what we might think of as potential claims. Whether any particular grievance starts a full-scale social problems process will depend on contingencies: whether the grievance can be packaged as a rhetorically powerful claim, whether claims-makers can mobilize sufficient resources, the nature of the other claims currently competing in the social problems marketplace, and so on.

The level of tension along societal fault lines can be understood as another contingency. Periods of higher tension probably increase the receptivity of the press, the public, and policymakers to claims. In some cases, these claims may even—at first glance—seem oblique. Late nineteenth-century America, for instance, witnessed an active claimsmaking campaign against the English sparrow, a bird that had been imported to the United States in hopes that it would eat insects that infested urban areas (Fine & Christoforides, 1991). The sparrow was widely denounced in moralistic terms: it was lazy and dirty. The intensity of the antisparrow campaign seems surprising, until it is understood as part of the period's larger anti-immigrant claimsmaking. In the late nineteenth and early twentieth centuries, the United States was experiencing one of its periodic waves of opposition to immigration, and claims about the influx of a foreign bird paralleled worries about the country's ability to accommodate human immigrants. Although complaints about bird species aren't all that common, the larger tensions of the time gave the antisparrow claims visibility.

In addition to cycles of concern regarding particular issues, we can note periods when American society seems particularly open to claimsmaking. Three major periods of intense reform activity appear in U.S. history. First, in the decades preceding the Civil War (roughly 1830–1860), there was considerable social movement activity: the abolitionist campaign to abolish slavery, of course, but also intense interest in women's rights, new religions, the temperance movement against strong drink, opposition to immigration (particularly focused on anti-Irish sentiments), and so on. Second, the late nineteenth/early twentieth-century period featured a revived women's movement, further opposition to immigration (particularly from southern and eastern Europe), prohibitionist campaigns against alcohol and other drugs, and all of the other causes associated with the Progressive Era. And more recently, beginning in the 1960s and continuing to the present, there has been intense claimsmaking regarding civil rights, women's rights, a war on drugs, renewed concern about immigration (now from Latin America and Asia), and many other issues.

A comparison of these three periods shows that concerns with such fault-line topics as race, women's issues, immigration, and drug use do not just recur, but tend to emerge at roughly the same times. This concurrence suggests that conditions in some historical periods seem to foster claimsmaking. We might speculate that the impending Civil War left people unsettled and more open to the social problems claims of the first period. In the more recent period—as noted in earlier chapters—a new media environment and increasingly sophisticated claimsmaking methods have helped foster contemporary claimsmaking (see Box 10.5). Again, examining the social problems process across time reveals surprising similarities and differences that can help us better understand our contemporary arrangements for constructing social problems.

THE PROBLEM OF PROGRESS

Comparisons of claims across time raise another comparative question: Do things ever get better? That is, can we speak of social progress, or are things actually getting worse? It seems possible to make a strong case that there has been progress on many fronts: During the twentieth century, life expectancy rose markedly (a newborn male's life expectancy—46 years in 1900—rose to 78 in 2010, the improvement for females was even greater, and life expectancies for nonwhites grew more than those of whites). The percentage of young people graduating from high school climbed (from about 6 percent in 1900 to, according to some calculations, over

Box 10.5 Food Activism in Two Eras

In the 1830s, followers of Sylvester Graham (recalled today as the inventor of the graham cracker) believed that eating minimally processed food could reduce the risks of spiritual and physical corruption. The 1960s and 1970s saw the emergence of a movement promoting natural—as opposed to artificial—foods. Haydu (2011) studied these two American food protests, separated by nearly 150 years. Both questioned the value of processed foods and both were connected to other social movements of their eras; however, their reasoning was rather different.

The Grahamites' links were to the larger religious revival—the Second Great Awakening—of the 1830s. They were concerned with self-discipline and moral decency (the graham cracker blandness was supposed to help control sexual appetites). They saw their claims about avoiding processed food as linked to other morality movements, such as the evangelical revival and the temperance campaign against alcohol.

In contrast, the natural food movement emerged in the context of the New Left's campaign to promote communalism over capitalism. The counterculture—typified by the hippies in the 1960s—promoted personal liberation from the ties of conventional society. Its rhetoric focused on the political significance of food choices, more than on morality.

Although both movements focused on eating natural—as opposed to processed—foods, they understood Nature in very different ways: the Grahamites associated it with keeping God's laws, while the natural food movement sought a world uncorrupted by technology. These examples remind us that all claims are rooted in the cultures of their times.

80 percent in recent years). The right to vote became more widely available (in 1900, few women, few African Americans in the South, and no one aged eighteen to twenty could vote). And the standard of living improved (so that, for instance, access to indoor plumbing,

electricity, and phone service—all relatively rare in 1900—became nearly universally available) (J. Best, 2001b). Isn't all this progress? Most people would say yes, but claims about troubling conditions tend to accentuate the negative. Claimsmakers' rhetoric often insists that things are worse than they seem and that they are deteriorating, that real catastrophe lies ahead, that progress is only an illusion. Claimsmakers rarely speak of progress; they seem to fear that acknowledging societal improvements may encourage complacency and discourage taking the actions needed to address troubling conditions. This worry is understandable: it is probably harder to arouse concern about a troubling condition if people are focused on how much things have improved. In addition, however, four aspects of the culture and organization of claimsmaking make it easier to downplay progress:

1. *Perfectibility.* Claimsmakers often invoke **perfectibility** as a standard. They declare that they won't settle for improving a particular troubling condition—that they are determined to eradicate the problem. As noted in Chapter 7, policymakers often "declare war" on social problems: heavily publicized wars have focused on such problems as poverty, cancer, drugs, and most recently, terrorism (J. Best, 1999). Similarly, our current education policy promises to "leave no child behind." But perfection is a very high standard; as long as one child is doing poorly in school, or one person is poor, there will be room for improvement—and therefore continued opportunities for claimsmaking.

2. *Proportion.* As big problems disappear, relatively smaller problems seem proportionally bigger than before. In 1900, many of the most common causes of death were infectious diseases. Vaccinations and antibiotics caused many of these threats to virtually vanish. Still, everyone is going to die from some cause, so attention can now focus on potentially fatal diseases—such as breast cancer—that received relatively little attention when influenza, pneumonia, and diphtheria were killing far more people. Similarly, ending the worst forms of

racial inequality (such as lynching and institutionalized segregation in the South) allows attention to focus on those less violent, less systematic forms of racism that remain. This means that claimsmakers need never run out of conditions that might be constructed as social problems.

3. **Proliferation.** Contemporary society encourages the proliferation of social problems claims. Chapter 5 discussed the growing number of arenas where claims can be mounted, including the increasing number of television channels and the Internet's endless reach, which have made it far easier to promote social problems claims. At the same time, most of these emerging arenas address segmented audiences, giving claimsmakers the advantage of being able to direct their rhetoric toward the homogeneous audience most likely to be receptive. Claimsmakers can therefore avoid confronting criticism and counterclaims, particularly during the early stages of a campaign, when they are seeking to mobilize support. The disadvantage, of course, is that in a world with more arenas, it is harder to gain general public attention for one's claims. For example, it has become easier to promote environmental causes by communicating in arenas filled with environmentalists, but harder to get the attention of the whole society and keep everyone focused on environmentalist concerns.

4. **Paranoia.** Finally, social progress fosters paranoia—fears of societal collapse. How can claimsmaking rhetoric be made compelling in a world characterized by social progress? One method is to warn that we are in terrible danger, that a collective catastrophe is on the horizon. Apocalyptic scenarios abound; claimsmakers warn about the threats of nuclear war, nuclear winter, climate change, overpopulation, pollution, resource depletion, epidemic disease, ethnic conflict, globalization, economic collapse, famine, genetic engineering, nanotechnology (tiny technological devices that might outcompete the natural biological system), or robotics (machines that might develop superior intelligence and eliminate people). Moreover, all

of these fears focus on troubling conditions that have *social* causes and are therefore suitable subjects for claimsmakers. They can argue that progress is a temporary illusion and warn that what seems to be progress will, in fact, lead to disaster.

In short, the experience of progress has, in some ways, made it easier to construct social problems: claimsmakers can insist that social arrangements remain imperfect; they find it easier to draw attention to previously neglected problems now that some of the big problems of the past have been resolved; they can target and reach audiences likely to be sympathetic to their claims; and they can warn that progress is illusionary, just a predecessor of far worse problems. At the same time, as people get used to social change, what once may have been constructed as an urgent problem may be normalized and no longer be the subject of alarming claims (see Box 10.6).

Given these patterns, it should not be surprising that social problems claims feature the most urgent rhetoric. Not only can claimsmakers draw attention to existing troubling conditions, but they also can predict alarming future problems. These are the secular equivalents of religious prophecies that the world will end on a particular date. It is worth noting that, in retrospect, these warnings often seem misguided. Consider alarmist warnings about AIDS in the late 1980s (in 1987, a leading television talk show host declared, "Research studies now project that . . . one in five heterosexuals could be dead from AIDS at the end of the next three years" [Fumento, 1990, p. 3]); and the furor about the Y2K problem (the concerns that the world's computers would be unable to cope when the calendar changed from 1999 to 2000, and that the resulting crisis might threaten civilization itself).

Apocalyptic rhetoric helps make claims stand out in the social problems marketplace. Every year brings a flu season, and it is always possible to speculate that this year's flu may turn into a devastating pandemic. Accentuating a positive record of progress rarely makes claims more competitive, whereas offering a dire forecast can

Box 10.6 Measuring Automobile Traffic Fatalities

Almost as soon as people began driving cars, there were traffic fatalities. Vardi (2014) notes that early critics denounced cars as almost demonic. Automobile enthusiasts sought to counter these claims with arguments that cars were valuable. One response to auto fatalities was to measure the problem, to develop statistical evidence that could help promote the spread of automobiles.

While it might seem that a rising death toll from cars would support claims that automobiles are a social problem, the car enthusiasts argued that the increase was distorted by the rapid increases both in the number of cars on the road and in the total distance they traveled. While the automobile's opponents pointed to the number of traffic fatalities (15,000 in 1922), its proponents argued that, when properly interpreted, the data showed that cars were actually becoming safer (that is, that the number of deaths per registered vehicle—or per million miles driven—was falling).

Over time, automobile deaths came to be redefined as a necessary cost of having cars. The United States covers a large area, and cars offered the freedom to travel different routes at relatively high speed and low monetary cost. Debate focused on ways to reduce traffic fatalities by setting speed limits, licensing drivers, and so on, rather than on defining auto fatalities as an evil that had to be eliminated. Note that such compromises are inherent in lots of social policies: vaccinations protect millions from serious diseases, but there are a few severe adverse reactions; alcohol and tobacco are enjoyed by millions, but they are calculated to cause hundreds of thousands of deaths. Deciding which costs society is willing to pay is central to many debates over social problems.

help grab the attention of media workers, the general public, and policymakers. Terrible fears make for good headlines, create good conversation topics, and offer policymakers opportunities to take a stand defending society from a threatening menace.

In short, the question is not whether there is or is not evidence of social progress. The point is that the social problems process pits claims against one another, and that claimsmakers can justify pessimistic rhetoric as a competitive strategy—the most effective way of arousing concern for their issues. This is one more way that the larger societal context shapes claimsmaking.

EXTENDING OUR FOCUS ACROSS SPACE AND TIME

Although the case study is the typical method for studying the social problems process, this chapter has suggested that there is much to be gained from studying more than one case at a time. Comparisons allow us to compare and contrast social issues across space and time—to recognize that there are various ways to construct the same troubling condition, and that claims morph as they diffuse from one country to another, or as a new wave of concern breathes fresh life into a once visible issue that has since fallen out of favor.

Typically, claims emphasize troubling conditions in the here and now—and in the future. Claimsmakers warn that this is why things are bad now, and that there are reasons to worry that things might get much worse. Expanding our focus—thinking about claims more broadly, by considering how social problems were constructed in other places or during other time periods—can help us place those claims in context, to locate the social problems process within a larger framework, so that we can better understand how that process operates. Without such bases for comparisons, it is difficult to assess any particular set of claims.

MAKING CONNECTIONS

- *Although many troubling conditions follow the six stages of the social problems process, often claims fail to attract media attention (discussed in Chapter 5) or public concern (covered in Chapter 6).*

- *Comparisons across time or between places are a useful way of evaluating social problems and the choices made by social problems workers and policymakers. See Chapters 7 and 8 for more about social policy and its implementation.*

- *Looking at cycles of concern across time or between different countries reveals how conditions in some historical periods foster claimsmaking. Chapter 3 explains how activists exploit cultural opportunities when conditions are optimal for drawing attention to their claims.*

CASE STUDY
IS SOCIAL PROBLEMS THEORY ETHNOCENTRIC?

Sociologists began publishing constructionist studies of social problems in the United States in the 1970s. The perspective spread in ways consistent with theories of diffusion—first to other English-speaking countries, such as Canada, the United Kingdom, and Australia, and then to other democracies in Western Europe and Japan. But sociologists in the United States continue to conduct the largest share of constructionist research. How has this fact affected constructionists' thinking about social problems?

All social constructions—including a book like this one—are products of their time and place. People who construct meanings—such as a book's author—are members of their cultures, and they inevitably allow assumptions from those cultures to shape their thinking. Anthropologists refer to this as **ethnocentrism**—the tendency to assume that one's own culture is correct, natural, normal. To some degree, all social constructions will be ethnocentric. While we can't eliminate ethnocentrism, we should be aware of its influence, and try to prevent it from overwhelming our thinking.

Consider, for example, the idea of the social problems marketplace introduced in Chapter 2. Contemporary Americans are used to thinking in terms of competition and the metaphor of the marketplace. Thus, Supreme Court decisions have referred to the importance of the "marketplace of ideas"—the notion that the free exchange of ideas will lead to the truth—and that metaphor has been used to justify freedom of religion, speech, and the press. By speaking of a social problems marketplace, sociologists of social problems have extended this line of thinking to the competition among claimsmakers for the attention of the press, the public, and policymakers. Similarly, speaking of claims as packages (see Chapter 5) evokes the imagery of marketing. In a country where protests by outsider claimsmakers are common enough that many find it difficult to attract attention to their causes, the metaphor of vendors competing in a marketplace is easily understood.

While sociologists in the United States may find the metaphor of the marketplace useful for thinking about claimsmakers struggling to be heard, that doesn't mean that the concept of a social problems marketplace works equally well in describing the social problems process in other societies. Consider Japan. Like the United States, Japan has a democratic government, but the Japanese government is less susceptible to claims by protesters. It is more difficult to mobilize resources for social movements or to make a career out of activism in Japan (Ayukawa, 2001). As a result, those who want to complain about social conditions—to make claims—find it easier to hire lawyers to sue on their behalf. Policy changes tend to follow lawsuits in which lawyers argue that their clients have been harmed. Thus, nonsmokers sued Japan National Railways (at the time operated by the government) to increase the number of nonsmoking cars on high-speed trains; although the plaintiffs' case lost in court, the railroad increased the number of nonsmoking cars.

A second pressure that leads to policy changes in Japan occurs when the Japanese government endorses some international agreement, such as the World Health Organization's Framework Convention on Tobacco Control, or statements from the European Convention on Human Rights (while not part of Europe, Japan sends observers to the European Court of Human Rights). Such international bodies may promote social policies, such as tighter restrictions on smoking, legal rights for children born out of wedlock, or eliminating capital punishment, that run counter to existing Japanese policies. In such cases, the awkwardness of seeming out of step with Western nations makes the Japanese government more willing to consider changing policies (Ayukawa, 2015). Japanese claims often are sorted out, not in the public square or the social problems marketplace, but in courts and other official circles, where policymakers decide whether new policies are needed or existing policies need modification. As a result, Japanese constructionist studies often focus on a sequence of policymakers' decisions, such as campaigns every few years to change the regulations regarding sexually explicit content in graphic novels (Akagawa, 2015).

Or take a second example: China. The government of China is authoritarian. In recent years, the government has permitted the expansion of private enterprise, but social control by the government remains powerful. The Chinese government attempts to block citizens' access to disapproved information on the Internet, news media content is closely supervised, and protesters can be arrested and punished. There may be a thriving economic marketplace, but there is no parallel free marketplace for social problems claims. In general, the Chinese government largely controls the social problems agenda, choosing which issues will receive attention, and setting the terms for how social problems will be constructed.

For instance, when the city of Guangzhou prepared to host the Asian Games in 2010, the government announced a goal of reducing reported crimes below 60,000 and, at the end of the year, the goal was met—there were only 59,900 reported crimes recorded. But accomplishing this goal involved a campaign to discourage citizens from calling the 110 police hotline (because those calls would be counted as crime reports); in fact, those who used the hotline were subject to fines. Rather, posters encouraged citizens to bring their complaints to local police stations; the posters gave out local police numbers, calls to which were not recorded as reported crimes. In response, the number of reported crimes fell, allowing the government to point to official statistics showing that crime was relatively uncommon in Guangzhou, presumably making foreign visitors less reluctant to attend the Asian Games (Xu, 2013). Or, to take another example, the government may decide at one point in time that motorcycles should be encouraged, only to later reverse itself and try to discourage them (Xu, 2015).

Nonetheless, the Chinese government encounters resistance. Whereas the government once controlled all mass media, there are now private newspapers that can—carefully—criticize some public policies. And, particularly in Hong Kong, young citizens have mounted protests against policies they view as threatening to bring the former British colony under the same sorts of tight controls that the rest of the country experiences (Adorjan & Yau, 2015). But such gestures fall far short of the country having a social problems marketplace.

QUESTIONS

1. How has the social problems process changed over time as new communications technologies have appeared?

2. Based on news reports, can you think of other countries where the social problems process seems to differ from that in the United States?

3. Identify some current concern. What factors might make it easy or difficult for claims about that social problem to spread through diffusion?

11

■

The Uses of the Constructionist Stance

■

Most of us find ourselves discussing social problems with friends or family members from time to time. In general, these everyday conversations focus on what we've called *troubling conditions*. People argue about the scope of conditions, or about what causes them (for instance, some may insist that poverty is caused by discrimination or a lack of good jobs, while others counter that poor people are at least partly to blame for their own problems). Reports from the media may be used to buttress one position or another (perhaps someone will refer to a radio talk show or a program on television about poverty). There may be disagreements about what should be done (should the government distribute more—or less—money to the poor?). In short, these conversations tend to treat social problems as though they are conditions that have an objective existence in our society.

Of course, this book has adopted a very different stance. It has been relatively uninterested in such social conditions, and has focused instead on what people think and say about social problems. Instead of treating social problems as social conditions, it has described a *process* in which people's ideas about social problems emerge and evolve.

Chapter 1 introduced a model of a social problems process with six basic stages: claimsmaking, media coverage, public reaction, policymaking, social problems work, and policy outcomes. That model (reproduced as Figure 11.1) provided the organizational framework for the chapters that followed, which, in general, dealt with successive stages in the social problems process.

While exploring the six stages in the social problems process, this book has remained focused on the subjective nature of social problems. Remember that what all phenomena that are considered social problems have in common is not a particular objective quality, some sort of harm or damage that they inflict on society. Rather, the one characteristic that all social problems share is subjective: people define them as troubling. Social problems are not conditions; they are *concerns*.

This subjective work—people's efforts to understand and draw attention to what they define as troubling conditions—occurs at every stage in the social problems process. It begins with claims-makers' efforts to construct claims that will convince others to share their concern about a troubling condition. And at each successive stage in the process, people—media workers, members of the public, policymakers, social problems workers, and those who evaluate and criticize policies—rework the claims that come to their attention, and reconstruct the problem again and again so that their new understanding will be appropriate for their purposes. News workers repackage primary claims into secondary claims to fit the demands and conventions of news coverage; members of the public respond by interpreting these secondary claims to correspond with their own understanding of how the larger world works; policymakers

Figure 11.1 Basic Model of the Social Problems Process

Claims-making ⟶ Media Coverage ⟶ Public Reaction ⟶ Policy-making ⟶ Social Problems Work ⟶ Policy Outcomes make further alterations so that the troubling condition can be addressed through a formal policy; social problems workers try to apply abstract policies to practical situations; and various evaluators redefine what is needed according to their assessments of how well policies work.

In other words, social problems construction is not something that happens all at once, through the actions of a single set of actors at one stage in the social problems process. Instead, it is an ongoing process, in which different people work out different ways of making sense of the situations they confront. Any phenomenon can be understood in lots of different ways, and social construction is a process of making choices—of people in a particular situation choosing one perspective among all the possibilities. Each effort to construct or understand a social problem needs to meet two criteria: first, it needs to make sense to—and be useful for—whoever is producing the construction; second, it needs to be able to convince others—whoever the audience for that construction may be.

Social construction is thus an *interactive* process. People present their constructions to an audience of others (as when an activist holds a press conference, a legislator tries to convince colleagues to vote for a bill, or a caseworker tries to persuade clients that taking a particular action will be in their best interest). Those others, however, may react in different ways (perhaps no reporters bother to attend the press conference, perhaps the legislature votes unanimously in favor of the bill, perhaps some clients reject the case worker's advice while others follow it). These reactions become feedback, and on the basis of the audience's response, the people offering the construction may continue pressing their claims, modify those claims to see whether a repackaged version might elicit a better response, or even decide to abandon the claims entirely. Although we may think of a claimsmaker addressing an audience, we should not imagine that that audience is passive. Rather, audiences react to claims, and claimsmakers are likely to revise their constructions in response to those reactions.

All of this means that our initial model of the social problems process, as illustrated in Figure 11.1, oversimplifies the process in some important ways. First, the arrows between stages imply that influence is unidirectional; they ignore the role of feedback and the interactive nature of the process. Second, the actors at the different stages in the social problems process do not necessarily limit their interactions to contacts with those in the next stage. Third, and very important, interactions also occur *within* each stage. That is, activists interact with others in their social movement organization, as well as with activists in rival SMOs, and with other sorts of claimsmakers, such as experts. Similarly, media workers interact with their colleagues and follow one another's coverage, and so on.

Moreover, when we look at interactions between actors in different stages, we realize again that the basic model's depiction of actors addressing only those at the next stage in the process is too simple. For example, the model suggests that claimsmakers will focus their attention on influencing media coverage, but claimsmakers may do far more. Sometimes claimsmakers bypass the media and directly address members of the public, policymakers, social problems workers, or even those who evaluate policy outcomes. There are many possible pathways through the social problems process. Figure 11.1 can be thought of as offering a simplified, fairly typical natural history—a framework for developing this book's argument. In contrast, Figure 11.2 gives a better sense of the complicated ways in which actors in different stages of the process can interact; it suggests the range of possible connections that might shape how social problems evolve.

Examine Figure 11.2 carefully, and note the following five features:

1. The five one-way stage-to-stage arrows found in the simplified model reappear in Figure 11.2 as thicker arrows—a reminder that these are particularly important links in the social problems process.

Figure 11.2 Interactions in the Social Problems Process

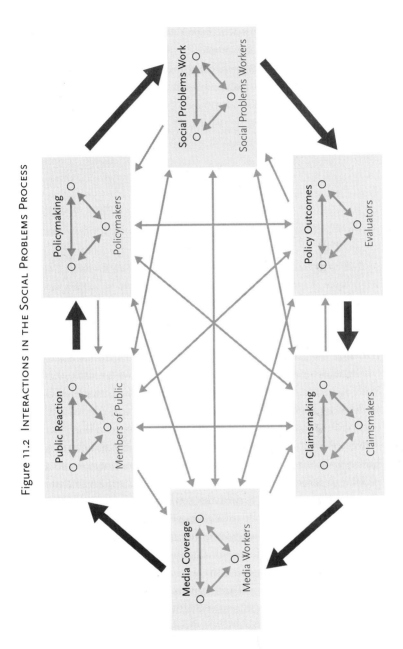

2. Each stage in the social problems process is now represented by a box, and small circles within each box denote the various actors in that stage (that is, different claimsmakers in the claimsmaking stage, and so on). In turn, those circles are linked by two-way arrows suggesting interactions among the people at each stage.

3. Arrows connect each stage with every other stage, illustrating possible connections, in that it may be possible for actors at any stage to communicate with people anywhere else in the social problems process.

4. The arrows linking all the different stages go in both directions, to illustrate that there is always the possibility of feedback and social interaction.

5. The figure is laid out as a circle, rather than along a straight line, and there is a thick arrow between "Policy Outcomes" (which the basic model presented as the final stage in the social problems process) and "Claimsmaking" (which was, of course, the first stage). This arrow denotes how reactions to social policies often lead to new claimsmaking campaigns (as discussed in Chapter 9). The figure's roughly circular shape reminds us that the social problems process need not end—that critiques of social policies often inspire new cycles of claimsmaking.

Figure 11.2 is complex, but that is because it reflects genuine complexities—the many possible pathways through the social problems process. The entire process is an example of what sociologists call a *complex system*, with many elements that affect one another (Watts, 2011). It is important to appreciate this complexity; spend some time examining Figure 11.2. Pick one particular arrow and consider the sorts of activities it might involve. Then pick another. Do this until you are comfortable, until you understand how this complex figure depicts the overall social problems process.

These complexities become especially apparent when we compare social problems processes across space and time (the subject of Chapter 10). For example, many campaigns raise concern about dangerous drugs. Some of these efforts are remarkably successful at attracting intense media coverage, arousing great public concern, and inspiring new policies; the 1986 campaign to warn Americans about the dangers of crack cocaine is an obvious example (Reinarman & Levine, 1995). On the other hand, some campaigns flop, such as the 1989 effort to draw attention to "ice" (smokable crystal methamphetamine), although later campaigns to raise alarm about this drug had more success; or the 1993 warnings about "Cat" (methcathinone, a drug that—so far—has not aroused great concern) (Jenkins, 1999). We can imagine a continuum of outcomes for antidrug campaigns that ranges from widespread, intense concern to indifference. Only by comparing antidrug claimsmaking campaigns—targeting different drugs, at different times, or in different places—can we begin to appreciate the many possible ways that the social problems process can unfold. And, of course, various claims about other troubling conditions—racial discrimination, ecological problems, and so on—will display similar variability in their outcomes.

In other words, our constructionist model—both the simpler version depicted in Figure 11.1 and the more complex version presented in Figure 11.2—should be understood as a tool, a framework that can be used to help us think critically about the social construction of social problems. Most days, news media present various stories that report on claimsmaking, policymaking, or social problems work; very often they also run stories about public reactions and evaluations of different policies. (And, of course, all of those stories are themselves examples of media coverage.) The constructionist model can be used to place all those stories in their broader context, to view them as parts of the larger social problems process. And that's worth doing, because we are constantly surrounded by examples of the social problems process.

IS THIS STUFF USEFUL?

As noted way back in Chapter 1, the constructionist stance for thinking about the social problems process is not the traditional approach to studying social problems. Most books about social problems have been—and continue to be—organized around a series of chapters that deal with various conditions considered to be social problems—crime, racism, and the like. Each chapter summarizes information about its problem: statistics about crime rates, theories of crime causation, and so on. This book has presented very little information of that sort.

The justification for this book's constructionist approach is that it is intellectually coherent. Rather than letting our attention drift as we examine, one at a time, crime and other specific phenomena that people consider social problems, this book has focused on the general topic of the social problems process—on the insight that the only thing the various conditions called social problems have in common is that they are socially constructed—and it has explored the ins and outs of that process.

This approach is intended to give you some tools for recognizing, thinking about, and responding to social problems claims. Ten years from now—or maybe twenty or thirty—you will encounter warnings about a terrible new social problem of some sort. There is no way of predicting exactly what the topic of those warnings will be—perhaps a new crime, or a new disease, or a new form of drug abuse. But we can be reasonably confident that you will run into such claims, because such claims have been an important part of the social landscape for a very long time, and there is no reason to expect that they will vanish—particularly not in a world where twenty-four-hour television news broadcasts, the Internet, and other forms of electronic communication make it incredibly easy to promote new claims. If anything, claims are likely to spread via ever more channels as new media evolve (consider, for example, the relatively recent emergence of Facebook pages as forums for claims, and of news bulletins transmitted to cell phones and other portable electronic devices). People who pay even minimal attention to the media can expect to spend their lives bombarded by such claims.

Moreover, the historical record is full of warnings about terrible problems that—in retrospect—seem mistaken. In the 1970s, some environmentalists warned that civilization was jeopardized by global climate change—that humans faced an impending ice age brought on by global cooling. Fifteen years later, fears about the threat of global cooling would be replaced by what seem to be their exact opposite—concerns over the danger of global warming. In another example, in the early 1990s some commentators warned that violent crime was about to spiral out of control—that a generation of "superpredators" would be coming of age. Instead, crime rates fell fairly steadily during the years that followed. These claims received plenty of respectful attention when they first appeared, even though their forecasts proved to be quite wrong.

There are many other examples of urgent claims that hindsight lets us see as exaggerated, if not silly. There is a long history of critics warning that the amusements of the young—games, toys, dances, movies, television, music, and on and on—endangered the next generation. Each successive style of rock music, for example, has been denounced as threatening the moral fabric of young people. There is an equally long history of commentators charging that the current wave of immigrants threatens the foundation of American society, that some new recreational drug is spreading out of control, and so on. Such claims often acknowledge that earlier claims about similar problems exaggerated the threat, yet the claimsmakers insist that this new problem is different—the real deal—that it presents a genuine danger that must be addressed.

At one extreme, it is possible to treat all social problems claims as correct, true, accurate. When claimsmakers warn that a particular troubling condition is this serious, affects that many people, and so on, we might simply accept those claims, even though we may realize that, in the past, many such claims have proved to be exaggerated or even false. In other words, every time we encounter a news story that warns we should be worried about a new problem, we could decide to worry. An alternative, but equally extreme stance might be to approach all claims cynically, to presume that they are wrong, false, bogus. We could suspect that claimsmakers are interested parties who are quite willing to say anything, that media workers are just trying to attract an audience, that politicians are cynically pandering to voters' concerns, and so on. Knowing that some social problems claims have been exaggerated in the past, we might simply discount and ignore any claims we encounter in the future. The first possibility encourages excessive credulity; the second fosters cynicism, apathy, and ignorance.

Obviously it would be desirable to find a middle ground between those extremes—a stance somewhere between credulousness and cynicism. That is, it would be better to approach claims thoughtfully—critically—so that we could weigh what we're told about social problems and make our own evaluations about the nature of those problems and the best ways of addressing them.

The constructionist model of the social problems process can help in this regard. Understanding that claims need to be made persuasive—that claimsmakers are competing to be heard in the social problems marketplace so that they can bring their claims to the attention of press, public, and policymakers—offers a useful foundation for thinking about social problems as a process. In particular, it can help us to think carefully about how the problem is being constructed, about the rhetoric of claimsmaking, about who is making which claims, and so on.

By adopting a constructionist stance, we can identify interesting questions that we might ask about a set of claims. Is the problem clearly defined, or are we encouraged to understand it primarily through typifying examples? Is there any reason to suspect that those typifying examples may not be all that typical? If the claims feature statistics, where do those numbers come from, and how likely is it that they are accurate? What sorts of warrants are being used to make the claims compelling? How are the media covering the issue? What sources are they drawing on, and how does what the media report differ from what the claimsmakers are saying? Are the media presenting different constructions of the problem, and what do those differences reveal?

Further questions arise at successive stages in the social problems process. Is the problem addressed in our everyday conversations? Is it a theme in stories or jokes that we hear from people we know, and if so, does the public seem to be constructing the problem in different terms from those that claimsmakers and the media are using? Which aspects of the problem do policymakers emphasize? Do their policy recommendations match their claims? Do they seem workable? How do social problems workers describe their activities and the clients with whom they work? Who criticizes social policies and why, and how do they frame their critiques?

Such questions give us tools that we can use to think critically about social problems. Note, however, that being critical sometimes does mean rejecting claims. The answers to some of the questions you ask may strike you as completely convincing; you may decide that some claims are quite correct, and you may even be moved to join some claimsmakers' causes. In other instances, though, questioning the claims might lead you to suspect that those claims are exaggerated or misguided. Thus, thinking critically can help you become a thoughtful consumer of social problems claims.

There is another way to use the constructionist approach. Studying how social problems are constructed—how some claims prove effective while others fall by the wayside—offers useful information for would-be claimsmakers. That is, constructionist research can be studied for its practical advice on how to arouse concern and mobilize action regarding whatever you might consider as troubling conditions (just as it can suggest how opposition to claims might be made more effective). Studying the social problems process offers lessons on how to assemble persuasive claimsmaking rhetoric, how to mobilize effective adherents, how to incorporate expert knowledge in campaigns, how to elicit media coverage and attract public attention, how to understand the concerns of policymakers and social problems workers, and so on. If you are inclined to take an active part in the social problems process, the constructionist stance can help you ask—and answer—very practical questions. It is a perspective that can benefit participants, as well as observers.

What constructionism cannot do is tell you which conditions ought to concern you. You have your own values, your own sense of what is or is not troubling, what needs to be changed, and what sorts of changes are needed. You may be attracted by the ideologies of liberals or conservatives, of feminists or fundamentalists. Those are choices you need to make, and the constructionist stance does not provide the grounds for preferring one choice over another. The goal of this book has not been to tell you *what* to think about various social conditions, but rather to offer guidelines for *how* to think about the social problems process. If this book advocates a moral position, it is that it is desirable for people to think critically about that process, to engage the claims they encounter.

I hope you will find these ideas useful in the years ahead. Good luck.

Glossary

abeyance A period when a social movement is relatively inactive.

activists Members of a social movement organization who make claims about social problems. Compare *experts*.

adopters The people who accept new innovations as part of the process of diffusion. Compare *transmitters*.

agenda setting Choosing which claims will receive the attention of media or policymakers.

arena A public venue where social problems claims can be presented.

audience The people whom claimsmakers seek to persuade with their claims.

audience segmentation Targeting media presentations for particular audiences.

beneficiaries People who stand to benefit from a social movement's success. Compare *constituents*.

bias A tendency for media workers' personal beliefs and views on an issue to interfere with balanced and impartial coverage.

biomedicalization The process of arguing that biological processes are the root cause of many troubling conditions.

carrying capacity The number of issues that can receive attention in an arena.

case An instance of a previously constructed troubling condition that requires attention through the application of appropriate policy.

case study An examination of a particular problem.

causal story A story that classifies a troubling condition in a familiar category according to the nature of its cause.

claim An argument that a particular troubling condition needs to be addressed.

claimsmakers People who seek to convince others that there is a troubling condition about which something ought to be done.

claimsmaking The process of making claims, of bringing a troubling condition to the attention of others.

commission A special, high-status group—often created at the national level—that evaluates policies and issues recommendations.

conclusion The part of a claim that specifies what should be done, what action should be taken to address a troubling condition.

condensing symbol A shorthand element—such as a landmark narrative, typifying example, slogan, or visual image—that evokes a package.

conscience constituents People who contribute money or even join demonstrations because they believe in a particular cause, although they do not expect to be direct beneficiaries of that cause. Compare *constituents*.

constituents People who support a social movement. Compare *beneficiaries* and *conscience constituents*.

constructionism A sociological approach that focuses on the process of social construction.

contemporary legend A story, also called an *urban legend*, spread from one person to another and believed to be true by teller and listener.

counterclaim An argument that directly opposes a particular claim.

countermovement A movement that opposes a social movement by promoting counterclaims that challenge the opponent's claims.

cultural opportunity A situation when a shift in popular ideas makes it possible to change how a particular troubling condition is addressed. Compare *political opportunity*.

cultural resources Cultural knowledge that can be incorporated in claims.

diagnostic frame A social movement's depiction of the nature of a problem. Compare *prognostic frame*.

dialog An exchange of ideas between two or more persons.

diffusion The process by which innovations spread.

domain expansion Redefining a troubling condition to encompass a broader array of cases.

ethnocentrism The assumption that one's culture is right or natural.

evaluation research A social scientific assessment of the effectiveness of a specific policy.

experts People—such as physicians, scientists, lawyers, and officials—who have special knowledge and claim to speak with special authority. Compare *activists*.

feedback The phenomenon in which a particular cause produces an effect that in turn affects the cause.

focus group A set of people that researchers select to discuss certain topics in order to learn what the public is thinking.

frame alignment Ways in which activists try to promote a social movement's frame to prospective members.

frame amplification Ways in which activists appeal to prospective members by arguing that a social movement's frame is consistent with popular beliefs.

frame bridging Ways in which activists appeal to prospective members thought to be already sympathetic to a social movement's frame.

frame dispute A disagreement between groups of activists about how to frame a particular troubling condition.

frame extension Ways in which activists appeal to prospective members by extending a social movement's frame to encompass the concerns of those prospective supporters.

frame transformation Ways in which activists appeal to prospective members by inviting them to reject familiar views of the world and adopt the activists' very different perspective.

framing The way in which claimsmakers construct claims about a troubling condition.

ground The portion of a claim that argues that a troubling condition exists.

ideology A system of beliefs regarding how society does and should operate.

inertia A reluctance to alter existing social arrangements.

insider claimsmakers Claimsmakers who have easy access to publicity and people in positions of power. Compare *outsider claimsmakers*.

joke cycle A set of jokes that share a form or topic and are popular for a period of time.

landmark narrative A typifying example that dominates news coverage of a troubling condition, shaping the terms in which the problem is covered and how the news audience understands the problem.

macrosociology Sociological studies concerned with whole societies. Compare *microsociology*.

master frame A broad construction that can be easily modified and applied to many troubling conditions.

media coverage Attention from mass media outlets, such as newspapers and television, that can bring claims to the attention of a wide audience.

medical model A general framework for thinking about medical matters as diseases that require treatment.

medicalization The process of defining a troubling condition as a medical matter.

microsociology Sociological studies concerned with interactions between individuals. Compare *macrosociology*.

motif A recurring thematic element in legends and jokes.

motivational frame A social movement's justification for taking action.

naming Coining a term to identify a troubling condition.

natural history A sequence of steps or stages often found in a particular process.

news work The job of locating and presenting news to the larger public.

nonrelational channel A link in diffusion that does not involve a personal connection between a transmitter and an adopter. Compare *relational channel*.

objectivism A school of thought that defines social problems in terms of objectively measurable characteristics of conditions. Compare *subjectivism*.

outsider claimsmakers People who lack easy access to publicity and to people in positions of power. Compare *insider claimsmakers*.

ownership Having one's construction of a troubling condition become widely accepted.

package A familiar construction of a particular troubling condition, including specifications of its causes and solutions.

perfectibility Using the eradication of a troubling condition—instead of its improvement—as the standard for evaluating a social policy.

pharmaceuticalization The process of defining prescription drugs as solutions to troubling conditions.

piggyback To link a new troubling condition to an already established social problem.

policy domain The part of the political system that focuses on a particular troubling condition.

policy outcome The result of how a particular social policy is implemented.

policy proposal stream A set of policy proposals that policymakers hear for addressing a troubling condition.

policymakers People who are able to establish a social policy of some kind.

policymaking The process of devising policy to address a particular troubling condition.

political opportunity A situation when a shift in power makes it possible to change how a particular troubling condition is addressed. Compare *cultural opportunity*.

political stream The current political situation recognized by policymakers in which a troubling condition might be addressed.

polity Groups and individuals who have easy access to policymakers.

popular culture Commercial entertainment.

population All those described by a statistic. Compare *representative sample*.

position issue A troubling condition about which people disagree. Compare *valence issue*.

primary claim One of the initial claims, usually presented by activists or experts, that begin the social problems process. Compare *secondary claim*.

problem recognition stream The set of claims that policymakers hear about a troubling condition.

prognostic frame A social movement's description of what needs to be done about a particular troubling condition. Compare *diagnostic frame*.

relational channel A link in diffusion that involves interpersonal contact between a transmitter and an adopter. Compare *nonrelational channel*.

representative sample A sample that accurately reflects the diversity of the population. Compare *population*.

resource Anything that can be drawn on to construct a claim.

resource mobilization Collecting and assembling money, members, and other resources needed by a social movement.

rhetoric The study of persuasion.

sample A subgroup used as a basis for statistical generalizations about a population.

sample survey A poll administered to a sample in order to generalize about opinions or other characteristics of a population.

secondary claim The media's transformation of a primary claim. Secondary claims are usually shorter and more dramatic than primary claims. Compare *primary claim*.

segmentation See *audience segmentation*.

semantic polling The use of software to classify the content of social media messages.

SMO See *social movement organization*.

social condition A social circumstance or arrangement.

social construction The process by which people continually create—or construct—meaning.

social issue A topic of social concern that is characterized by disagreement or debate.

social movement A general cause that motivates activists and social movement organizations to address a particular troubling condition.

social movement organization (SMO) A particular organization that belongs to a social movement.

social problems cluster Claimsmakers who take similar positions on similar social problems.

social problems marketplace The public forum where claims are presented and discussed.

social problems process The process through which particular troubling conditions come to be constructed as social problems.

social problems work The application of constructions of a troubling condition or a social policy to practical situations.

social problems workers People who do social problems work.

sociological imagination The ability to see private troubles in terms of larger public issues.

statistic A number that measures or characterizes a particular situation.

subjectivism A school of thought that defines social problems in terms of people's subjective sense that something is or isn't troubling. Compare *objectivism*.

subjects The people (variously called addicts, clients, defendants, offenders, patients, suspects, victims, and so on) who in some way embody a socially constructed social problem.

target population The group of people intended to be affected by a social policy.

theorization The presentation of claims using abstract principles and arguments.

topical joke cycle A joke cycle about a particular event.

transmitters The people who promote new innovations as part of the process of diffusion. Compare *adopters*.

trope A common rhetorical element.

troubling condition A condition that becomes a subject of claims.

typifying example A particular instance chosen to illustrate a troubling condition—often a dramatic, disturbing, or memorable case.

urban legend See *contemporary legend*.

valence issue A troubling condition about which there is general agreement. Compare *position issue*.

variant A version of a contemporary legend or joke.

warrant The portion of a claim that justifies doing something about a troubling condition.

References

Abraham, J. (2010). Pharmaceuticalization of society in context: Theoretical, empirical, and health. *Sociology* 44: 603–622.

Adams, J. T. (1941 [1931]). *The epic of America*. Garden City, NY: Blue Ribbon Books.

Adorjan, M., Christensen, T., Kelly, B. & Pawluch, D. (2012). Stockholm Syndrome as vernacular resource. *Sociological Quarterly.* 53(3): 454–474.

Adorjan, M., & Yau, H. L. (2015). Resinicization and digital citizenship in Hong Kong: Youth, cyberspace, and claims-making. *Qualitative Sociology Review* 11(2): 160–178.

Akagawa, M. (2015). Regulating pornocomic sales to juveniles in Japan: Cycles and path-dependence of a social problem. *Qualitative Sociology Review* 11(2): 63–73.

Åkerström, M. (2006). Doing ambivalence: Embracing policy innovation—at arm's length. *Social Problems* 53: 57–74.

Alterman, E. (2003). *What liberal media? The truth about bias and the news.* New York: Basic Books.

Anstead, N., & O'Loughlin, B. (2015). Social media analysis and public opinion: The 2010 UK general election. *Journal of Computer-Mediated Communication* 20: 204–220.

Appleton, L. M. (1995). Rethinking medicalization: Alcoholism and anomalies. In J. Best (Ed.), *Images of issues: Typifying contemporary social problems* (2nd ed., pp. 59–80). Hawthorne, NY: Aldine de Gruyter.

Ayukawa, J. (2001). The United States and smoking problems in Japan. In J. Best (Ed.), *How claims spread: Cross-national diffusion of social problems* (pp. 215–242). Hawthorne, NY: Aldine de Gruyter.

Ayukawa, J. (2015). Claims-making and human rights in domestic and international spheres. *Qualitative Sociology Review* 11(2): 110–121.

Bacon, R. J. (2013). In the shadow of saturated fat: The struggle to get trans fats noticed. In J. Best and S. R. Harris (Eds.), *Making sense of social problems: New images, new issues* (pp. 233–250). Boulder, CO: Lynne Rienner.

Badano, S. E., Burgermeister, S. J., Henne, S., Murphy, S. T., & Cole, B. M. (2014). Legitimacy concerns in animal advocacy organizations during the Michael Vick dogfighting scandal. *Society and Animals* 22: 111–134.

Barker, K., & Galardi, T. R. (2015). Diagnostic domain defense: Autism spectrum disorder and the *DSM-5*. *Social Problems* 62: 120–140.

Barnes, F. (2004, May 28). Liberal media evidence. *The Daily Standard*. Retrieved from www.weeklystandard.com.

Bartley, T., & Child, C. (2014). Shaming the corporation: The social production of targets and the anti-sweatshop movement. *American Sociological Review* 79: 653–679.

BBC. (2015, June 12). Ebola: Mapping the outbreak. *BBC.com*. Retrieved from http://www.bbc.com/news/world-africa-28755033.

Becker, H. S. (1995). The power of inertia. *Qualitative Sociology* 18: 301–309.

Beckett, K. (1994). Setting the public agenda: "Street crime" and drug use in American politics. *Social Problems* 41: 425–447.

Beckett, K. (1996). Culture and the politics of signification: The case of child sexual abuse. *Social Problems* 43: 57–76.

Bell, K. (2014). Science, policy and the rise of "thirdhand smoke" as a public health issue. *Health, Risk & Society* 16: 154–170.

Benford, R. D. (1993). Frame disputes within the nuclear disarmament movement. *Social Forces* 71: 677–701.

Benford, R. D., & Hunt, S. A. (2003). Interactional dynamics in public problems marketplaces: Movements and the counterframing and reframing of public problems. In J. A. Holstein & G. Miller (Eds.), *Challenges and choices: Constructionist perspectives on social problems* (pp. 153–186). Hawthorne, NY: Aldine de Gruyter.

Benson, R. (2013). *Shaping immigration news: A French–American comparison*. New York: Columbia University Press.

Berger, P. L., & Luckmann, T. (1966). *The social construction of reality: A treatise in the sociology of knowledge*. Garden City, NY: Doubleday.

Berns, N. (2004). *Framing the victim: Domestic violence, media, and social problems*. Hawthorne, NY: Aldine de Gruyter.

Best, J. (1990). *Threatened children: Rhetoric and concern about child-victims*. Chicago: University of Chicago Press.

Best, J. (1999). *Random violence: How we talk about new crimes and new victims*. Berkeley: University of California Press.

Best, J. (Ed.). (2001a). *How claims spread: Cross-national diffusion of social problems.* Hawthorne, NY: Aldine de Gruyter.

Best, J. (2001b). Social progress and social problems: Toward a sociology of gloom. *Sociological Quarterly* 42: 1–12.

Best, J. (2011). If this goes on . . . : The rhetorical construction of future problems. In T. van Haaften, H. Jansen, J. de Jong, & W. Koetsenruijter (Eds.), *Bending opinion: Essays on persuasion in the public domain* (pp. 203–217). Leiden, Netherlands: Leiden University Press.

Best, J. (2013). *Damned lies and statistics: Untangling numbers from the media, politicians, and activists* (updated ed.). Berkeley: University of California Press.

Best, J. (2015). Beyond case studies: Expanding the constructionist framework for social problems research. *Qualitative Sociology Review* 11(2): 18–33.

Best, J., & Best, E. (2014). *The student loan mess: How good intentions created a trillion-dollar problem.* Berkeley: University of California Press.

Best, J., & Bogle, K. A. (2014). *Kids gone wild: From rainbow parties to sexting, understanding the hype over teen sex.* New York: New York University Press.

Best, J., & Furedi, F. (2001). The evolution of road rage in Britain and the United States. In J. Best (Ed.), *How claims spread: Cross-national diffusion of social problems* (pp. 107–127). Hawthorne, NY: Aldine de Gruyter.

Best, R. K. (2012). Disease politics and medical research funding: Three ways advocacy shapes policy. *American Sociological Review* 77: 780–803.

Bloom, J. (2015). The dynamics of opportunity and insurgent practice: How black anti-colonialists compelled Truman to advocate civil rights. *American Sociological Review* 80: 391–415.

Blumer, H. (1971). Social problems as collective behavior. *Social Problems* 18: 298–306.

Bogard, C. J. (2003). *Seasons such as these: How homelessness took shape in America.* Hawthorne, NY: Aldine de Gruyter.

Bowman, K., Marsico, J., & Sims, S. (2014, December 15). Is the American Dream alive? Examining Americans' attitudes. *American Enterprise Institute.* Retrieved from https://www.aei.org/wp-content/uploads/2014/12/Is-the-American-Dream-Alive_Dec2014.pdf.

Bracey, G. W. (2007). "The first time everything changed." *Phi Delta Kappan* 89(2): 119–136.

Bristow, J. (2015). *Baby boomers and generational conflict.* London: Palgrave Macmillan.

Bronner, S. J. (1988). Political suicide: The Budd Dwyer joke cycle and the humor of disaster. *Midwestern Folklore* 14: 81–89.

Brooks, C., & Manza, J. (2013). A broken public? Americans' responses to the Great Recession. *American Sociological Review* 78: 727–748.

Brown, J. D. (1991). The professional ex-. *Sociological Quarterly* 32: 219–230.

Brown, P. (1992). Popular epidemiology and toxic waste contamination: Lay and professional ways of knowing. *Journal of Health and Social Behavior* 33: 267–281.

Brunsma, D. L. (2004). *The school uniform movement and what it tells us about American education*. Lanham, MD: Scarecrow Education.

Burgess, A. (2004). *Cellular phones, public fears, and a culture of precaution*. Cambridge, UK: Cambridge University Press.

Burstein, P. (1991). Policy domains: Organization, culture, and policy outcomes. *Annual Review of Sociology* 17: 327–350.

Burstein, P. (2014). *American public opinion, advocacy, and policy in Congress: What the public wants and what it gets*. New York: Cambridge University Press.

Calabresi, M. (2015, June 15). "Why America can't kick its painkiller problem: The price we pay for relief." *Time* 185: 26–33.

Campion-Vincent, V. (2005). *Organ theft legends*. Jackson: University Press of Mississippi.

Chambliss, D. F. (1996). *Beyond caring: Hospitals, nurses, and the social organization of ethics*. Chicago: University of Chicago Press.

Clarke, A. E., Shim, J. K., Mamo, L., Fosket, J. R., & Fishman, J. R. (2003). Biomedicalization: Technoscientific transformations of health, illness, and U.S. biomedicine. *American Sociological Review* 68: 161–194.

Cohen, J. W., & Brooks, R. A. (2014). *Confronting school bullying: Kids, culture, and the making of a social problem*. Boulder, CO: Lynne Rienner.

Cole, S. A. (2015). A surfeit of science: The "CSI effect" and the media appropriation of the public understanding of science. *Public Understanding of Science* 24: 130–146.

Conrad, P. (2007). *The medicalization of society: On the transformation of human conditions into treatable disorders*. Baltimore: Johns Hopkins University Press.

Daniels, J. (2009). Cloaked websites: Propaganda, cyber-racism and epistemology in the digital era. *New Media and Society* 11: 659–683.

Davenport, M. (2014, July 24). Reflections on the American Dream. *Liberal Beef*. Retrieved from http://liberalbeef.com/2014/07/24/reflections-american-dream/.

Davis, P. W. (1994). The changing meanings of spanking. In J. Best (Ed.), *Troubling children* (pp. 133–153). Hawthorne, NY: Aldine de Gruyter.

de Vaus, D. A. (1986). *Surveys in social research*. London: Allen & Unwin.

Del Rosso, J. (2015). *Talking about torture: How political discourse shapes the debate*. New York: Cambridge University Press.

Dickson, D. T. (1968). Bureaucracy and morality: An organizational perspective on a moral crusade. *Social Problems* 16: 143–156.

Doering, J. (2014). A battleground of identity: Racial formation and the African American discourse on racial intermarriage. *Social Problems* 61: 559–575.

Doherty, B. (2011). "Just a matter of when?" *Reason* 42(9): 32–39.

Downs, A. (1972). Up and down with ecology—The "issue-attention cycle." *Public Interest* 28: 38–50.

Dundes, A. (1987). *Cracking jokes*. Berkeley, CA: Ten Speed Press.

Dundes, A., & Pagter, C. R. (2000). *Why don't sheep shrink when it rains? A further collection of photocopier folklore*. Syracuse, NY: Syracuse University Press.

Eaton, M. (2010). Manufacturing community in an online activist organization: The rhetoric of MoveOn.org's e-mails. *Information, Communication and Society* 13: 174–192.

Eccles, R. (2015, April 13). The American dream is for dreamers. *Lonely Conservative*. Retrieved from http://lonelyconservative.com/the-american-dream -is-for-dreamers/.

Ellis, B. (1991). The last thing said: The *Challenger* disaster jokes and closure. *International Folklore Review* 8: 110–124.

Ellis, B. (2001). *Aliens, ghosts, and cults: Legends we live*. Jackson: University Press of Mississippi.

Ellis, B. (2003). Making a Big Apple crumble: The role of humor in constructing a global response to disaster. In P. Narváez (Ed.), *Of corpse: Death and humor in folklore and popular culture* (pp. 35–79). Logan: Utah State University Press.

Emerson, R. M. (2015). *Everyday troubles: The micro-politics of interpersonal conflict*. Chicago: University of Chicago Press.

Erikson, K. T. (1976). *Everything in its path: Destruction of community in the Buffalo Creek flood*. New York: Simon & Schuster.

Feder, E. K. (2014). *Making sense of intersex: Changing ethical perspectives in biomedicine*. Bloomington: Indiana University Press.

Ferdik, F., Rojek, J. & Alpert, G. P. (2013). Citizen oversight in the United States and Canada: An overview. *Police Practice and Research*. 14:104–116.

Fine, G. A. (1992). *Manufacturing tales: Sex and money in contemporary legends*. Knoxville: University of Tennessee Press.

Fine, G. A., Campion-Vincent, V., & Heath, C. (Eds.). (2005). *Rumor mills: The social impact of rumor and legend*. New Brunswick, NJ: AldineTransaction.

Fine, G. A., & Christoforides, L. (1991). Dirty birds, filthy immigrants, and the English sparrow war: Metaphorical linkage in constructing social problems. *Symbolic Interaction* 14: 375–393.

Fine, G. A., & Turner, P. A. (2001). *Whispers on the color line: Rumor and race in America*. Berkeley: University of California Press.

Fischer, D. H. (1989). *Albion's seed: Four British folkways in America*. New York: Oxford University Press.

Francis, A. (2015). *Family Trouble: Middle-class parents, children's problems, and the disruption of everyday life*. New Brunswick, NJ: Rutgers University Press.

Fraustino, J. D., & Ma, L. (2015). CDC's use of social media in a risk campaign—"Preparedness 101: Zombie Apocalypse." *Journal of Applied Communication Research* 43: 222–241.

Frawley, A. (2015). *Semiotics of happiness: Rhetorical beginnings of a public problem.* London: Bloomsbury.

Freidson, E. (1986). *Professional powers: A study of the institutionalization of formal knowledge.* Chicago: University of Chicago Press.

Fujiwara, L. H. (2005). Immigrant rights are human rights: The reframing of immigrant entitlement and welfare. *Social Problems* 52: 79–101.

Fumento, M. (1990). *The myth of heterosexual AIDS.* New York: Basic Books.

Furedi, F. (2001). Bullying: The British contribution to the construction of a social problem. In J. Best (Ed.), *How claims spread: Cross-national diffusion of social problems* (pp. 89–106). Hawthorne, NY: Aldine de Gruyter.

Gallo-Cruz, S. (2012). Negotiating the lines of contention: Counterframing and boundary work in the School of the Americas debate. *Sociological Forum* 27: 21–45.

Gallup. (2015). Gay and lesbian rights. *Gallup.com.* Retrieved from http://www.gallup.com/poll/1651/gay-lesbian-rights.aspx.

Gamson, W. A. (1992). *Talking politics.* New York: Cambridge University Press.

Gamson, W. A., & Modigliani, A. (1989). Media discourse and public opinion on nuclear power: A constructionist approach. *American Journal of Sociology* 95: 1–37.

Gamson, W. A., & Sifry, M. L. (Eds.). (2013). The #Occupy movement [special section]. *Sociological Quarterly* 54: 159–228.

Gauchat, G. (2012). Politicization of science in the public sphere: A study of public trust in the United States, 1974 to 2010. *American Sociological Review* 77: 167–187.

Gengler, A. M. (2012). Defying (dis)empowerment in a battered women's shelter: Moral rhetorics, intersectionality, and processes of control and resistance. *Social Problems* 59: 501–521.

Gitlin, T. (1983). *Inside prime time.* New York: Pantheon.

Gitlin, T. (2012). *Occupy nation: The roots, the spirit, and the promise of Occupy Wall Street.* New York: HarperCollins.

Goedeke, T. L. (2005). Devils, angels, or animals: The social construction of otters in conflict over management. In A. Herda-Rapp & T. L. Goedeke (Eds.), *Mad about wildlife: Looking at social conflict over wildlife* (pp. 25–50). Boston: Brill.

Goldstein, D. E. (2004). *Once upon a virus: AIDS legends and vernacular risk perception.* Logan: Utah State University Press.

Gormley, W. T., Jr. (2012). *Voices for children: Rhetoric and public policy.* Washington, DC: Brookings Institution Press.

Gould, D. B. (2009). *Moving politics: Emotion and ACT-UP's fights against AIDS.* Chicago: University of Chicago Press.

Griffiths, H. and Best, J. (2016). Social problems clusters as contexts for claimsmaking: Implications for the study of off-campus housing. *Sociological Spectrum* 36: 75–92.

Gusfield, J. R. (1967). Moral passage: The symbolic process in public designations of deviance. *Social Problems* 15: 175–188.

Gusfield, J. R. (1981). *The culture of public problems: Drinking-driving and the symbolic order.* Chicago: University of Chicago Press.

Haines, H. H. (1984). Black radicalism and the funding of civil rights. *Social Problems* 32: 31–43.

Hamilton, J. T. (2004). *All the news that's fit to sell: How the market transforms information into news.* Princeton, NJ: Princeton University Press.

Harris, S. R. (2010). *What is constructionism? Navigating its use in sociology.* Boulder, CO: Lynne Reinner.

Haydu, J. (2011). Cultural modeling in two eras of U.S. food protests: Grahamites (1830s) and organic activists (1960s–70s). *Social Problems* 58: 461–487.

Heath, C., Bell, C., & Sternberg, E. (2001). Emotional selection in memes: The case of urban legends. *Journal of Personality and Social Psychology* 81: 1028–1041.

Hilgartner, S., & Bosk, C. L. (1988). The rise and fall of social problems. *American Journal of Sociology* 94: 53–78.

Holstein, J. A., & Gubrium, J. F. (Eds.). (2008). *Handbook of constructionist research.* New York: Guilford.

Holstein, J. A., & Miller, G. (2003). Social constructionism and social problems work. In J. A. Holstein & G. Miller (Eds.), *Challenges and choices: Constructionist perspectives on social problems* (pp. 70–91). Hawthorne, NY: Aldine de Gruyter.

Horowitz, R. (2013). *In the public interest: Medical licensing and the disciplinary process.* New Brunswick, NJ: Rutgers University Press.

Houston, J. B., Seo, H., Knight, L. A. T., Kennedy, E. J., Hawthorne, J., & Trask, S. L. (2013). Urban youth's perspectives on flash mobs. *Journal of Applied Communication Research* 41: 236–252.

Irvine, J. M. (2002). *Talk about sex: The battles over sex education in the United States.* Berkeley: University of California Press.

Jenkins, P. (1998). *Moral panic: Changing concepts of the child molester in modern America.* New Haven, CT: Yale University Press.

Jenkins, P. (1999). *Synthetic panics: The symbolic politics of designer drugs.* New York: New York University Press.

Jenkins, P. (2000). *Mystics and messiahs: Cults and new religions in American history.* New York: Oxford University Press.

Jenkins, P. (2001). *Hidden gospels: How the search for Jesus lost its way.* New York: Oxford University Press.

Jenkins, P. (2006). *Decade of nightmares: The end of the sixties and the making of eighties America.* New York: Oxford University Press.

Jenness, V. (1993). *Making it work: The prostitutes' rights movement in perspective.* Hawthorne, NY: Aldine de Gruyter.

Jenness, V., & Grattet, R. (2001). *Making hate a crime: From social movement to law enforcement.* New York: Russell Sage Foundation.

Jenness, V., & Grattet, R. (2005). The law-in-between: The effects of organizational perviousness on the policing of hate crime. *Social Problems* 52: 227–259.

Johnson, J. M. (1995). Horror stories and the construction of child abuse. In J. Best (Ed.), *Images of issues: Typifying contemporary social problems* (2nd ed., pp. 17–31). Hawthorne, NY: Aldine de Gruyter.

Johnson, K. R. (2013). Murdered mothers: The social construction of troubling statistics. In J. Best and S. R. Harris (Eds.), *Making sense of social problems: New images, new issues* (pp. 135–151). Boulder, CO: Lynne Rienner.

Kempner, J. (2014). *Not tonight: Migraine and the politics of gender and health.* Chicago: University of Chicago Press.

Kiel, D. C., & Nownes, A. J. (1994). Political language, causal stories, and pesticide regulation. *American Review of Politics* 15: 491–506.

Kindy, K., & Kelly, K. (2015, April 12). Thousands dead, few prosecuted. *Washington Post*, p. A1.

Kingdon, J. W. (1984). *Agendas, alternatives, and public policies.* New York: HarperCollins.

Kirk, S. A., & Kutchins, H. (1992). *The selling of DSM: The rhetoric of science in psychiatry.* Hawthorne, NY: Aldine de Gruyter.

Kleykamp, M., & Hipes, C. (2015). Coverage of veterans of the wars in Iraq and Afghanistan in the U.S. media. *Sociological Forum* 30: 348–368.

Kollmeyer, C. J. (2004). Corporate interests: How the news media portray the economy. *Social Problems* 51: 432–452.

Kretschmer, K. (2014). Shifting boundaries and splintering movements: Abortion rights in the feminist and New Right movements. *Sociological Forum* 29: 893–915.

Kubal, T. (2008). *Cultural movements and collective memory: Christopher Columbus and the rewriting of the national origin myth.* New York: Palgrave Macmillan.

Kurti, L. (1988). The politics of joking: Popular response to Chernobyl. *Journal of American Folklore* 101: 324–334.

Lafer, G. (2002). *The job training charade.* Ithaca, NY: Cornell University Press.

Langlois, J. (1983). The Belle Isle Bridge incident: Legend, dialectic and semiotic system in the 1943 Detroit race riots. *Journal of American Folklore* 96: 183–196.

Lee, E. (2003). *Abortion, motherhood, and mental health: Medicalizing reproduction in the United States and Great Britain.* Hawthorne, NY: Aldine de Gruyter.

Letukas, L. (2013). Global policy outcomes: Comparing reactions to post-tsunami aid. In J. Best and S. R. Harris (Eds.), *Making sense of social problems: New images, new issues* (pp. 265–281). Boulder, CO: Lynne Rienner.

Letukas, L. (2014). *Primetime pundits: How cable news covers social issues.* Lanham, MD: Lexington.

Link, M. W., Battaglia, M. P., Frankel, M. R., Osborn, L., & Mokdad, A. H. (2007). Reaching the U.S. cell phone generation: Comparison of cell phone survey results with an ongoing landline telephone survey. *Public Opinion Quarterly* 71: 814–839.

Lipsky, M. (1980). *Street-level bureaucracy: Dilemmas of the individual in public services.* New York: Russell Sage Foundation.

Lipsky, M., & Smith, S. R. (1989). When social problems are treated as emergencies. *Social Service Review* 63: 5–25.

Lofland, J. (2003). *Demolishing a historic hotel: A sociology of preservation failure in Davis, California.* Davis, CA: Davis Research.

Loseke, D. R. (2003). *Thinking about social problems* (2nd ed.). Hawthorne, NY: Aldine de Gruyter.

MacCoun, R. J., & Reuter, P. (2001). *Drug war heresies: Learning from other vices, times, and places.* New York: Cambridge University Press.

Macionis, J. J. (2013). *Social problems* (5th ed.). Upper Saddle River, NJ: Pearson.

Madianou, M. (2013). Humanitarian campaigns in social media. *Journalism Studies* 14: 249–266.

Malinen, K. (2014). "This was a sexual assault": A social worlds analysis of paradigm change in the interpersonal violence world. *Symbolic Interaction* 37: 353–368.

Malloy, T. F. (2010). The social construction of regulation: Lessons from the war against command and control. *Buffalo Law Review* 58: 267–354.

Maratea, R. J. (2014). *The politics of the Internet: Political claimsmaking in cyberspace and its effect on modern political activism.* Lanham, MD: Lexington.

Maurer, D. (2002). *Vegetarianism: Movement or moment?* Philadelphia: Temple University Press.

McAdam, D. (1983). Tactical innovation and the pace of insurgency. *American Sociological Review* 48: 735–754.

McAdam, D. (1994). Culture and social movements. In E. Laraña, H. Johnston, & J. R. Gusfield (Eds.), *New social movements: From identity to ideology* (pp. 36–57). Philadelphia: Temple University Press.

McAdam, D. (2015). Be careful what you wish for: The ironic connection between the civil rights struggle and today's divided America. *Sociological Forum* 30: 485–508.

McAdam, D., & Rucht, D. (1993). The cross-national diffusion of movement ideas. *Annals of the American Academy of Political and Social Science* 528: 56–74.

McCarthy, J. D., & Zald, M. N. (1977). Resource mobilization and social movements. *American Journal of Sociology* 82: 1212–1241.

McCombs, M. (2004). *Setting the agenda: The mass media and public opinion.* Cambridge, UK: Polity.

McCright, A. M., & Dunlap, R. E. (2011). The politicization of climate change and polarization in the American public's views of global warming, 2001–2010. *Sociological Quarterly* 52: 155–194.

McGarty, C., Thomas, E. F., Lala, G., Smith, L. G. E., & Bliuc, A.-M. (2014). New technologies, new identities, and the growth of mass opposition in the Arab Spring. *Political Psychology* 35: 725–740.

Medvetz, T. (2012). *Think tanks in America.* Chicago: University of Chicago Press.

Meyer, D. S., & Rohlinger, D. A. (2012). Big books and social movements: A myth of ideas and social change. *Social Problems* 59: 136–153.

Miller, G., & Holstein, J. A. (Eds.). (1997). *Social problems in everyday life: Studies of social problems work.* Greenwich, CT: JAI Press.

Mills, C. W. (1959). *The sociological imagination.* New York: Oxford University Press.

Morris, P. (2012). *Blue juice: Euthanasia in veterinary medicine.* Philadelphia: Temple University Press.

Murray, C. A. (1994). *Losing ground: American social policy, 1950–1980.* New York: Basic Books.

National Highway Traffic Safety Administration. (2014, December). 2013 motor vehicle crashes: Overview. *NHTSA National Center for Statistics and Analysis.* Retrieved from http://www-nrd.nhtsa.dot.gov/Pubs/812101.pdf.

Nelson, B. J. (1984). *Making an issue of child abuse: Political agenda setting for social problems.* Chicago: University of Chicago Press.

Newport, F. (2014, October 21). Americans' confidence in government to handle Ebola drops. *Gallup.com.* Retrieved from http://www.gallup.com/poll/178760 /americans-confidence-government-handle-ebola-drops.aspx.

Nichols, L. T. (1997). Social problems as landmark narratives: Bank of Boston, mass media and "money laundering." *Social Problems* 44: 324–341.

Nichols, L. T. (2003). Voices of social problems: A dialogical constructionist model. *Studies in Symbolic Interaction* 26: 93–123.

Nichols, L. T., Nolan, J. J., III, & Colyer, C. J. (2008). Scorekeeping versus storytelling: Representational practices in the construction of "hate crime." *Studies in Symbolic Interaction* 30: 361–379.

Obama, B. (2013, December 4). Remarks at the Town Hall Education Arts Recreation Campus. *American Presidency Project.* Retrieved from http://www .presidency.ucsb.edu/ws/?pid=104522.

O'Brien, P. K. (2013). Medical marijuana and social control: Escaping criminalization and embracing medicalization. *Deviant Behavior* 34: 423–443.

Oring, E. (1987). Jokes and the discourse on disaster. *Journal of American Folklore* 100: 278–286.

Parilla, P. F. (2013). Cell phone use while driving: Defining a problem as worthy of action. In J. Best and S. R. Harris (Eds.), *Making sense of social problems: New images, new issues* (pp. 27–46). Boulder, CO: Lynne Rienner.

Parsons, N. L. (2014). *Meth mania: A history of methamphetamine.* Boulder, CO: Lynne Rienner.

Pawluch, D. (1996). *The new pediatrics: A profession in transition.* Hawthorne, NY: Aldine de Gruyter.

Pearson, G. (1983). *Hooligan: A history of respectable fears.* London: Macmillan.

Pellow, D. N., & Brehm, H. N. (2015). From the new ecological paradigm to total liberation: The emergence of a social movement frame. *Sociological Quarterly* 56: 185–212.

Pfohl, S. J. (1977). The "discovery" of child abuse. *Social Problems* 24: 310–323.

Pielke, R. A., Jr. (2007). *The honest broker: Making sense of science in policy and politics.* New York: Cambridge University Press.

Pierotti, R. S. (2013). Increasing rejection of intimate partner violence: Evidence of global cultural diffusion. *American Sociological Review* 78: 240–265.

Polletta, F., & Tomlinson, C. (2014). Date rape after the afterschool special: Narrative trends in the televised depiction of social problems. *Sociological Forum* 29: 527–548.

Preston, R. (1994). *The hot zone.* New York: Random House.

Putnam, R. (2015). *Our kids: The American Dream in crisis.* New York: Simon & Schuster.

Rank, M. R., Hirschl, T. A., & Foster, K. A. (2014). *Chasing the American Dream: Understanding what shapes our fortunes.* New York: Oxford University Press.

Ravitch, D. (2003). *The language police: How pressure groups restrict what students learn.* New York: Vintage.

Reinarman, C. (1994). The social construction of drug scares. In P. A. Adler & P. Adler (Eds.), *Constructions of deviance* (pp. 92–104). Belmont, CA: Wadsworth.

Reinarman, C., & Levine, H. G. (1995). The crack attack: America's latest drug scare, 1986–1992. In J. Best (Ed.), *Images of issues: Typifying contemporary social problems* (2nd ed., pp. 147–186). Hawthorne, NY: Aldine de Gruyter.

Rosenberg, I. B. (2009). Height discrimination in employment. *Utah Law Review* 2009: 907–953.

Rossi, P. H., Lipsey, M. W., & Freeman, H. E. (2004). *Evaluation: A systematic approach* (7th ed.). Thousand Oaks, CA: Sage.

Rudy, D. R. (1986). *Becoming alcoholic: Alcoholics Anonymous and the reality of alcoholism.* Carbondale: Southern Illinois University Press.

Saad, L. (2013, August 2). In U.S., 38% have tried marijuana, little changed since '80s. *Gallup.com*. Retrieved from http://www.gallup.com/poll/163835/tried-marijuana-little-changed-80s.aspx.

Saad, L. (2014, November 17). Ebola ranks among Americans' top three healthcare concerns. *Gallup.com*. Retrieved from http://www.gallup.com/poll/179429/ebola-ranks-among-americans-top-three-healthcare-concerns.aspx.

Saguy, A. C. (2003). *What is sexual harassment? From Capitol Hill to the Sorbonne.* Berkeley: University of California Press.

Saguy, A. C. (2013). *What's wrong with fat?* New York: Oxford University Press.

Saletan, W. (2003). *Bearing right: How the conservatives won the abortion war.* Berkeley: University of California Press.

Sanders, C. B., Christensen, T., & Weston, C. (2015). Constructing crime in a database: Big data and the mangle of social problems work. *Qualitative Sociology Review* 11(2): 180–195.

Sasson, T. (1995a). African American conspiracy theories and the social construction of crime. *Sociological Inquiry* 65: 265–285.

Sasson, T. (1995b). *Crime talk: How citizens construct a social problem.* Hawthorne, NY: Aldine de Gruyter.

Schneider, A. L., & Ingram, H. M. (1993). Social constructions of target populations: Implications for politics and policy. *American Political Science Review* 87: 334–347.

Schneider, A. L., & Ingram, H. M. (Eds.). (2005). *Deserving and entitled: Social constructions and public policy.* Albany: State University of New York Press.

Schudson, M. (2011). *The sociology of news* (2nd ed.). New York: Norton.

Schwartz, H. (2011). *Making noise: From Babel to the Big Bang and beyond.* Cambridge: MIT Press.

Scotch, R. K. (2001). *From good will to civil rights: Transforming federal disability policy* (2nd ed.). Philadelphia: Temple University Press.

Shibutani, T. (1966). *Improvised news: A sociological study of rumor.* Indianapolis, IN: Bobbs-Merrill.

Shifman, L., Levy, H., & Thelwall, M. (2014). Internet jokes: The secret agents of globalization? *Journal of Computer-Mediated Communication* 19: 727–743.

Silver, I. (2006). *Unequal partnerships: Beyond the rhetoric of philanthropic collaboration.* New York: Routledge.

Silver, I., & Boyle, M.-E. (2010). Constructing problems by promoting solutions: Corporate advertisements about U.S. poverty. *Journal of Poverty* 14: 347–367.

Smith, A., & Pollack, H. (2003). Understanding the Diallo case: The trial, the community and the police. *Criminal Justice Studies* 16: 355–361.

Snow, D., & Benford, R. (1988). Ideology, frame resonance, and participant mobilization. *International Social Movement Research* 1: 197–217.

Snow, D., & Benford, R. (1992). Master frames and cycles of protest. In A. D. Morris & C. M. Mueller (Eds.), *Frontiers in social movement theory* (pp. 133–155). New Haven, CT: Yale University Press.

Snow, D. A., Rochford, E. B., Jr., Worden, S. K., & Benford, R. D. (1986). Frame alignment processes, micromobilization, and movement participation. *American Sociological Review* 51: 464–481.

Sobieraj, S. (2011). *Soundbitten: The perils of media-centered political activism.* New York: New York University Press.

Spector, M., & Kitsuse, J. I. (1977). *Constructing social problems.* Menlo Park, CA: Cummings.

Staller, K. M. (2006). *Runaways: How the sixties counterculture shaped today's policies and practices.* New York: Columbia University Press.

Starr, P. (1982). *The social transformation of American medicine.* New York: Basic Books.

Stewart, J. (2012). Fiction over facts: How competing narrative forms explain policy in a new immigration destination. *Sociological Forum* 27: 591–616.

Stone, D. A. (1989). Causal stories and the formation of policy agendas. *Political Science Quarterly* 104: 281–300.

Strang, D., & Meyer, J. W. (1993). Institutional conditions for diffusion. *Theory and Society* 22: 487–511.

Suarez, E., & Gadalla, T. M. (2010). Stop blaming the victim: A meta-analysis on rape myths. *Journal of Interpersonal Violence* 25: 2010–2035.

Taylor, V. (1989). Social movement continuity: The women's movement in abeyance. *American Sociological Review* 54: 761–775.

Toulmin, S. E. (1958). *The uses of argument.* Cambridge, UK: Cambridge University Press.

Tuchman, G. (1978). *Making news: A study in the construction of reality.* New York: Free Press.

Turow, J. (1997). *Breaking up America: Advertisers and the new media world.* Chicago: University of Chicago Press.

Tyson, N. deGrasse. (2009). *The Pluto files: The rise and fall of America's favorite planet.* New York: Norton.

U.S. Census Bureau. (1975). *Historical statistics of the United States: Colonial times to 1970.* Washington, DC: U.S. Government Printing Office.

Useem, B., & Zald, M. N. (1982). From pressure groups to social movement: Organizational dilemmas of the effort to promote nuclear power. *Social Problems* 30: 144–156.

Vardi, I. (2014). Quantifying accidents: Cars, statistics, and unintended consequences in the construction of social problems over time. *Qualitative Sociology* 37: 345–367.

Vasterman, P. L. M. (2005). Media-hype: Self-reinforcing news waves, journalistic standards, and the construction of social problems. *European Journal of Communication* 20: 508–530.

Vaughan, D. (2006). The social shaping of commission reports. *Sociological Forum* 21: 291–306.

Walgrave, S., & Wouters, R. (2014). The missing link in the diffusion of protest: Asking others. *American Journal of Sociology* 119: 1670–1709.

Watts, D. J. (2011). *Everything is obvious: Once you know the answer.* New York: Crown Business.

Weinberg, D. (2014). *Contemporary social constructionism: Key themes.* Philadelphia: Temple University Press.

Weisner, C., & Room, R. (1984). Financing and ideology in alcohol treatment. *Social Problems* 32: 167–184.

Welch, M. (2000). *Flag burning: Moral panic and the criminalization of protest.* Hawthorne, NY: Aldine de Gruyter.

White, L. (2000). *Speaking of vampires: Rumor and history in colonial Africa.* Berkeley: University of California Press.

Whittier, N. (2009). *The politics of child sexual abuse: Emotions, social movements, and the state.* New York: Oxford University Press.

Whittier, N. (2014). Rethinking coalitions: Anti-pornography feminists, conservatives, and relationships between collaborative adversarial movements. *Social Problems* 61: 175–193.

Wilcox, M. M. (2014). Lgbttsqqiaa . . . *Contexts* 13(1): 12–14.

Xu, J. (2013). Politics and the production of crime data in China: A case study of Guangzhou. Unpublished paper presented at the annual meeting of the Society for the Study of Social Problems, New York.

Xu, J. (2015). Claims-makers versus non-issue-makers: Media and the social construction of motorcycle ban problems in China. *Qualitative Sociology Review* 11(2): 122–141.

Yukich, G. (2013). Constructing the model immigrant: Movement strategy and immigrant deservingness in the New Sanctuary Movement. *Social Problems* 60: 302–320.

Zegart, A. B. (2004). Blue ribbons, black boxes: Toward a better understanding of presidential commissions. *Presidential Studies Quarterly* 34: 366–393.

Index

statistics
  to establish grounds for a claim, 33
  policy outcomes and, 278, 279
  "wars" over, 52
stereotypes, 188, *189*
Stockholm syndrome, expanding domain
    of, *56*
Stone, Deborah A., 216
student loans, modifying, *292–94*
Student Nonviolent Coordinating
      Committee (SNCC), 17,
      20, 68
  confrontational activities and, 89
  resources of, 79
subjectivist definitions of social
      problems, 8–10, 16,
      330
subjects of social problem workers,
      232–33, 246–52
  battered women, *250*
  case construction and, 240–46, *245*
  classifying, 243
  coercion of, 249
  evaluation of policy outcomes by,
      275–76
  repeaters, 251
  resistance of, 251–52
Supreme Court
  legalization of abortion, *90*, 200
  on "marketplace of ideas," *325*
  on same-sex marriage, *228*
surveys, *see* public reaction
symbolic politics, rhetoric of, 220, 222

T

talk shows, 149, 151–52
target populations, 218–19
teachers' unions, 254
technological change, case studies on,
    161–64
television, *see* media and media coverage

terminology of constructionist approach,
      14–16
terrorism, *see* September 11, 2001,
      terrorist attacks
theorization, 307
think tanks, 119, *120*
thirdhand smoke, 277
Time, 34
time as basis for comparative research,
      299
tobacco industry, *127–28*
tobacco smoking, 118, 277, 307
topical joke cycles, 188–90
torture, 222
total liberation frame, 76
toxic waste sites, health problems living
      near, 124
traffic fatalities, 224, 322
trans fat, *270*
transmitters, 304–5, *306–7*
trope, *63*
troubling conditions, 329
  as basis for comparative research,
      299
  definition of, 15–16
  persistence of, 265
tsunami 2004 relief efforts, Indian
      Ocean, 267
twelve-step programs, 106, 248–49
Twenty-First Amendment, 265
Twitter, 154, 178
two-spirits, 12
typifying example, 32

U

UFO abductions, social construction of,
      12–13
undocumented immigrants, 280
urban legends, *see* contemporary
      legends
Utah, immigration policy of, 280